SET SAIL
≫AND≪
LIVE YOUR DREAMS

SET SAIL
AND
LIVE YOUR DREAMS

Follow a Young Family Sailing Over the Horizon on the Adventure of a Lifetime

APRIL AND BRUCE WINSHIP

Seaworthy
PUBLICATIONS

SEAWORTHY PUBLICATIONS, INC. • MELBOURNE, FLORIDA

SET SAIL AND LIVE YOUR DREAMS
Follow a Young Family Sailing Over the Horizon
on the Adventure of a Lifetime

Published in the USA and distributed worldwide by:
Seaworthy Publications, Inc.
6300 N. Wickham Rd
Unit 130-416
Melbourne, FL 32940
Phone 310-610-3634
email orders@seaworthy.com
www.seaworthy.com

Library of Congress Cataloging-in-Publication Data

Names: Winship, April, 1957- author.
Title: Set sail and live your dreams : follow a young family sailing over the
    horizon on the adventure of a lifetime / April and Bruce Winship.
Description: Melbourne, Florida : Seaworthy Publications, Inc., [2019]
Identifiers: LCCN 2018056820 (print) | LCCN 2019013528 (ebook) | ISBN
    9781948494199 (E-book) | ISBN 1948494191 (E-book) | ISBN 9781948494182
    |
    ISBN 9781948494182¬(Paperback : alk. paper) | ISBN 1948494183-(Paperback
    : alk. paper)
Subjects: LCSH: Sailing--Anecdotes. | Winship, April, 1957---Travel. |
    Winship, April, 1957---Family. | Families--Travel.
Classification: LCC GV811 (ebook) | LCC GV811 .W56 2019 (print) | DDC
    797.124--dc23
LC record available at https://lccn.loc.gov/2018056820

DEDICATION

We dedicate this book with infinite love to our courageous daughters Kendall Clare Elizabeth and Quincy Rose Michelle who made our journey an unforgettable kaleidoscope of memories.

And to *Chewbacca*, our magic carpet.

CONTENTS

PROLOGUE

"I braced for the inevitable cry of splintering fiberglass against the sea swept reef and was helpless to stop time and the drift towards the end of our dream... a dream that had only just begun."

We were not new to voyaging when we left our land life behind and embraced our dream. We fell in love with the sea on our first 3,300-mile journey across the Pacific Ocean. As a young married couple looking for an adventure to paradise we would never have guessed the first overnight sail of our lives would last 32 days. Our escapades hitchhiking throughout the South Pacific on several sailboats ended two years later in Panama when we land trekked home vowing to someday return to paradise on our own boat. But first we had to overcome tragedy.

These are the chronicles of our 10-year sabbatical at sea cruising Mexico, Central and South America as a family, on a shoestring budget with our young children on our catamaran *Chewbacca*. It's about how we rekindled the cruising dream, prepared our boat and ourselves for life afloat, mastered seamanship, homeschooling and raising a family on 33-feet in both idyllic and dangerous times.

CHAPTER 1

TIME FOR A CHANGE

"There are two options in a person's life: reflections and actions. One is an opportunity to think, the other is an opportunity to live."

-Author unknown

THEY SAID THAT HOLDING YOUR CHILD AFTER A MISCARRIAGE IS THE BEST way to begin the healing process. However, all I felt was a numbness, a loud drumming in my ears, a hollowness. I peered at our daughter's lovely face and felt so sorry that I would never see her living life as we had hoped.

I languished in a deep sadness knowing our goals of having a family and sailing to paradise had vanished. I forgot what it was like to smile, or even laugh out loud. Life seemed cruel, unfair and unbearable. We had lost ourselves and now I wasn't even sure if I had the will or desire to recapture our dream.

Where did our happy life go?

From my hospital bed it seemed a lifetime ago that Bruce and I were young carefree college students poised to join the yuppie life in Los Angeles upon graduation. With two careers and no kids on the horizon we fell squarely into the category of DINKS; (Double Income No KIDS). For several years we worked hard and played hard and as proof our spare room was littered with downhill skis, roller blades, tennis rackets and a smattering of scuba diving gear. Life was good, and like Disneyland we thought SoCal was "The happiest place on earth."

We didn't live far from the beach, so it made perfect sense to join a sailing club. We had both learned to sail dinghies in college, but neither of us progressed much beyond a novice sailor. One club offered a free introductory open ocean sailing class and we took the bait. BAM! We were both hooked before we even left the harbor.

Over the next couple years Bruce and I earned certificates in basic sailing, boat handling and coastal navigation so we could check out the club boats on our own. With passing grades, our instructors encouraged us to participate in "Sunday races around the harbor" and admittedly it was a great way to hone our skills... but neither of us was much into the thrill of competitive sailing. Shortly after the starting gun sounded, Bruce would set a downwind course, coasting right past the rounding markers and out into the open ocean. I would radio back our regrets, pop the Beach Boys into the cassette player and retrim the sails for a gentle cruise along the coast. As I rummaged through the ice chest for our picnic Bruce often joked, "Let's turn left here... next stop Hawaii!" With the gentle breeze at our backs, we'd sail contentedly just outside the surf line with a backdrop of glistening sun worshippers lining Malibu Beach. *Why race when we could cruise?*

Through the club newsletter we read about a string of lectures sponsored by the local community college entitled *Sailing Adventure Series*. The title captured our imaginations and we faithfully attended all the monthly presentations. The speakers shared their nautical wisdom and fascinating sailing stories reaching the far corners of the earth to a rapt audience. Beautiful color slides illuminated the auditorium with scenes of gorgeous yachts anchored in front of lush tropical islands as we sat back and escaped to unknown paradises.

What a concept: Work hard, retire and sail to the South Pacific. We'd been on the 9-to-5 treadmill for nearly five years, so paradise was only 35 years away and waiting just for us.

One presentation featured world cruisers, Lin and Larry Pardey. These were sailing purists; they had built their own wooden boat, didn't need "no stinkin' engine" and thought an oak bucket made a dandy toilet. They cooked gourmet meals on a kerosene stove... always served with the proper wine.

Unlike previous speakers, Lin and Larry weren't rich retirees or flashy round-the-world racers hawking their mega yacht designs. They didn't insist we needed a pricey 65-footer with a carbon fiber mast and enough electronic gizmos to run the space shuttle to sail your way to paradise. The images I had come to associate with the perfect cruising yacht were totally changed that evening. The Pardey's built their boat themselves out of mahogany, oak and teak. *Seraffyn* cost $7,765 and although she was a simple boat, they lived a joyous life aboard their stout 24-footer. For 11 years Lin and Larry voyaged over 45,000 miles exploring the Pacific, Atlantic and Indian oceans and the Caribbean, Mediterranean and South China Seas. *Seraffyn* had circled the globe and looked capable to go around again.

Something wasn't right. Somehow, they were doing it... and doing it now. *Would paradise wait for us?*

"Go small, go simple, go now," was the Pardey's mantra and by the end of the evening we were nodding our heads in agreement along with the rest of the mesmerized crowd. But perhaps, we were nodding our heads a little more enthusiastically than our fellow attendees, because three months later we had quit our jobs, sold our cars and rented out the condo.

We were bound for Paradise.

CHAPTER 2

HITCHHIKING TO PARADISE

"Following the sun, we left the old world."

-Christopher Columbus, Italian Explorer

"**W**HY NOT GO NOW?" BRUCE ASKED ON THE DRIVE HOME. "WE'VE ALWAYS HAD the travel bug, we've got some savings and we could rent out the condo." Lin and Larry had the plan all worked out, we just had to follow in their wake.

But the idea of building a boat terrified me. I flat out lacked the skills to erect a doghouse from a prefab kit, let alone build a sailboat. Besides, the project would certainly take more than five years... more likely forever! After discussing it further we concluded that if we wanted to go now, we would just have to buy a boat.

The next weekend we drove over to the marina district and knocked on a few doors. Every yacht broker claimed they had the perfect boat for us. One mast, two masts, fiberglass and wooden boats all bobbing along the sales docks begging for a new owner. Being relatively new to the world of cruising sailboats, I wasn't exactly sure what we were looking for but the one attribute all these boats had in common: they were all well beyond our means. Even with two incomes, buying a long-range cruising boat, especially one in decent shape, was out of the question. Perhaps our cruising dream was unattainable. Frustration set in like a dark cloud as we trudged away from the dock.

Walking back to the parking lot Bruce picked up several local boating magazines hoping to find an economical cruising boat for sale by owner. We slid into a booth at the marina café and started scouring the *SAILBOAT* classified ads. The boats were listed by size, but may as well have been grouped by price, because as the boat length increased, the costs jumped exponentially. Most of the boats we could afford began with *Perfect Day Sailor... Race Ready... No Amenities...* or *Needs TLC. How could it be that everything in our price range was incapable of crossing an ocean?*

The waiter approached our table and my concentration was shattered as he blurted out, "You guys looking to crew?" From behind the magazine I mumbled something about looking to buy a boat to get us to the South Pacific then paused. *Wait, what did he mean by the term crew?* Bruce chimed in and asked, "Could we crew on a sailboat for something more than just day sailing around the bay?" "Oh, hell yes," the waiter replied enthusiastically. "People are looking for extra hands all the time. It's right there in that sailing rag. There, turn the page and you'll see."

He took our drink order and we dug back into the magazine, our concentration refocused on the section entitled *CREW WANTED*:

"Semi-fit captain mid 60's seeking 18 - 35 female first mate for extended world cruise and possible LTR."

"Long-term Relationship." Really? Are these captains only looking for offshore romances? I was beginning to get truly discouraged in between laughs. Luckily, further down the page there were several ads placed by captains genuinely looking for competent crew to help them sail to distant locations. We focused on the "serious" ads, crossing out some, circling others and underlining a few possibilities. Excitement bubbled within me. I thought we probably looked like a couple of jittery bookies scouring the track sheet for our winning pony. This just might be the hot ticket to paradise.

What a concept! Free passage in exchange for helping sail someone else's boat to exotic destinations. This sounded like a way to gain experience without first taking the expensive plunge into boat ownership. Heck, I didn't even know if I would like cruising, so what better way to find out than as crew? We quickly narrowed the list down to boats bound for the South Pacific with eminent departure dates. One ad stuck out:

"Crew wanted. Sail to Tahiti. Share expenses. Well-found boat departing in 10 weeks. Daytime phone # …"

We chugged down our drinks and headed straight for home. The front door had barely closed behind us and Bruce made a bee-line for our bookshelf. He brought over a map of the world stuffed inside a worn *National Geographic* magazine. South Pacific… Society Islands… Tahiti. Bruce looked up grinning like a Cheshire cat, "Bingo, smack in the middle of paradise." I nodded my head and reread the ad. Crewing wasn't our original focus, but it was a possible path to our dream. I could hear my father's words playing out in my head; *"Be stubborn with your goals, but flexible in your journey."* I looked up at Bruce and said with bold conviction, "I'm in."

The next afternoon found us motoring down Highway 101 to meet Deiter. The traffic pressed forward like a steady lava flow of crimson lights converging on San Diego. Riding the brake pedal I turned off the radio chatter and focused my thoughts to what we were heading for.

It was just past dinnertime when we pulled into the marina parking lot creeping beside a forest of aluminum masts in search of D Dock. After a few passes, I noticed a fellow peering expectantly out of an unmarked barred gate. He had a graying goatee and a Portuguese fisherman's cap smartly squared atop his head. "I bet that's Deiter," I pointed as we coasted to a stop. The lone figure waved us over, silently unlocked the gate and stiffly raised his hand to meet Bruce's. "Deiter" he said then nodded his cap towards me and repeated his name just in case I had missed it. Bruce recalled that beneath his strong grip, his hand felt like a bundle of dry twigs in a well-worn brown paper bag. We introduced ourselves and were led down a corrugated steel ramp towards a sea of bobbing boats.

I imagined how the next phone conversation with my parents would begin:

"Hi Mom, you'll never guess what Bruce and I are going to do…"

If we had said we were taking a break, buying rail passes and heading to Europe for six months, that would have been imaginable... but we were skirting the "we've never heard of such a thing" scenario and I understood the trepidation our parents might feel.

It was only 12 weeks since we had first met Deiter and before I knew it, we were standing in the marina parking lot with two duffle bags at our feet. A quarter mile away the chariot that would carry us to the South Pacific lay waiting at the dock and I slung my heavy duffle over my shoulder and maneuvered between the parked cars towards my future.

The next morning Bruce and I uncoiled *Journey's* dock lines and stepped aboard as Deiter stood behind the wheel and steered us past the breakwater. Just like that, we were on our way, actually bound for Paradise.

Facing the first overnight sail of our lives, Bruce and I turned to each other searching for anxiety. Fortunately, we were young, inexperienced and had no worries. Worst case; if we hated cruising we could always fly home from Tahiti on a jumbo jet. Just over the bow lay 3,300 miles of open ocean separating us from paradise.

Neither of us had ever been on an overnight sail, yet here we were. Our first shakedown sail on *Journey* was about to turn into a 32-day nonstop trek across the Pacific Ocean!

We did make it to Tahiti, and despite more than a few misadventures serving as crew on several sailboats…two years and five countries later, like wayward adolescents gone temporarily insane, we made our way back home.

Re-entering the corporate world was not much tougher than kicking off the flip flops and lacing up a pair of wing tips. Bruce landed back with his previous company and I secured my dream job even after divulging I took off for a couple years to "bum around hitching rides on sailboats." It was almost as if everyone secretly desired to have an "adventure or two" but could not bring about the necessary sacrifices to "just do it" and our risk taking was viewed as a positive, in and out of the workplace.

Very soon we were both melded back into the 9-to-5 working world. Bright and early every morning we tramped off to the train station to rejoin the mainstream like a herd of lemmings dashing for the cliff, clutching our travel mugs of coffee and morning papers. Akin to everyone else we had the mortgage or rent, food, insurance and other bills to pay. We had schedules. On the surface we resembled normal, all-American, income generating, tax paying, productive citizens working towards the gold watch and pension plan. But deep down there smoldered a dream. All our focus was towards the new goal of buying our own boat; our escape pod back to Paradise.

We returned to the same old society, restarted our careers but not our old lifestyle. It was time to get serious about living our dream, but first we needed a plan, so we put pencil to paper.

Bruce jotted down on the first line:

1. Identify your dream.

He looked up and said, "What do we want to do? It doesn't matter if our goal is to buy a boat and sail back to Paradise on our own boat, or get a dinghy and putter around the Bay. Either way we first have to realistically define our dream."

2. Make a plan.

"We need a plan to move our dream to reality." I reminded Bruce of one of his favorite sayings; "A goal without a time frame just remains a dream." So we discussed what a workable time frame would look like.

3. Stay focused.

"You know we're a little outside of the box here and we will have to make some serious lifestyle changes and sacrifices to achieve our goal." I nodded, not quite comprehending what sacrifices we would need to make.

The next line simply read;

4. Go for it.

Bruce looked at me, "In for a penny..." I countered with a chuckle, "In for a pound." *God help us.*

Although the Pardeys' philosophy of "Go small, go simple, go now" struck a chord in me, my maternal time clock was ticking. Loudly. I turned to Bruce and said, "Want to hear something crazy?" We reviewed our life and our love of cruising and boldly agreed to have a family first and share the cruising lifestyle with our children. I blame my parents for this idea. When I was four years old my parents immigrated to Australia and their courage exposed me to the possibilities of living a life outside of the box. The experience led me to believe that we could create an awesome adventure with our future family.

We had a plan. This time around we bought second and thirdhand cars and turned the LA condo profits into a sizable down payment on a small house in the suburbs. We pinched our pennies twice and "Goodwill" became my store of preference. When friends stopped by, I would jokingly explain that our good furniture was out being cleaned. Wine came in a box and eating out became a rarity and even then, usually entailed a drive-through window.

We held ourselves accountable and taped our "Boat Fund" goals to the bathroom mirror. They smiled back at us each morning. We were on a mission and every month we would excitedly chart our progress. We didn't reach our financial goals every month but thankfully we never stopped trying.

If we could stick to a savings plan we would buy our boat, then build a cruising kitty and return to paradise with our kids in no time. It seemed like such an easy plan.

Three years after our Pacific hitchhiking adventure ended, the test strip turned blue and we were over the moon with joy. I would be an older mother at 35 but I wasn't alone. My pregnancy progressed, and our favorite pastime was watching our baby girl move from one side of my belly to the other. "Sort of like Alien," said Bruce, awestruck, as he touched my swollen belly where an elbow or knee poked up. I studied the new ultrasound pictures after our visit to the doctor and fell hopelessly in love with the budding life within me; perfect little feet with every toe accounted for and tiny fingers reaching for a beautiful face.

In the sixth month, I awoke in the dead of night to a twinge. Bruce lay in the curve of my back, and we were stacked like spoons in a drawer, Bruce, me and baby. By morning our stillborn girl was handed to me wrapped in a warm receiving blanket. Our world was shattered. But I was assured by my doctor that our misfortune was a fluke and the odds of another miscarriage were very remote, so we were encouraged to dust ourselves off and get back in the saddle again. We regrouped and within several months, baby number two, a son, was on the way. Our happiness almost obliterated the painful memories of our first loss and the three of us flourished. But sadly, lightening "can" strike the same place twice. At the sixth month mark, Bruce, ashen faced and sobbing, rushed me to the hospital as reality sunk in that a second nightmare had begun.

All of our dreams were shattered. Pointless to continue on.

CHAPTER 3

THE WOOKIEE WINS

"Whatever boat you own, your heart should skip a beat every time you row up to her."

-Captain of the sailing vessel *Raven*

S OMEWHERE DEEP WITHIN ME A SPARK IGNITED. THE TRAUMA OF OUR misfortunes never dulled, yet I discovered a determination and fearlessness that wasn't there before. The only encouraging thought was that a medical term was now attached to my second miscarriage. Incompetent Cervix. With a cervix too weak to hold a growing fetus I would miscarry during the last trimester. It was a cruel fact that doctors do not often pin a first miscarriage on the cervix, but a second one prompted a closer look. I found renewed hope and confidence in a team of doctors specializing in cases like mine. I was prescribed surgery, bed rest, new medicines and constant monitoring that stacked the odds of a successful pregnancy in our favor.

After many months of anxiety we joyously welcomed our daughter Kendall into our world. Following my doctor's same recipe, two years later our second daughter Quincy was born. We learned that nothing was impossible or insurmountable with a realistic plan, sacrifice, courage and teamwork. When Quincy was delivered Bruce leaned over the hospital bed and whispered, "I believe we have our crew. Now, all we need is a boat." Even though I will never completely heal from losing my babies, their loss taught me that life is precarious and more than ever I wanted to reach for an extraordinary life and share it with our new family.

We were easily spotted as the couple pushing a double-wide baby stroller along the sales docks and boat storage facilities from one end of San Francisco Bay to the other. We were on a mission. We were looking for a gem someone had forgotten, a diamond in the rough that had been replaced by a fancier model or a higher priority.

In addition to scouring the boatyards, we attended boat shows, checked the classifieds and talked to every yacht broker from San Diego to Seattle. We kept an open mind and considered fiberglass, steel and aluminum hulls, fin keels, full keels, even twin keels. We contemplated sloops, ketches and yawls and once eyed a Chinese-junk rigged boat. Most of the boats we looked at were conventional single hull sailboats but over time we were sold on the stability, interior space and speed of a catamaran. Unfortunately, most cruising catamarans dwelled in a land far beyond our financial means.

Our friend once told us, "Whatever boat you own, your heart should skip a beat every time you row up to her." Although not exactly technical, his sage advice became our yardstick above all others. But we'd been searching, turning over every rock, and still we were coming up empty. Was there really a boat out there for us?

On a drizzly October afternoon, while commiserating with a yacht broker about the futility of our boat search, Bruce gazed down the estuary and noticed a sleek racing catamaran sailing our way. "Now, if I could turn a beast like that into a small cruising catamaran, we would have something," he mused out loud, just as the captain dropped her sails and ghosted along the sales dock. While the owner was securing the dock lines he informed the broker that he was being transferred to Singapore and was looking for a buyer.

As if on cue, the cloudy skies cleared, and we were invited aboard. The owner followed and shared a few details with us. "She is a Locke Crowther open-ocean racing design. She's constructed of fiberglass, with a lightweight foam and balsa core, built for speed. She's a proven competitor in her home waters of Australia and I brought her here to campaign in the San Francisco Bay. She took first place in the Double-Handed Farallones Race, clocked at 23 knots beneath the Golden Gate Bridge!" Laughing, the broker chimed in, "OK, that's four times faster than the average cruising boat, but these 10-meter catamarans are a popular racing class "Down Under" and I've been trying to beat this boat over the past few years with my own racing trimaran. She's a fast, capable racer and I'll admit I'm more familiar looking at her stern, as I always seem to be chasing her!"

Up close the catamaran was even more of a racing rig than I had first thought. A row of winches lined the cabin top like a column of soldiers awaiting a firm command. A spider web of lines sprang forth from chocks, blocks, cams and cleats. Six sheets ran forward to handle the spinnaker gear, five more tamed the massive mainsail and four worked the jib. What the others were used for I had no idea! Add an experienced racing crew of six and I imagined this boat was an intimidating adversary. At the bow there was no windlass for the anchor chain…hell, there wasn't even any anchor chain or anchor for that matter. This was obviously a full-fledged racing boat, not a boat designed for cruising.

I went below to check out the "spacious" accommodations. Entering the main cabin, I had to stoop over because the ceiling height was only four feet high. I'd have to learn to live life bent over if I ventured far in this contraption. Just inside the door was a kitchen table suitable for a couple of friendly adults sitting Japanese style on floor cushions. Proceeding left or right I could step down into either hull which contained a full-size bed and a row of open shelving to store sailing gear. The kitchen was in the forward part of the left hull and held only a double-burner camp stove and no oven. There was no fresh water tankage, so a foot pump was set up to deliver saltwater to a miniscule kitchen sink. Somewhat hidden behind a threadbare curtain sat a solitary toilet that appeared nonfunctioning from the growth sprouting within the bowl.

Seriously, this boat lacked just about every piece of cruising equipment we required for an extended voyage with our young family. Why were we looking at her? Common sense said NO… but my heart skipped a beat.

A few days later, with great expectations, we marched down the dock to where our new boat awaited us. The marina was bathed in a swirl of fog as I hugged six-month-old Quincy to my hip and a wiggly two-year-old Kendall was perched high on Bruce's shoulders. With a congratulatory smile the broker held aloft a bottle of chilled California Champagne.

Bruce's hands trembled as he handed over the check that represented our entire life savings. I peeked at what was left in our checkbook and grimaced. I silently counted on my fingers how many days until Bruce's next paycheck.

I stepped aboard and surveyed our purchase. Somehow, she wasn't as perfect as I'd remembered, and the dank aroma of mildew greeted me as I opened the door. *No new car smell here*. Bruce and I sat knee to knee at the salon table and trying to push my uncertainties aside, we brainstormed and came up with a barebones project list that I hoped would turn this Arabian into a Clydesdale of a cruising boat. The list was long.

Now, where to start? We were in unanimous agreement to strip out every item aboard that wasn't bolted down... and even some that were. High on my list was to yank out the pumpkin orange shag carpet followed by peeling off the mold streaked brown corduroy cloth covering the walls. I emptied out every cupboard and scrubbed out the icebox while Bruce got on his knees and took a hacksaw to the bolts on the non-functioning head. Relentlessly we exorcised memories of the past.

Enormous racing sails that once pushed our boat to trophy winning speeds were spread out on the marina lawn, folded and set aside for resale. Outdated electronics and corroded light fixtures were snipped free and placed to the side of the dumpster for some lucky treasure hunter. Now an empty shell, our boat awaited her future as the pages of a fresh notebook held our ambitious projects list.

For the next few months we simply referred to our catamaran as *"The Boat."* "She really is overdue for a name, but she needs something easy for the girls to remember" I commented to Bruce as we walked along the marina docks getting ideas. "OK, I get it, so no *Moon Shadow* or *Knotty Buoy*" he countered. We batted around a long list of cartoon cats including *The Lion King's* Simba, *Winnie the Pooh's* Tigger and the *Pink Panther*. Although popular with catamarans, names containing the word "cat" such as *Catfish*, *Catnip* and *Caterpillar* left me cringing. *Stray Cat* and *Purrfection* were already cruising and so was the aircraft carrier *USS Kitty Hawk*. At last Kendall came to the rescue with the name of her favorite Star Wars character.

"We christen this ship *CHEWBACCA*. May she bring fair winds and good fortune to all who sail upon her."

CHAPTER 4

METAMORPHOSIS OF CHEWBACCA

"There is nothing - absolutely nothing - half so much worth doing as simply messing about in boats."

-Kenneth Grahame, *Wind in the Willows*

"WHAT HAVE WE GOTTEN OURSELVES INTO?" I HEARD BRUCE MURMUR AS HE reread the article. He had immersed himself in the few books and articles written about cruising catamarans, for like us, catamarans were a relative newcomer to the boating scene. Propped up in bed, he read aloud that a proper cruising catamaran should be longer than 40 feet in length. Half asleep I wondered, *why didn't you read this before we bought our 33-footer!* The text rambled on...

> *"... the longer waterline is critical because today it's not unheard of to see massive water and fuel tanks, oversize engines, washer and dryers, trash compactors and electrical systems that could power a small village, all packed aboard the modern catamaran."*

"Obviously, they haven't met our little *Chewbacca*," I mumbled as I rolled over.

We recognized from the start that her inherently slim racing hulls meant limited weight carrying capacity and we strived to keep *Chewbacca* light. In the process, we chose to forgo some of the systems that made modern catamarans more comfortable. Water tanks, pressurized water systems, hot water heater, freezer and a water-maker didn't make the cut.

A 12-volt refrigerator/freezer would have been nice, but we couldn't afford the weight of the additional batteries required to keep a unit running nor the initial cash outlay.

We admired Lin and Larry Pardey, who are known as "America's first cruising couple," and their mantra of "Go small, go simple, go now" but we weren't anywhere near the experienced world sailors they were. They logged over 50,000 miles using only the power from their sails, but we agreed that for us, a reliable engine was a necessity… but it wasn't going to be cheap. As we prioritized the list, hard decisions were made on what we were willing to live without.

Chewbacca's original power came from a worn out two-stroke outboard motor that swung down from a nacelle or pod beneath the cockpit floor. Hot on Bruce's list was replacing it with a 9.9 horsepower outboard engine designed specifically for sailboats. While most cruising boats boasted a diesel engine of 100 or more horsepower, *Chewbacca's* torpedo like racing hulls were so efficient, a small dinghy motor was all the power required.

With the new engine installed, we practiced our docking, but even with the oversized propeller offering better maneuverability the words adrenaline-laced described our efforts to glide effortlessly into our double wide slip. Most cruising boats are 10 feet wide, but *Chewbacca* had a rather extreme 22-foot beam, which made for a stable racing platform, but presented several challenges. "OK, it's gotta be easier than this. I'm asking Gary for advice" was Bruce's response as he coiled the lines and sought out a fellow catamaran owner. A half hour later, he returned, we untied the lines, circled the marina basin and when we docked, Bruce backed her in stern first. "Who would have thought backing into our slip would be the way to go? Now… I wonder if Gary has any advice on how to tack this beast more efficiently than we've been doing it," and with that question hanging in the air, Bruce was off again.

Over the next five years our weekends were split between day sailing, nautical swap meets and marine stores looking for a deal on cruising gear. My favorite hangout was our local marine store's "bargain basement" where last year's models or returned items could be had for half price. Saturday mornings were dedicated to early morning dumpster diving at the neighboring boatyards where Bruce braved the smells to score discolored but perfectly good boat fenders, discarded pieces of teak and mostly functional boat gear. You never knew when someone else's junk was another's prize. For the girls, it was the ultimate Easter egg hunt.

Our spending escalated as we started to upgrade equipment, electronics and safety gear. To transform our racer into a cruising boat we bought and installed:

- *GPS*
- *Cruising mainsail and headsail*
- *Depth sounder*
- *Auto pilot*
- *VHF radio (line of sight, short distance)*
- *Ham radio (short wave, long distance)*
- *EPIRB (Emergency Position Indicating Radio Beacon)*
- *Life raft*
- *Safety netting around the lifelines*
- *A tri-color navigation light atop the mast*
- *Standing and running rigging with heavier gauged wire*
- *1 Fortress everyday anchor*
- *1 Fortress storm anchor*
- *100 feet of chain*
- *Manual anchor windlass*

Before we could head out to the tropics we needed a fresh coat of anti-fouling bottom paint. The nearest boatyard that could accommodate a catamaran as wide as *Chewbacca* was in Napa, so we made the 12-hour journey up the Napa River to take her out of the water. It was a long day and when I went to bed, we were perched eight feet up in the air on jack stands.

During the ensuing week, even though *Chewbacca* rested in the heart of the beautiful California wine country, I rarely looked up to take in the picturesque vineyards. An Indian summer lingered but it was lost on me with all the work at hand. Time is money in the world of boatyards and we vigorously attacked our list of chores from sun up to sun down. I wrote in my journal:

"Sometimes I feel weighted down and completely overwhelmed by our "To-Do" lists. They dominate my life. It would be so much easier to forego the dream and just stay put... but I really want to give the girls a chance to live an extraordinary life and experience paradise as we've seen it, so suck it up. No whining."

By the end of the second week, *Chewbacca* sported several new coats of bottom paint in addition to a new wind generator and a short-wave radio. To accommodate for full-time living Bruce built additional cabinets in the galley and shelving in the staterooms. Two new hatches were also installed for additional light and ventilation and thankfully Bruce's motto of "measure twice, cut once" was adhered to and the new hatches slid in perfectly.

Finally, satisfied with the fruits of our hard labor we launched *Chewbacca* back into her watery home where all boats belong.

Later that evening as I walked alone along the dock, the changes to *Chewbacca* were evident. The old racer now had a lived-in cruiser look. A second-hand windsurfer was lashed to the lifelines that were covered with fluttering dish towels left out to dry in the last of the sun's rays. A customized sunshade covered the once exposed cockpit, the wind generator whirled off our stern and an inflatable dinghy trailed behind serving as our family car. Our cheery salon was dotted with family photos and school crafts. The racing machine we had purchased was slowly morphing into a modest cruising catamaran but more importantly, *Chewbacca* was becoming our family home.

Just before we pushed off from the boatyard dock, we received our Vessel Documentation Number from the U.S. Coast Guard. In the cruising world, this was equivalent to trading in *Chewbacca's* California Driver's License for a U.S. Passport. It was a pivotal moment and she was now cleared to sail the world.

Chewbacca was ready... but were we?

CHAPTER 5

DOLLARS AND SENSE

"A small boat and a suitcase full of money beats a 40-footer tied to the bank every time."

-Unknown cruiser

I T WOULD BE CONSIDERED IN BAD TASTE TO ASK SOMEONE HOW MUCH MONEY they make, how much savings they have or how they could afford that luxury car, house on the ninth tee or a ski cabin at Lake Tahoe. But when you're 42, intentionally unemployed and living your dreams everyone wanted to know: HOW DID YOU DO IT?

- *"How could you both retire so young and take your kids sailing?"*
- *"Did you sell off one of those start-up dot com companies?"*
- *"Did a rich relative die and leave you money?"*
- *"Did you sell your house and everything to do this?"*
- *"Did you hit the lottery?"*
- *"Oh, how can you be so lucky?"*

Yeah, so lucky. We had more pocket money as poor college students than we had after handing over the check for *Chewbacca…* but we had our boat.

Long before we started looking for our dream boat, we decided we didn't want to finance a boat, but rather purchase one outright. The truth is, it limited our choices of boats and would drain our savings, but if we wanted to embark on an open-ended adventure, we thought we'd be more successful if we didn't have a boat mortgage hanging over our heads in addition to our house.

I was thankful that our passion to fulfill our dream and our material sacrifices had seen us clear to purchase a boat, yet we hadn't completely figured out just how we were going to create the finances that would sustain us during our planned adventure. I stared at Bruce across the dinner table and said, "So, what's the program?" Just like we had tackled so many other decisions in our young married lives, we approached the problem by taking pen to paper and formulated a plan.

We debated on how we should structure our cruising kitty. We could either:

A) *Build a large enough cruising kitty to live off of until we drew it down to zero, or*

B) *Bank enough principle so we could live off the interest and not touch the nest egg.*

Pros and cons. I leaned towards option B. I realized that this would be a greater temporary financial hardship, but I felt in my heart that it was the right thing to do. I wanted the option to cruise open-ended without a set end date. Could we live solely off the bank interest if we invested enough? I came up with a WAG (wild-ass-guess) as to our monthly expenses and then Bruce built in a little fudge factor and ran some calculations to figure out just how much money we needed to squirrel away to pay out enough interest to support ourselves:

$$12 \ E/RT = S$$

Where:

E = Estimate of monthly cruising expenses

R = Expected rate of return on investment

T = Anticipated months of savings

S = Monthly savings required to reach nest egg goal

I sat quietly watching Bruce run the calculations, then rerun the calculations. I could see by the look on his face that our adventure plans might come crashing to a halt right then and there. "Is it doable?" Bruce shook his head, "I don't know." He turned the calculator around so that I could see the display. The monthly savings requirements to build a realistic cruising kitty would consume well over half of Bruce's paycheck each month. Even for our frugal family that was a pretty steep climb.

Bruce spun the calculator around and started punching more numbers. I watched in silence knowing we were going to come up short. *Is this where it would end?* For five minutes, I sat and listened to the clicking of the calculator keys and observing Bruce shake his head. Suddenly he looked up with a grin "I think we can do this." He paused and went back to his scribbled notes and his finger ran across the calculator keys one more time. "We gotta get serious and find some fat rabbits in here." OK, no one else understood Bruce's lingo but I got it. Bruce was hunting for the easy target areas where we could trim our expenses and at the same time, try to uncover forgotten assets. The fat rabbits.

Out came a clean sheet of graph paper. I sharpened my pencil and captured our actual current financial commitments and determined to the penny how much we were truly living on per month. I had an idea but was a little surprised when I broke it down into categories and columns. Bruce had basically two columns; *Essentials vs. Nonessentials* or what I referred to as *Needs* vs. *Wants*. Food and utilities went into column #1, while eating out and new furniture went into column #2. This didn't mean we couldn't eat out, it only highlighted that it was "nonessential" and it was up to us to make that choice. I could already tell where my shoe fund was going to land. As the columns filled in, Bruce highlighted which costs or outlays would not be following us on our adventure. House insurance, mortgage payment and car insurance were highlighted but they were soon replaced in the bottom column by boat insurance, boat maintenance and estimated marina expenses.

Bruce paused when it came to the house mortgage payment. Was it essential? We could sell our three-bedroom house and really boost the cruising kitty, but then we would lose our stake in the strong California housing market. I feared that once we sold, we would never be able to buy our way back in. Bruce made some additional notes and looked up wanting to know if I was ready for a really crazy idea. "We could downsize the house. We could look for a smaller fixer upper, sell the bigger house and bank the difference. It's the best of both worlds." I added "OK, a smaller house would be easier to rent, especially if it had no yard, and if we were careful, the rental income would cover the mortgage and property taxes and our net outlay would be zero." That's a lot of "If's" but as the pencil moved from column to column, I could see our plan coming into focus.

Once we figured our barebones living expenses without any frills, I trusted that our basic needs and wants wouldn't drastically change after we set off cruising. I also trusted that we could maintain self-control when it came to our spending. However, like everyone else starting a new endeavor, I only had a general idea of how much we needed while cruising and wouldn't know for certain until we were out there and living the life.

Hardly a piece of romantic bedroom décor, a not so subtle three-foot tall fundraising thermometer hung behind the door that measured our monthly financial progress. Some months it was hard to save. Decembers were especially tough to maintain our budget. We didn't want Mr. Grinch to steal Christmas so we learned to shop for Christmas year-round. We didn't rule out shopping at garage sales and second-hand stores for clothing and household items. I was astounded how simple cost cutting practices added up month after month and year after year. The months when our property tax and home/car insurance policies came due were the most difficult, so I couldn't always color in our savings thermometer and there were times when progress seemed painfully slow... but we pressed on. *Stay focused and keep your eye on the prize*, was my unwavering mantra.

We spent every free weekend aboard *Chewbacca*. I often walked along the deck with a notepad in hand while Bruce dictated what gadget or gizmo he thought we needed to install. Sometimes I would question him if this was a *want or a need*. When he reached the end, we switched places and I would add my vision for our home on the water while Bruce scribed and asked if this or that was an *essential or nonessential* item. Our combined ideas began the process of turning our racing boat into the ultimate spartan cruising boat. While doing this exercise one autumn evening we had the good fortune to meet our marina neighbors.

Lounging in his cockpit with his wife Sally, Bobby shouted a "Howdy neighbor." Leaning over his lifelines he continued, "Looks like you kids are prepping your cat for a big cruise." Looking back, he toasted to his own boat, "We left in *Sally Ann* and cruised around Mexico... got as far as Puerto Vallarta."

"Did you like it?" I asked, edging closer wanting to hear more. "Well, we loved it... but we made a mistake that I hope you won't make." Bruce and I exchanged glances wondering what was coming. Sally stepped onto the dock and confessed in a somber voice, "We spent all our time in marinas and before we knew it, our cruising kitty was depleted, and we had to come back home to work. We were having such a good time, we forgot to pace ourselves and our money ran out."

They both looked so wistful, it was heartbreaking. "We only lasted a year. But it was a great year of partying on the *Sally Ann* with friends."

I couldn't picture us toting our youngsters to nightclubs and bars, partying with friends. But Bobby and Sally's serious message gave me pause. It was an early wakeup call that living too extravagantly could reduce our time in paradise.

CHAPTER 6

THE ODD COUPLE

"Procrastination is the graveyard of most dreams."

-Edmond Mbiaka, Writer

T HE CLOCK WAS TICKING. IF WE WANTED TO GO CRUISING WHILE THE GIRLS were still young enough to want to go on an adventure with their parents, we had to get moving. For safety reasons, we couldn't go before they were mature enough to understand the responsibilities and dangers of living at sea and be proficient swimmers. Quincy was now six months old and Kendall two and a half, so that left us the next five years to build our cruising kitty, outfit *Chewbacca* and now the hardest phase was about to begin… preparing ourselves.

Maybe we could have postponed the adventure and completed our tasks at a more leisurely, sane pace, but we were aiming for that sweet spot of opportunity before the girls reached their teens and before our aging parents needed our assistance. I had witnessed too many dreams abandoned by others to dally.

I stared at our initial *THINGS TO-DO* list in disbelief and I tried not to feel defeated before we had even crossed the first item off:

- *Swim lessons for the girls*
- *Prepare myself to homeschool*
- *Advanced First Aid*
- *Ham radio advanced class*
- *Create a Living Trust*
- *Apply for passports*
- *Contract a property manager*

- *Meet with a financial planner to set up an account and ATM card to draw a monthly allowance*
- *Meet with family physician to plan and create a comprehensive medical kit*
- *Immunizations*
- *Get new house ready to rent*

And the list kept growing. Our bedroom wall became the project board with dozens and dozens of yellow sticky notes. We divided the wall into *THINGS TO BUY*, *BOAT PROJECTS*, *CLASSES TO TAKE* and a special category for *NON-BOAT PROJECTS*, such as immunizations, swim lessons and house projects to be completed before Departure Day or D-Day, as we called it. We also had to categorize the list with a timeline. Immunizations had to be administered over a period of months, so we couldn't save that until a week before departure. As we completed the tasks we tossed a coin to see who got to rip down the note and tear it to pieces. We felt a sense of shared accomplishment as we steadily plucked off the notes and inched ever closer to realizing our dream.

To prepare for home-schooling, I gained experience teaching a small group of preschoolers. When Kendall progressed into Kindergarten I assisted in her classroom and as part of the bargain I was allowed to bring along three-year-old Quincy to be a part of the class. Homeschooling was still out-of-the-box thinking at the time, then add in sailing to foreign lands and I seemed quite the renegade to Kendall's principal when I explained why both our girls wouldn't be coming to school anymore. The principal was flabbergasted and the look of disbelief on her face was heart wrenching. *Was I that bad of a mother?* Everyone looked at me like I was gambling with my children's future. I felt like a delinquent and worried that a social worker would come knocking on our door.

Deviating from the main-stream didn't feel irresponsible to me; on the contrary, I thought it brought a deeper and richer life. But our choices were swiftly scrutinized, and judgement passed. Our future was speculated upon and others' opinions hailed down from out of the blue. Why didn't everyone believe as I did; *All the good fruit is out on the limbs.* But the critics weighed in; usually beginning with "Are you crazy?"

- *Homeschooling is unproven.*
- *What about the girl's lack of interaction with their peers?*
- *Won't they be socially stunted?*
- *How can you leave your career?*
- *You obviously haven't thought this thing through.*

I remained undeterred by the naysayers and as my confidence rose in my own decision making I realized that it was unnecessary, and in fact, potentially harmful to be held back by others' opinions.

We had the only boat in the marina with a playpen in the salon and a baby gate across the companionway. A Johnny Jumper was slung over the boom and hung through the overhead hatch, becoming a perfect high chair for our crammed quarters. The intimate salon with its four-foot headroom became the ultimate playhouse or "Hobbit Hole" for *Chewbacca's* pint-sized crew.

We continued to prepare ourselves by attending sail repair demonstrations, engine maintenance clinics and by taking classes on advanced first aid and coastal navigation. We had our used life raft inspected and re-certified. Bruce deployed it with a strong tug on the moldy pull tab and the bright orange igloo inflated with a whoosh on the workshop floor. The kids bounced on the musty orange tubes while we sorted through dead batteries, expired flares, emergency rations, rusty fishhooks and deteriorated first aid supplies circa 1970. Climbing in with the girls, I prayed we would never need to see the inside again.

Amidst all these preparations we sold our house and purchased a smaller townhome that was better suited as rental property. We moved in and Bruce stopped installing boat gear just long enough to tile, carpet, paint and do some remodeling on what we hoped would be a small stake in the housing market when we returned.

If we thought downsizing from a bigger house to a smaller one was brutal, we were in for a rude awakening when six months later we moved from the townhome to the boat. I hadn't a clue what we would have to leave behind when we moved from a three-bedroom, two-bath house to a 33-foot sailboat. That's right. THIRTY-THREE FEET! We should have tried living in our walk-in closet as a test!

Procrastination, more than personal health, family emergencies or natural disasters is most often the stake driven into the heart of many well-intended cruising plans. I didn't want to end up a statistic like so many, so we decided to draw a line in the sand and commit to a cast-off date. Determined to keep on schedule we signed up with a fun rally sailing from San Diego, California to Cabo San Lucas, Mexico. We plunked down the $100 entry fee and made a promise to be there. D-Day was marked on the calendar in ink and was closing in fast.

We basked in the positive vibes and encouragement from family, friends and marina neighbors and felt their enthusiasm carrying us ever closer towards the starting line.

Six months before D-Day, all our belongings fit inside our garage. We agreed that any item that could be easily purchased upon our return would be sold or given away.

At three months and counting, our "land life" belongings had shrunk significantly, while our "sea life" pile began to grow.

With less than one month remaining, we had finally reached our financial and personal goals for our great escape. The project wall was bare, and the paper savings thermometer was colored to the top.

At our final garage sale, we sold everything left in the house, including our beds, kitchen table and chairs. But I wasn't sad. I felt free and energized.

We sat Indian style that evening in our hollow kitchen, eating a takeout pizza. The girls ran unbridled through the open rooms, their laughter bouncing off the sterile walls. Clearing away the grease stained cardboard box and empty paper cups, I realized we'd sold our beds. Oops. The house had become an empty shell while *Chewbacca* waited for us at the dock.

CHAPTER 7

BLAST OFF

"Nothing diminishes anxiety faster than action."

-Walter Anderson, American painter & writer

I WONDERED HOW I WOULD LIKE THE CRUISING LIFE THE SECOND TIME AROUND. This time was different. It wasn't just Bruce and I crewing on other people's boats hitchhiking our way across the Pacific. We had a young family and our own boat. If things went awry, we couldn't simply fly home or change boats for a new destination. New fears began to nibble around my periphery.

Would we have enough money month after month? What if we hated this endeavor? What if the girls hated it? What if we wrecked *Chewbacca*? What if one of us got injured or worse yet, we could all die.

I harbored secret fears of us contracting some tropical illness that a swig of Pepto-Bismol, a slathering of antibiotic cream and a band-aid couldn't cure. And my fears were not totally unfounded. During a boat show seminar, I learned that it wasn't uncommon for circumnavigators to have their appendix and tonsils removed in preparation for facing the open ocean, far from medical support. Jeez! And here I was worried about my family getting their tetanus shots and teeth cleaned.

My biggest concern was keeping the girls safely onboard *Chewbacca*. It was serious business and we practiced boat safety at the dock and while sailing. Whenever the girls were topsides, each wore a life vest with their safety harnesses clipped onto a stainless-steel bar welded under the cockpit chairs. The tether was long enough to allow movement within *Chewbacca's* small cockpit, but not long enough to reach the edges of the boat. They each had their favorite Beanie Baby tied with a tether through a buttonhole on their jacket.

Everyone, including stuffed pets needed to stay safely aboard while at sea. Growing up around boats the girls viewed these safety measures and the small living quarters as perfectly normal.

One day it dawned on me that our kids were about to embark on a Carnival Cruise, while Bruce and I were literally driving the boat. The girls, being only five and seven, had some advantages during this chapter of our adventure:

- *They were oblivious to parental concerns.*
- *They only enjoyed each moment for what it was…a time to play and explore.*
- *Both girls were too young to stand watch or fully participate in trimming the sails or maintaining the boat, so they happily went along as contented passengers.*

Some people thought we were crazy traipsing off into the wild blue yonder, taking a chance on an adventure, and exposing our children to a nontraditional life. Were we realistic about potential cruel realities of life at sea? On one side of my brain, thoughts of potential disasters lurked. Why were we exposing ourselves to all these dangers? But the other half reasoned that Bruce and I were armed with enough sailing experience to succeed…at least to Mexico.

Sobering questions danced before me. *Would I be competent in my roles as teacher, parent and first mate? Would the girls need remedial education when we returned? Would they be social outcasts as so many hinted? Which of us would need therapy? Were we sufficiently prepared? What about Chewbacca?*

I made a pact with myself to become more than merely Bruce's assistant or homemaker on the water. I vowed to become an equal partner with Bruce in the sailing and maintenance of our home… but only time would tell.

Before we pushed *Chewbacca* away from the dock, I asked Bobby of the *Sally Ann* to take a family picture. I heard the camera shutter click like an exclamation point at the end of a sentence enticing me to turn the page to a new chapter. We cast off the dock lines and Bruce steered us out of the marina. A wave of fulfillment finally broke through my jumble of feelings, quelling most of my anxious thoughts. I cracked open a brand new journal and made my first entry.

"October 3rd: We're really doing this!"

We were all gathered in the cockpit, bundled against the cold as *Chewbacca* slipped by the San Francisco waterfront and I wondered when we would see this familiar skyline again. To our starboard lay Alcatraz with a swirling layer of fog cloaking its cold concrete facade. An hour later, the shadow of the Golden Gate Bridge passed overhead and then silently fell behind us. We entered the Pacific Ocean, took a left turn and so began our sabbatical at sea.

CHAPTER 8

FINALLY LIVIN THE DREAM

"It is so hard to leave-until you leave. And then it is the easiest goddamned thing in the world."

-John Green, Author

WE HAD THREE WEEKS TO MAKE OUR WAY TO THE RALLY STARTING POINT in San Diego. It would have been a 90-minute flight, but we weren't flying. It would have been an eight-hour drive, but we weren't driving. With an average speed of five knots, *Chewbacca* could only cover a little over 100 miles per day... if everything went perfectly. So, three weeks seemed about right.

We were only two days down the coast and topping off our gas cans at the fuel dock when a sleek, shiny new sailboat pulled up behind us. As we caught their dock lines I instantly recognized the distinctive markings of a "kid" boat. Stuffed toys in the cockpit and kids sized shoes outside the companionway door. Like us they were beginning their cruising adventure heading south for warmer weather. But that's where the comparison ended.

Leaning over the lifelines we shared expectations and apprehensions of this new lifestyle. The mom mapped out an aggressive schedule to tour as far south as Panama, and then sail back and return to work the following year. A 12-month tour. She literally held up her hand and ticked off ports of call on her fingers in a well-rehearsed succession. Truthfully, most of the ports I never heard of as I nodded along with the geographical tour. Who was I to confess I learned my geography of cruising ports by watching reruns of *"The Love Boat."*

When she inquired about our plans, I confessed that we hadn't planned much past Cabo San Lucas but would probably see how

Mexico went the first year or so. I could see in her eyes as they roamed over *Chewie* that she didn't believe our scruffy little boat and our lack of planning would even see San Diego, much less Mexico. In a flash their fuel tanks were topped off, honey colored teak decks sprayed down with fresh water, monogrammed fenders briskly pulled aboard, and their matching lines retrieved and nautically coiled. We were left waving goodbye to their wake.

Maybe we weren't planning this right. They seemed so together, mapped out, so… scheduled. And here we were drifting along. Doubt crept into my mind. "Maybe we should make a plan, commit to a schedule, and draw a route past Mexico," I posed. Bruce just shrugged and said that it didn't matter where we were the next year. In 12 months the other family would be back at work and we would be sipping margaritas on a white sand beach somewhere warm. OK, this wasn't exactly the schedule I was looking for, but you gotta love a man with a plan.

Once back on the "road" Bruce reached over and adjusted *Han Solo*, our trusty autopilot. *Han* was a Godsend and took over the tedious task of steering *Chewbacca* as she slipped into the night. *Han* never suffered from the cold, never got hungry or tired, always steered with a steady hand… and never needed a pee break. The girls had already shed their bulky winter clothes for zip up one-piece pajamas and said good night. With not a care in the world they snuggled beneath their covers and the waves sang a lullaby of their own as *Chewbacca* rocked them to sleep.

I checked our GPS course, heading and depth, while Bruce marked our progress on the paper chart spread out on the salon table. We couldn't be too careful. I'd heard too many horror stories that ended tragically due to navigational errors to be complacent. I felt like a surgeon in the operating room as I laid out our night watch instruments neatly on the salon table:

- *Chart*
- *Binoculars*
- *Flash light*
- *Hand held compass*
- *Pencils*

- *Ruler*

- *Dividers*

Besides losing someone overboard, my next greatest fear was striking a barely submerged steel shipping container lost off a cargo ship.

Settling in for my first night watch on *Chewbacca*, my mind drifted back to another night watch 10 years earlier while we were hitchhiking our way across the Pacific. We were sailing in the same ocean but a few hundred miles to the southwest of where *Chewbacca* was now. And like this night, there was nothing around, so I stargazed with a sliver of moon as my only companion. At night, there are no references in the sea to guide you. No street signs, no lane markers, no guard rails. It's like moving along in a black void unless you are lucky enough to have a full moon keeping you company. I should have felt lonely, but I only felt contentment being on the open ocean. We were safe, away from everything, and I could relax. I scanned ahead like always not expecting to see anything. I was making a second pass when my eyes caught a reflection off the water. A split-second glint of something. I stood up from behind the wheel to get a better look as *Journey* slipped across the flat water. Silver ripples shimmered from the moonlight flickering across the surface, but little else. Maybe it was nothing. Or was it? The hairs stood up on the back of my neck as I clicked the autopilot 15° to starboard. Nothing. Just my stupid, overactive imagination working overtime on a lonely stretch of ocean. I kept staring into the darkness… and there it was. *Journey* glided silently by a half-submerged cargo container with only feet to spare. An unlit specter.

Recalling that night, even a decade later was unsettling, and it didn't matter to me that we were sailing well away from the shipping lanes, I still harbored a fear of striking a half-submerged object. The truth was our light balsa-cored racing construction was no match for any collision.

My journal entry that night simply read:

> *Midnight. Bruce is off watch catching some sleep which leaves me in charge. Two hours of keeping a constant watch scanning the*

waters, keeping our boat and ourselves out of harm's way is more of a strain than I remembered. I can't wait for sunrise.

With the bitter cold offshore weather, I voted for two-hour watches. My attention started to drift when the cold seeped up through my tennis shoes, past my thick woolen socks and into my bones. As I stood in the cockpit not even my earmuffs, stocking hat and a fleece scarf were able to keep the warmth in. A freezing tail wind broke through my layers of T-shirts, sweat shirts, jacket and foul weather gear. I shivered. *Chewbacca's* open cockpit was designed for a warm tropical climate in the southern hemisphere, not for the California coast in October. I waddled through my watch routine looking like an Emperor Penguin tottering across an Antarctic ice floe rather than a sailor heading south. Southern waters couldn't come fast enough I thought, as another arctic like blast hit my already numb face. At long last my two hours were up, and I reached down and tapped Bruce's leg to signal it was his turn to stand watch.

The variable coastal winds gave us plenty of opportunities to practice changing the sails. The accelerator and brake pedal on a sailboat are the sails, and to keep the boat in control and balanced they require constant tending, and even switching to different sized sails when the weather conditions change. Our mainsail had reef points or tie-off points that allowed us to shorten a sail big enough to cover a driveway down to a mere bedsheet, all without removing the sail. It took both of us to wrestle down and reef the powerful mainsail to keep *Chewbacca* under control in storm conditions. But when we reduced the mainsail, we also needed to reduce the headsail to keep the boat balanced.

In heavy weather it was Bruce's job to go out alone on the tramp to change the headsail. He had to first clip into the safety line to keep from being thrown off our little bucking bronco as he crawled his way along the deck getting doused with frigid salt water with each dip of *Chewbacca's* bows into the cresting waves. After he made his way to the bow I would release the halyard from the safe confines of the cockpit and watch Bruce claw down the angry sail and secure it to the tramp with bungie cords before it could be blown overboard. He then dragged the smaller sail from the locker and clipped it onto the headstay and then signaled for me to hoist it skyward. He really had the short end of the stick as the "snotty-weather-headsail-changer guy." When the squall passed, the process was reversed.

It didn't take me long to conclude that this aspect of sailing was anything but romantic.

The decision to shorten sail was made quickly when the sky darkened, the wind increased and the once little ripples on the water were whipped up into white caps. An old sailor's adage is *"If you have to ask if it's time to reef the sail, it's already too late."* In one brutal stretch of squally weather that lasted five hours, I counted eight sail changes.

While Bruce and I tackled the sailing, the girls busied themselves crafting, reading and preparing the watch snacks. They delivered up trays of chunky peanut butter on Ritz crackers and bags of nuts, hard candy, trail mix and granola bars…until their bedtime called.

Bruce sharpened his coastal navigational skills and penciled little X's on the paper charts every half hour to mark our progress. The GPS display gave our latitude and longitude, but Bruce also took bearings off landmarks ashore to confirm our position. The chart began to look like a cross stitch sampler memorializing our tracks south.

We tag-teamed the sailing duty so the off-watch person could doze on the cockpit bench and stay sort of warm wrapped in a layer of blankets, keeping nearby and available for a sail change or a second opinion if another boat's course came into question.

During my second night shift, I noted the navigation lights of an approaching ship changing from red to green, back to red and then green again. For 15 minutes, I watched with growing nervousness as this ship zigzagged its way inbound of us. The green light revealed his starboard side, then the red light exposed his port side. *Why was this fool tacking back and forth in front of me?* He was getting closer and I tried to hail him on the VHF radio but got no response. He continued to get closer and finally I jabbed Bruce awake and pointed out the misguided ship to our port. Still groggy, he snatched the binoculars for a closer look and after a while noted the stranger's navigation light went from GREEN-YELLOW-RED-GREEN-YELLOW-RED. Wait, there is no YELLOW navigation light. My "freighter" turned out to be a traffic light along the Pacific Coast Highway. "Perhaps it's time we change watch," noted Bruce chuckling.

CHAPTER 9

A ROCKY START

"You know, Hobbes, some days even my lucky rocket ship underpants don't help."

-Bill Watterson, American Cartoonist

W E WERE TWO DAYS SOUTH OF MONTEREY WHEN THE WEATHER SUDDENLY deteriorated. The wind increased, whipping the seas into a choppy froth. VHF radio chatter between the offshore fishing boats said a gale was headed our way. The National Weather Service defines a gale as a strong wind packing 34-47 knots. "That's 50 miles an hour" said Bruce as he hastily consulted our chart and without hesitation I started the engine and we high-tailed it to the nearest protected harbor, Port San Luis.

Bruce calculated that we were only three hours from shelter. Only. But when your boat is running from a storm into sharp headwinds time has a funny way of standing still. Finally, I could make out the sanctuary of the protected harbor just ahead and soon we would be safe. We were so close.

BANG. The engine gave a sudden jolt and then…SILENCE. I spoke too soon.

Lying on his belly with his head dipping below the frigid water with each wave, Bruce spied the problem. Our prop was entangled in thick yellow rope from a submerged crab pot. I ran to the galley and grabbed the nearest knife, so Bruce could cut the rope free. As my hand found Bruce's beneath the cold salt water I thought perhaps I should have reached for one of my crappier steak knives instead of my prized burled Maplewood handled bread knife! After the rope was cut free he stood up shaking the seawater from his head and shoulders. Shivering he lowered the motor down and restarted it. *Chewbacca* moved forward another few yards… BANG!

It happened again. "Damn. We're almost there and some crazy fisherman figured it would be more convenient to set his crab pots across the harbor entrance" muttered Bruce. He reached down and cut the second line but when he engaged the motor our propeller shook like a wheel badly out of alignment. It was bent and we didn't have a spare. Not so good planning. We had no choice but to limp the engine the last half mile into the harbor where it appeared the entire Pacific Coast fishing fleet was also seeking shelter from the storm. Bruce steered to an open mooring and leaning over the bow I snagged the slimy rope with the boat hook on my first try. From a distance it might have even looked like we knew what we were doing.

Now that we were safe from the storm we had to solve our propeller problem. Bruce hitched a ride to shore with the Harbor Master to check in and radioed back that a Yamaha dealer was right on the harbor property. "That's great," I said, my spirits rising just a bit. Then he radioed back, "OK there's no replacement propeller in stock but he can have one shipped out of Los Angeles. Take about a week." "Shit," I said too late to retract the word over the radio. "So, what do we do now?" Two minutes later, Bruce was back on the VHF. The dealer realized the predicament we were in or maybe he just heard the exasperation in my voice over the radio because he graciously offered to remove the prop off his showroom model and sell it to us. I stood grinning and nodding into the radio mic. Bruce broke the spell and came back with even more good news. As a bonus, the shop owner took our old bent prop to his repair shop and with a little heat, beat it back into reasonable shape.

Bruce arrived back to *Chewbacca* like a returning conqueror with not one but two props in his hands. He got to work reinstalling our new replacement propeller while I began to unpack and inflate our dinghy for a trip ashore to let the girls burn off some energy. Our destination was a dilapidated floating dock tethered under the pier. As Bruce motored around looking for a space to nudge into, I noticed that all the fishermen's skiffs were metal and looked quite robust but even they showed signs of hard use. Scanning the wooden dock I discovered why. It was thick with dagger sharp barnacles and a halo of rusty nails protruded from its perimeter.

This would be the first and last stop for our pretty little inflatable if we tied up here. Kendall even pointed out, "It'd be like rubbing against a porcupine." Only temporarily defeated we motored back to *Chewbacca* and unveiled our secret weapon…our bulletproof Porta-Bote. Admittedly ugly, this sturdy, kidproof, plastic folding dinghy stood a better chance at surviving than our inflatable dinghy any day. We motored back in our "plastic-fantastic" and nudged our way amongst the armored dinks.

It took nearly a week, but the forecasted calm weather finally arrived. I awoke at first light to find the fishing fleet was already crossing the horizon. Must be time to go. We hoisted our storm sails and cautiously followed the armada, setting our course for the infamous Point Conception. The prominent land mass jutted out from shore like too big of a nose on too small of a face. We had been warned that the waves could stack up around the point making for an especially treacherous rounding. I crossed my fingers.

As we drew closer into the arms of the open ocean, the seas crested at 12 feet. I wasn't so sure this was a good time for our little sailboat to have left the protected harbor. I sat frozen in the cockpit gripping my seat as the waves towered high above our stern like a foreboding wall. Bruce surveyed our surroundings and confirmed that with the storm's passing, both wind and sea were combining forces propelling us swiftly towards our destination. The severe conditions called for Bruce to hand steer through the liquid slalom course as *Chewbacca* surfed down the steep waves. We were approaching three times our normal cruising speed, and I found the sensation of speed both big-time frightening and a little exhilarating.

I watched Bruce's face closely for any apprehension. I guessed we were OK because a grin stretched across his face as hour after hour we surfed along bundled up against the cold. My rule of thumb; if Bruce kept smiling, I knew our situation was manageable. I slowly relaxed my grip on the cabin top as the nautical miles ticked off rapidly under the rudders and I felt myself smiling. Better than any carnival ride, the girls faces expressed only sheer exuberance galloping with the waves. A few hours later, *Chewbacca* left Point Conception in her wake and I danced a little jig inside that I could cross off our first major milestone.

We sailed through the moonless night and by dawn the wind and seas had smoothed out and by lunch we were in a dead calm. Welcome to Southern California. This was the first dead calm I had experienced aboard *Chewbacca* as she bobbed uncomfortably in the placid water. I cranked on the engine to get us moving and felt lucky this wasn't the doldrums. That band of miserable weather lurked a thousand miles away along the equator and I reflected on the most annoying days of my first long ocean passage aboard *Journey* in the B.K. days. Before Kids.

We were two days south of the equator when the steady trade winds abandoned us and the doldrums enveloped *Journey*. Our progress was numbingly slow. Beyond slow. A couple of my watch entries logged zero miles as the sails hung limp against the mast. *Journey's* rigging creaked in the stagnant air and grew beyond annoying. I looked hopefully to the horizon for a tug of wind. Nothing. I sat on sweat soaked cushions hording the precious shade of the cockpit awning and was too lethargic to even fetch a pail of tepid ocean water to pour over my burning head. I had to put my book aside as sweat dripped from my nose and blurred the words on the page. Night gave little relief as we drifted in a vacuum. Time stood infuriatingly still.

I thought perhaps this was where our Pacific hitchhiking adventure would end; marooned in the middle of the ocean. *Would someone find our lifeless bodies adrift on this cloudless sea, or would the currents carry our bleached skeletons to some distant shore?*

Journey's little diesel engine provided us with enough battery power for running our nighttime navigation lights and to power the ham radio, but we didn't carry enough fuel to motor our way out of the doldrums. We were way off the shipping lanes and no other sailboats were in our area. In fact, our nightly check-in with the Maritime Net essentially told the other boats to stay out of this wind void. We were on our own. I kept a keen eye on our fresh water supply and our food lockers, but as far as getting out of this hole, we would just have to wait it out.

I was half asleep in the cockpit when I felt the slightest cooling breath of air on my cheek. I sat up and scanned the horizon. The sun's glare was blinding as I confirmed the seas remained a glassy pond. Yet there was a slight movement in the air… or perhaps it was just my imagination. I grabbed the binoculars and scanned the horizon again. Two distant puff balls were rising from the ocean where just before placid water only reflected empty sky. I called Bruce on deck to confirm what might just have been a desert mirage. We drifted and waited and watched intently for two more days praying for the clouds to come nearer.

Eight days after being swallowed up by the windless band of blue, Mother Nature finally released her grip on us and the trade winds filled the sails and coaxed us towards our South Pacific island destination.

I was shaken out of my daydream as the steady drone of *Chewbacca's* engine began to sputter and gasp. *CRAP! NOW WHAT?* I was on watch and responsible to ensure we didn't run out of fuel. Before Bruce could reach the cockpit I quickly checked the little five-gallon plastic tank and confirmed that we were more than half-full. Thank God, not my fault. Bruce thought the sputtering sounded as if junk was lodged in the carburetor choking the flow of fuel. Every time I lowered the RPM or shifted the engine into neutral it died. Our only option was to motor the engine at full throttle. My imagination ran into overdrive as an image unfolded of *Chewbacca* docking at full speed… like an emergency landing on an aircraft carrier. Double crap!

As the shoreline came into view, Bruce hailed the marina office on the radio and explained our situation to a very mellow voice at the other end. "No problem Dude…just pull up to the fuel dock… we'll get you a slip." Bruce replied, "OK, I just want you to understand that we have engine problems and we will be coming in full throttle, so we will need help on the dock with our lines." "Dude you'll be fine, don't worry," repeated the sleepy voice.

Chewbacca swept in parallel to the empty fuel dock at warp speed. Bruce cut the engine and we both leapt off the runaway boat in unison.

We each threw a quick knot on the nearest dock cleat and *Chewbacca* jerked to an abrupt stop. I felt the sudden rush of adrenalin pumping through my veins and sat down, head between my knees, to stave off the dizzying effect. They say cruising is 98% boredom and 2% sheer terror and I think I just used up my 2%! My knees were still shaking as we entered the Harbor Master's office. From behind the counter I instantly recognized the voice. "Dude, you guys rock! Like watching Maverick doing a carrier landing." If only he knew.

"Mr. Mellow" turned and surveyed his wall map of available slips. He pointed to one, even after Bruce explained we preferred to remain where we were, at least until we got our engine sorted out. "Here's a perfect end tie just up the way," he replied proudly, tapping to a spot up the fairway. Reluctantly, we untied and at full throttle ran up the narrow channel of the marina. I wasn't looking forward to another carrier landing.

As we approached the assigned slip, low and behold, there was another boat parked there. Mr. Mellow's master map was obviously not up to date. Bruce made a hard 180 in the tight space, which was no small feat for a sailboat with a 22-foot beam. I informed Mr. Mellow of the situation over the radio while Bruce continued to steer *Chewbacca* in tight circles dodging other sailboats and a weekend daredevil kayaker trying to sneak between our hulls. Didn't the idiot realize there was a 12-inch razor sharp propeller under there churning white water like a giant margarita blender? Maybe my high-pitched voice over the radio lit a fire under Mr. Mellow's butt because moments later the offending boat zipped away. We repeated our high-speed docking maneuvers and by then my nerves were frayed rope.

Was this the cruising life I had bargained for? I'd been out of my comfort zone so much lately that it was becoming the new normal. We were only halfway to San Diego and already we had to take shelter from a gale, busted a propeller and now our brand-new engine was broken-down. I was cold, tired, hungry and beyond grouchy. Things weren't going as smoothly as I had fantasized. Bruce and I slumped in our tiny cockpit confronted with the darker realities of the cruising life the last few days had brought.

Dejected, Bruce stared off the stern where his eyes caught a small metal sign displaying the Yamaha logo. With my arms folded and my back to him, I gazed through the columns of masts and spotted the bright neon signs of a laundromat AND a grocery store. Minutes later, the aroma of baking pizza wafting across the water brought the girls into the cockpit. "This place is great" exclaimed Kendall excitedly and my pessimistic mood began to thaw. *Maybe it wasn't time to quit just yet.*

CHAPTER 10

THE CAPTAIN'S CHAIR

"Life shrinks or expands in proportion to one's courage."

-Anais Nin, Author

STALKING OUR TAIL WAS A DULL BLACK FIN SLICING THE WATER...A 20-FOOT TALL black fin.

We were just approaching the harbor entrance when the girls let out a squeal of excitement. I was focused on reading the depth sounder and pointing out the channel markers to Bruce when I looked back to see where the girls were pointing. Rarer, but just as exhilarating as having a Humpback Whale overtake our little boat, a matte black semi-submerged nuclear submarine silently glided past. As the girls waved enthusiastically from the cockpit of *Chewbacca*, the officers gave a crisp salute from their sleek conning tower. I couldn't have imagined a more exciting welcome to San Diego.

Scrutinizing our harbor chart, I located the free anchorage reserved for boats in transit simply marked A-9. The uninspiring name suited the location and an image of a seedy truck stop in Bakersfield sprung into my head. I wasn't far off. The designated square was squeezed full of sailboats and it took several passes around the perimeter to find even a single tight parking spot.

A true confession... in the five years we had owned *Chewbacca*, we had never anchored her. Never. We had all the gear, but never had occasion to actually set the hook. In the Bay, we would leave the dock, day sail and return. I had observed Bruce anchoring countless times while crewing in the South Pacific, but it's very different when you are the one standing all alone on the bow. I was thinking; *Maybe we should have practiced this a bit before now.*

I muscled the heavy forged steel anchor off its storage stand and just barely had it positioned on the bow roller when Bruce ghosted up to the drop site and hollered, "THIS LOOKS LIKE A GOOD SPOT… DROP IT HERE." Before I could comply, he gave the engine a little nudge in reverse to stop all forward motion. Whoa. I instantly lost my footing and as I stumbled to right myself the anchor slipped from my grasp, plummeting over the side. Forty-five pounds of solid steel belly flopped in the water and 100 feet of unbridled chain paid out between my gloved hands. Half a second before the runaway chain pulled me into the drink I released my death grip and allowed the rest of it to spill over into one big dog pile on the sludgy bottom. Not the proper way to set an anchor. My face glowed red with embarrassment and my heart pulsated from the adrenaline rush. First thought: *I hope nobody saw that fiasco.* Second thought: *I could have been seriously hurt had the chain wrapped around my foot and dragged me overboard to lay with the anchor.*

After composing myself I shouted to Bruce that I was OK. I was safe, but soon I felt the tears welling up in my eyes as I realized that I was not capable to do this job. The truth of the situation hit me like a sharp slap across the cheek… I had failed.

Being equal partners in our endeavor was important to me but the reality was clear; there were some duties that required more brawn than my 110 pounds possessed. I took a deep calming breath as I wiped the burning tears from my face. I clenched my hands in frustration and vowed: *This is OUR voyage, OUR joint endeavor damn it, and I want to play a crucial role and become an indispensable cruising partner.*

Bruce called me back to the cockpit. We had to anchor again and properly. An anchor has no holding power just resting on the sea bottom with the chain piled on top of it. I knew this. "Let's get that chain back on deck and I'll handle the anchor," he said gently as I pulled off my gloves and fetched his from the sail locker. We switched places. I took *Chewbacca's* helm while he began pulling up the heavy chain, hand over hand. Once everything was aboard I steered a circle around the anchorage and returned to our spot amidst 25 other boats. SLOW, SLOW… ALL STOP. NOW, SLOW REVERSE," Bruce called back instructions over his shoulder so I could hear them above the drone of the engine. As *Chewbacca* slowly backed up the anchor and subsequent chain slid overboard into the gooey mud bottom setting firmly. After she had settled comfortably into place, we talked. From that day forward Bruce took over setting the hook while I moved into the captain's chair for our "take-offs and landings." I knew I had to step up and hone my skills at the helm. As helmsman, I had to leave behind my old ways. In my new world there was no left or right, only port and starboard. God help me.

We had made it to the start of the fun rally that would mark our true departure from land life. The days of limitless hot showers, ice cubes at the press of a button, a pantry brimming with familiar food and a Walmart just five minutes down the road would vanish in our wake. Was I really ready for these sacrifices? "Last chance." I turned to face Bruce and he repeated, "Last chance. Are you in or do you want to turn back?" I responded, "In for a penny, in for a pound." *Let's do this*.

We were topped off with fuel, water and food. Our boat was ready, as was her crew. *Chewbacca* was the smallest boat registered in the cruisers rally and I steered her on a light breeze to meet up with the gathering fleet. She was in the company of 137 other vessels all bound for the same destination, 780 nautical miles away. The finish line lay six days ahead on what would hopefully be an easy downwind run.

We crept along under full sail towards the imaginary start line. I was just beginning to relax and settle into cruising mode when I glanced astern and spotted 90-feet of runaway fiberglass about to mow us down in their haste to be the first to pass the committee boats. This titan's crew was oblivious to our presence in their path and I instinctively jerked the tiller and peeled away as the behemoth smashed through the middle of a rolling Pacific swell. *Shit, they just barely missed us!*

This wasn't how I envisioned our adventure starting... with near catastrophe. All the joy was snatched from within me and replaced by fury. Wasn't anyone paying attention over there? My mind and body were on high alert, as I switched to *DEFCON 1*. There was no going back to my happy place, not just yet. I was beginning to realize this wasn't a casual fun sailing rally for many of these boats. Some captains were going for blood and wouldn't let any boats get in their way. The responsibility of keeping our boat and family safe weighed heavily on me as I shifted my senses into Mama Bear mode. *Chewbacca* had the pedigree and look of a serious racing catamaran, but she was a sheep in wolf's clothing. Only after the competing captains got close enough to see half of *Chewbacca's* crew were wearing Barney emblazoned life jackets and gleefully waving teddy bears did they deem us no threat.

The starting gun sounded and with spinnakers flying, the colorful fleet gradually spread out to the horizon. Some skippers choose to hang in tight and skirt the rocky shoreline while others like us preferred to sail 5 to 10 miles offshore. I wholeheartedly opted to leave more sea room between us, the fleet and land but remained on edge and wary of anyone encroaching in our space.

Once we were clear of the starting line I ducked below to prepare a simple lunch of tuna fish sandwiches. The first few days of any passage were set aside to gather my sea legs and adjust to new sleep patterns. The cabin felt especially confining and stuffy and I spent as little time as possible below, especially in the galley. I tried to enjoy the wide ocean view from the galley sink but I felt queasy even on our relatively stable platform. Gathering my goods, I headed topside. Initially it was better to do all prep work above decks, in the airy cockpit before taking food to the galley below to cook. In a few days, I would be able to spend unlimited hours below, but for now I was content to prepare food on deck. While I retrieved plates, the girls set up the cockpit table and we dined al fresco under the brilliant sky.

Night was approaching, signaling our ritual to shorten sail. I stood watch in the cockpit while Bruce went forward to change the headsail to a smaller one. Scanning the horizon something in the distance caught my eye. I could just make out a rectangle slab of white concrete on shore that denoted the U.S.-Mexican border passing to our left... or I should say on our port side. Ten years of preparation for this moment and without fanfare *Chewbacca* entered her first foreign waters propelled by gentle waves. As tradition dictated, we ceremoniously hoisted the small Mexican courtesy flag up to the spreaders as soon as the X on our chart put us in foreign waters. Seen as a gesture of respect and courtesy, all visiting ships must fly their host country's flag while in their territorial waters.

We set our course due south towards Turtle Bay along Mexico's Baja coast. Three days and nights of nonstop sailing lay before us. With steaming mugs of tea in hand we took turns standing watch over our new world. With the sun gone, we were flying blind on a black sea.

The sensation of sailing at night is like no other. Our silhouettes were framed by the greenish glow of the cockpit instruments and the only sounds I heard were the wind passing through the sails and the whoosh of the ocean as it was parted by *Chewbacca's* bows. We talked as only people talk when the outside world is at a distance and life is in focus. Once we left land, society as we knew it didn't exist. What did exist was our little ship and family wrapped securely in Neptune's arms. It was a heady feeling to have stayed our course all these years and although I was anxious to finish this passage, I wanted the moment to last forever.

Void of any scenery to use as a reference point I turned my head to embrace the company of the stars. Along the horizon, bright tri-color lights of white, red and green shone from each sailboat's mast, denoting their position on the black seas. The lights spread out joining the heavens in a moving constellation and served as a perpetual reminder that we were not alone.

I was snoozing in the cockpit when I felt Bruce tap my foot. "Time for your watch." "Uh, so soon?" I shifted into the helmsmen chair and took over as Watch Commander. Bruce gave me an update on our course and heading then greedily replaced my warm spot on the cockpit bench and pulled the blanket over his head. At least he was close if I needed help. I'd wait till he was just dozing before I tapped his foot in retaliation. I adjusted my harness and double checked that I was securely clipped into the cockpit.

I stared out into the darkness. The kitchen timer was set for seven minutes and when the alarm dinged, I stood up from the cockpit chair and made a complete scan of the black horizon to search for any other ships. I continually kept an eye on the compass course, GPS, depth sounder and wind conditions in case we needed to adjust or change out the sails. At night we relied solely on the instruments to feel our way across the ocean. At the end of each shift it was the responsibility of the person on watch to plot our GPS position on the chart. Throughout the night a line of neat little X's marched southward but for now only the eerie green glow of the GPS provided a strange comfort to me when all else was black.

Journal Entry:

> *2:00 a.m. Wind 12 knots from SSE, 2-foot seas, Speed 5.5 knots. Heading 185°. Crescent moon. I'm exhausted. two more nights to go.*

For me the sounds of the night are eerily amplified. Every slap of a wave, every creak of the boat, every breath exhaled by a visiting dolphin was as loud as a clap of thunder. Darkness magnified life and my senses were on edge. Primitive man was clearly at a disadvantage at night and modern man, for all his technology, is no better off. I pined for the warm glow of dawn and the first caress of the sun. My imagination was fueled as if on steroids and my evening coffee with its robust boost of caffeine didn't help!

When the girls woke, we shared a breakfast of instant oatmeal topped with granola and passed around a can of fruit cocktail with a communal spoon sticking out. Not gourmet, but a hit with the girls. I showed them where we had travelled during the night by tracing a pencil line down our X's on the chart. I then shared with them what sounds I'd heard, what I smelled and who stopped by to play in our wake while they were snug under their covers dreaming. "We had two pods of dolphins that streaked across the bows and I smelled the fishy exhale of a whale's breath just off the port stern. He didn't stay long though and rushed off to meet his lady friend." I often spun whimsical tales of our nautical encounters to the delight of the girls, but I didn't want to frighten them, so I left out the voices I heard while alone on watch… the indistinguishable voices in the dark.

CHAPTER 11

NOSEDIVE INTO THE PACIFIC

"Life is either a daring adventure or nothing at all."

-Helen Keller, Author

THE DAYS FLOWED BY AND THE MILES UNRAVELED BENEATH OUR HULLS IN THE comfort of routine. I was just finishing reading aloud the last chapter of *Little House in the Big Woods* when we merged with the fleet to drop anchor in Turtle Bay. I took my place at the helm and steered *Chewbacca* into the placid cove dotted with sailboats while Bruce pulled on his leather work gloves and made his way to the bow. The girls were perched on the cabin top and watched the new proceedings with interest. Tiller in hand, I listened for Bruce's instructions and guided *Chewbacca* into place as he released the anchor.

With the anchor down, Quincy assisted in cleaning up the foredeck and Kendall came down to the cockpit to read the GPS coordinates as I jotted them in the log book. We were beginning to formulate a post-passage routine not much different than unpacking the family car after a long road trip. I breathed a deep sigh of relief that we had completed the first leg of the rally unscathed.

Not fully comprehending the fact that Bruce and I had been up for 72 hours or the stress of our first long passage as a family, I went below for a short nap… and woke up 14 hours later!

Rejuvenated from my hibernation, I was raring to hit the beach. We ate a hearty breakfast and then prepared our dinghy to go ashore. As is tradition in the yachting world, dinghies have names and ours was a nod to our favorite movie, *Star Wars*. The *Blaster* had already survived a nail infested dock and now she was about to meet her first foreign shore. Through the binoculars, I spied neat rows of dinghies already pulled up on the sand and was looking forward to joining the party.

We had all dressed in our brand new, matching day-glow orange rally T-shirts. I pulled on my multi-pocketed heavy-duty cargo shorts and slid my feet into my new Teva sandals. We looked like cruisers ready to join in the festivities and I couldn't wait to feel my toes dig into the pristine white sand. Without a second thought we jumped in the dinghy and headed to shore.

Everything was going so right… before it went so wrong. Within a stones-throw from the beach the first wave crested below us twisting us sideways. This probably wasn't good because then the surf picked the dinghy up and rolled us like four tennis balls in a clothes dryer. Over and over the dinghy cart-wheeled through frothing seas. Each time we were upright I sputtered and gasped for air. After about five tosses we were spit up on the beach. NEWBIE was plastered on our foreheads as I gathered our family and tried to calm Kendall and Quincy who were understandably hysterical. I sat at the surfs edge and wiped dripping hair from the girls faces. I checked for blood, then signs of a concussion and felt their limbs. Nothing broken. Several cruisers ran to our assistance and grabbed onto the dinghy and wrestled it ashore. Thank God that sometimes the ignorant are spared from serious harm.

I guess we'd missed the "Surf Landing for Dummies" seminar and that aspect of the cruising life had proved a disastrous "learn by doing" exercise. Our light 2.7 outboard was great when I needed to lift it off *Chewbacca's* rail and hand it down to Bruce. But as we had just proven, it didn't have the horsepower to ride the waves safely ashore. Likewise, leaving the beach, I surmised that we didn't have the oomph to punch through the incoming surf and reach the flat water beyond. We were doomed both coming and going.

Instead of enjoying the festivities, Bruce spent time cleaning the dinghy engine of sand and used precious fresh water to flush out the carburetor.

"OK, let's not have a repeat performance," remarked Bruce hours later as us three girls hesitantly climbed into the dinghy and pointed it towards the pounding surf. "I got a plan," said Bruce reassuringly. With that he pushed us out into waist deep water, just inside the breaking surf line. "It's all about timing." *Like hell.* We were bobbing around in a plastic toy of a boat with an already proven inadequate weed-whacker of an engine and a terrified crew. Bruce patiently watched the rollers as they went ashore, pushing us further and further away from the beach. *What was he waiting for?* Then I saw it too. That lull in between sets of waves was our only way out. By now Bruce was almost up to his armpits in the surf and with one hard thrust upwards, pulled himself into the dinghy shouting, "START THE ENGINE, START THE ENGINE. GO, GO, GO." I pulled the starter cord, pushed the throttle forward, and we surged over the top of the wave before it crested and broke into white foam behind us. Success by a hair.

Clearly, we had a lot to learn about our new lifestyle and I hoped the learning curve was a short one.

CHAPTER 12

A DARK LANDFALL

"The lovely thing about cruising is that planning usually turns out to be of little use."

-Dom Degnon, Author

URTLE BAY FADED AS WE PREPARED FOR ANOTHER TWO DAYS AND NIGHTS at sea. Once again, we found ourselves in the thick of the cruising fleet. On this passage Bruce suggested we hang in close to shore to take advantage of the southern flowing current to help propel us along the race route. But with the image of the near miss at the starting line seared into my brain, Mama Bear voted to maneuverer further offshore to lose the crowd. Guess who won?

Aboard *Chewbacca* I assumed the role of quartermaster and watchful steward of our meager resources. I was hyper conscious of consuming our limited supply of fresh water and food too fast. We were surrounded by an ocean of water but ironically Coleridge penned it right in his poem *The Rime of the Ancient Mariner*:

"Water, water, everywhere,
And all the boards did shrink;
Water, water, everywhere,
Nor any drop to drink."

Of all our supplies, water was our most precious commodity. It was more precious than electricity. If we ran our battery banks low, all we had to do was fire up the engine to top off the batteries or more likely go without the few things that needed power, but if we ran out of water… that would spell disaster.

Our fresh water supply was restricted to what we could carry and any rainwater we could catch along the way, so this valued resource was rationed to drinking, cooking and brushing our teeth. I thought back to when I used to let the faucet run while I leisurely brushed my teeth. Seemed like ages ago. Luckily, I had learned all about the subject of fresh water conservation from our first cruising experiences in the South Pacific. Thumbing through my old journal I got a chuckle when I thought of what I sacrificed when it came to freshwater:

> Day 14: *"Halfway across the Pacific. I'm running out of clean underwear and haven't washed my hair in two weeks. Now I'm brushing my teeth and swallowing the rinse water just like Bruce. Yuck. I wish it would rain."*

You'd think with all the water surrounding us that taking a bath would be easy and it was, as long as you didn't mind salt water. The girls loved the challenge of pouring endless buckets of cool sea water over each other at bath time. By the time one of them was lathered up, another cold deluge came raining down from the bucket poured by the other. They were only strong enough to lift their little beach pails full of water, so it took a lot of dipping from a bigger bucket to complete the routine. Salt water leaves your skin dry and itchy, so an allowed luxury was a quick rinse of fresh water from a spray bottle.

With bathing lessons finished, we tucked the girls into their bunk and Bruce and I settled into our night time passage routine. As the hours passed, the masthead lights of our neighbors began to spread further and further apart and soon joined the twinkling stars on the horizon. Finally, I could relax and enjoy the serenity… for a moment. I say a moment because as often happens at sea, the wind changed, and my introspection was broken by Bruce's voice asking me to help him tuck another reef in the mainsail. As I moved out of the shelter of the cabin the cold wind sent a chill down my spine and my hair flying. Sometimes I wished we could just pull over and stop, but unlike a hiker stopping to pitch his tent for the evening, a sailboat never stops just because night falls. I fantasized about pulling up to a 7-11 barge anchored to the sea floor for dinner and a good night's sleep… but alas, there was no such thing.

We had enjoyed two days of gentle rolling seas with a steady 18-knot breeze pushing us comfortably downwind. I was thankful that the girls were quite happy no matter where they were aboard *Chewbacca*.

Below decks they engaged in all kinds of craft projects, puzzles and card games and when above decks, nature never disappointed. An interesting gathering of clouds, a pod of dolphins, a flyover by curious seabirds, a Humpback whale breaching or even the rugged coastal landscape passing by kept them in awe. I am certain being raised without a television encouraged the girls to learn how to occupy themselves without the constant stimulation of artificial entertainment. I also liked the fact that they enjoyed being alone and silence was not an uncomfortable sensation for either of them.

After the girls cleared the last of the morning cereal bowls from the cockpit I began tidying up *Chewbacca* anticipating anchoring later that afternoon. Bruce went below to recalculate our arrival time and reported that at our present speed, we wouldn't reach Bahia Santa Maria until well after dusk. He pointed to the chart and I could see the penciled X's marking our progress paralleling the coastline 20 miles offshore. *Shit, maybe we should have stuck a little closer to shore.* Tracing the line with my finger I saw that we were 60 miles from the entrance of the bay. Bruce added, "The dilemma is that we have another 12 hours of sailing and by then we will be entering the anchorage after dark." I thought about this for a moment and then asked, "Should we attempt anchoring in the pitch black or do we break away from the rally and continue sailing? Maybe we could find a suitable anchorage further down the coast in the daylight." But even I could hear the lack of conviction in my voice.

We were at the crossroads and debated the most prudent game plan. Sometimes our decision-making was muddied by lack of sleep and I felt the familiar fuzziness creeping in. We agreed a sound sleep was what we needed, not another night at sea, especially with the uncertainty of finding a safe anchorage somewhere down the line.

We pushed on for Bahia Santa Maria and if the favorable winds kept up, we just might win the race with the sun. But the weather Gods weren't playing fair. They sent a blanket of clouds to blot out the sun and I felt the temperature drop as the edge of a cold front approached. A steady grey drizzle soon enveloped my world. We pulled the now useless sails down and I slipped the engine into gear pointing *Chewbacca* towards shore.

Quite suddenly I became chilled to the bone. I handed Bruce the tiller and went below with the excuse to start a pot of rice for dinner, but I think everyone knew my main objective was to warm up over the stove. Being chef had certain advantages but all too soon, I was called on deck and the girls took over in the galley serving up a cold can of Dinty Moore stew poured directly over the pot of steaming rice with four spoons sticking out. This was probably a learned trait to get out of doing dishes, and it worked. After the somewhat hot meal, they scampered to their bunk burrowing deep under the covers. I drew the hood of my fleece lined sweatshirt tight to ward off the chill and huddled close to Bruce as *Chewbacca* ventured on.

Closing in on the fleet seemed painfully slow, but we finally picked up VHF radio chatter as boats converged on the bay's entrance. As *Chewbacca* drew closer the drizzle dissipated, and I could make out a field of tiny white lights twinkling in the distance. These were the boats already anchored and they seemed to wave at me as their masts swayed side to side in the ocean swell. It was impossible to discern where the sky, land and water met without the light of day. I felt just like a rookie airline pilot attempting her first night approach instrument landing. Bruce tightened his headlamp around his forehead, pulled on his gloves and readied the anchor. "As soon as we hit 20 feet let's drop the hook. I don't know how fast the bay shoals up and we don't want to be too close to shore." The meager light from his headlamp splashed across the black abyss as we crept on. When we reached 20 feet I called out and watched for Bruce's hand signals. As his fist went up, I notched the motor into neutral and then gave her a shot in reverse to stop all forward progress. A moment later, the splash of the anchor and the familiar clatter of chain paying out over the bow roller was music to my ears. I gradually increased reverse throttle pulling *Chewbacca* steadily backwards until I felt the anchor grab hold. Bruce signaled me to cut the engine.

I'd only played helmsman for a short time, but the new role was beginning to feel natural and I breathed a deep sigh of relief that our first night entrance was over. Sometimes a sailors best laid plans could be altered by Mother Nature and that day was a fine example.

We fell into bed surrounded by a fleet of boats, but when I awoke, *Chewbacca* was alone in a deserted bay. We had overslept another start. Cabo San Lucas was just 180 miles south. Bruce calculated two full days of sailing lay ahead so we ate a leisurely breakfast and enjoyed the solitude while we could. "We'll catch the fleet soon enough" said Bruce as he turned his face to the sun and enjoyed the moment. The girls went below to choose another book to read on this last leg of the rally while I poked around the cupboards to assess how much food we had left. I found, well... not much and I became acutely aware that my provisioning skills needed drastic improvement. My heartbeat quickened, and my palms started to sweat as I ticked off the remaining meals on my fingers. By my calculations, we could make it to Cabo, but without any delays. With little food and a dwindling water supply we couldn't put off our departure. It was time to hit the road.

Bruce adjusted and tweaked the sails, while I set *Han* back to work steering *Chewbacca*. The girls joined us in the cockpit and clipped in. Wearing their harnesses and tethers had become second nature to them and I was thankful they adapted so well to this new regimen. While their peers were sitting cross-legged on carpet squares in the classroom, they sat with the open sea at their feet and listened intently to Charlotte the spider and Wilbur the pig work out the meaning of life.

Besides devouring 11 books on our journey, the girls had built Lego castles and fantasy figures, strung beads and wove potholders from strips of cloth. Our supply of paint, crayons and Play-Doh also dwindled along the route. Action figures and fuzzy Beanie Babies fought wars and negotiated peace treaties as the Baja coastline slipped by to port.

The tip of the Baja Peninsula appeared on the horizon signaling that we were almost there. Recognizing the last meal of the rally was near, the girls brought forth their favorite playmates and lined them up neatly on the cockpit bench. It seemed the whole crew was hungry and looking forward to celebrating the rally's end. With a flourish, I shook out a brightly colored tablecloth as all eyes followed my movement. I was certain anticipation ran high that I surely must have squirreled away a few special delicacies to celebrate our arrival.

I set out a can of black olives, a squeeze bottle of mustard and a tin of corned beef. Undisguised disappointment appeared on the crew's faces and even the beanie babies looked downcast at the scanty offerings. As the famous arches of Cabo San Lucas passed, I remarked, "This is it, the cupboards are bare. How's that for perfect provisioning?"

CHAPTER 13

ANCHORING DANCE

"Anchor as though you plan to stay for weeks, even if you intend to leave in an hour."

-Tommy Moran, Royal Naval Reserve

CELEBRATORY AIR HORNS BLASTED AS WE CROSSED THE FINISH LINE WHICH only emphasized my desire to get off the "rally schedule" and begin cruising. But first we had to get some pesos, check into the country with the Port Captain and Immigration offices then restock our bare cupboards.

I crossed my fingers praying to God. *Here I am in a foreign country, sticking my only ATM card into a strange machine. We are totally screwed if this doesn't work.* I reluctantly let the plastic card be sucked from my fingers into the machine. I waited and seconds later heard a whirling sound. *OK, this is good.* The welcome screen stuttered then blinked alive. RETIRO, CUENTA DE CHEQUES, CUENTA DE AHORROS, EL SALDO. *Damn, everything is in Spanish.* I held my breath hopefully selecting the correct buttons. Silence. The machine was thinking. Then more churning sounds and the machine spat out a stack of colorful pesos. I exhaled. We're rich. Well, not really, our thick stack of pesos was only $30, but it worked.

Twenty-four hours later with our business completed and cupboards restocked we parted with the rally crowd and made our escape to one of the secluded anchorages a half day sail north to fully embrace our cruising life.

I was astounded when we rounded into the picturesque bay. I guess we weren't the only ones wanting to escape from the big town. The anchorage was bursting with every breed of boat imaginable: big, small, fancy, not so fancy and everything in between. There were fiberglass boats, wooden boats, a homebuilt boat, a trawler and a few swanky high dollar boats. Nothing here resembled the monolithic cruising community portrayed by the boat shows back home.

You wouldn't know it by looking at me, but I am a recovering boat show junkie. Years before our departure, I attended every cruising seminar on topics ranging from *The Care and Feeding of the Sailing Crew* to *Popular knots for Sailors*. While Bruce lingered at booths displaying the latest electronic doo-dads, I sat absorbing wisdom spewed by cruising culinary aficionados. I listened intently filling my notepad detailing how to dehydrate or can food and where to buy powdered eggs, canned butter and other specialty items. It seemed that everything that wasn't freeze-dried or vacuum-packed was brined, painted with a layer of grease or wrapped in aluminum foil. *Couldn't we eat the same food as the locals in the countries we were planning to visit? Couldn't I skip the mail order canned fruitcake that would keep for years and feed my family Prego and Chips Ahoy like normal people?* Besides, *Chewie* would sink under the weight of all the cruising supplies the experts deemed necessary. A more urgent question was: *How were we going to afford all these specialized goods?*

A few of the lecturers assumed that my galley was set up just like theirs… the dishwasher just starboard of the trash compactor next to the icemaker. Surprise! We had no refrigerator or freezer, just an icebox. And assuming I had their cruising "necessities," where was I supposed to plug in the Cuisinart and espresso machine?

I wondered; *Was anyone cruising around happily with a two-burner propane camp stove? Were there others who stored food in plastic Rubbermaid crates under the salon table instead of beneath the polished teak planks of their cavernous bilges?* As we circled the anchorage I had no idea that I would learn the answer to all these questions and much more.

We had barely set the anchor when a raging north wind swooped down from the mountains and unleashed itself on the isolated bay. Building whitecaps just beyond the anchorage compelled the fleet to stay put within the protected confines of the bay and it was like we were snowbound, but instead, we were wind bound. From this sanctuary, we had the opportunity to begin making new friends, who like us, were trapped by nature's grip. Like the unstoppable force of a glacier, the social life of the anchorage moved to the rocky beach… if you were hearty enough to brave the trip.

It took all hands to lower the *Blaster* from the deck into the water. The ferocity of the winds would have launched the dinghy skyward if Bruce and the girls hadn't climbed in to add ballast. The trickiest part was handing the outboard motor down to Bruce who had to clamp it onto the bracket as both boats surged up and down out of time. I trusted his abilities, yet I still tied a line around the motor just in case it got away from him… and either one or both went for a dive.

Bruce volunteered to drive which left us girls sitting in front forming a human shield to catch the brunt of the wind and cold ocean spray as we bashed through choppy seas. It was a roller coaster ride and the girls laughed and giggled and Bruce whooped it up with each wave breaking over us. At least three of us were having fun.

Once ashore I settled in and mingled, absorbing the first-hand wisdom shared by my more seasoned comrades. Some were veterans cruising the Sea for a second or third summer and I listened to their descriptions of the unique weather patterns in our new cruising grounds and where they deemed the safest and most protective anchorages were. I highlighted my cruising guidebook and took copious notes of exotic sounding destinations such as Isla Espiritu Santo, (Spirit of the Saint Island) Isla Danzante (Dancing Island) and Bahia Coyote (Coyote Bay). I networked the crowd like a hungry cub reporter listening to open debates on which towns offered the best provisioning options. Now that we were in Mexico I had to learn what local vegetables and fruits were abundant and durable in the intense heat. Show me a carrot or a potato and I'd know what to do with it, but some of these Mexican fruits and vegetables were completely alien to me. I tried to soak up their knowledge until my brain was overflowing. But I'd be back the next day because there was always something new to learn.

That night gale force winds screamed across *Chewbacca's* deck and rocked her like a hobbyhorse ridden by an angry child. Unable to sleep with the wind tearing through the rigging I sat in the salon thumbing through a cruising guide. Suddenly I felt a sharp jolt as *Chewbacca* leapt back a few feet and then abruptly stopped. I dashed barefoot into the cockpit and was met head on by what felt like the blast from the tail end of a jet engine. I half expected to see the bowsprit of a neighboring boat speared into *Chewbacca's* side, but it was just the black night who greeted me. Bruce was on my heels with the big spotlight in his hand and dashed to the bow sweeping the yellow beam across the water to check our position in the tightly packed fleet. I couldn't hear his words, but he turned around and flashed me a thumbs-up after a few sweeps. Relief washed over me. *Chewbacca* was safe. But the seeds of doubt took root. *Did our anchor pop out? Had it reset?*

A look around us and I knew 33 anchors clung tenaciously to the sandy bottom and we couldn't put *Chewbacca* or the other boats around us at risk if we were to "drag our anchor." There was no way I could remain below, so I put a kettle on for tea and joined Bruce in the cockpit. Clenched tight in the weather's grasp, we stood anchor watch anxiously waiting for dawn and formulated our re-anchoring plan step by step.

Before we left the safe confines of our dockside marina life for the open water we invested in a variety of anchors. Our everyday anchor was a 45-pound CQR or plow anchor, a classic among the cruising community. We also carried a smaller "day" anchor as well as our three-foot tall "Big Boy" storm anchor. The storm anchor was rated for a 60-foot heavy displacement boat, so Bruce figured it would hold our 33-foot lightweight catamaran in the severest of weather.

At first light nothing had changed. We were in the same place, but the wind was not abating. It was time to test that "Big Boy." I started the engine and as it warmed up I double checked the display on the depth sounder. Sitting nervously in the helmsman chair, I tightened my grip on the tiller and waited for Bruce's signal. He positioned himself on the bow, knees bent to absorb *Chewbacca's* up and down motion and pulled on his leather gloves. Language was useless as the words were stolen from our mouths by the howling wind. Bruce flashed me the "OK" sign and I responded with a thumbs-up.

Bruce pointed forward, pinching his thumb and forefinger slightly together. Uh-oh, maybe we should have reviewed our hand signals beforehand because I wasn't crystal clear on what he wanted. I put the engine in gear and gave it a little throttle. I could see him nodding, so I must have done it right. As the wind whistled in my ears, I was keenly aware that we hadn't had months and months of anchoring practice and that we had never anchored in such extreme conditions. Slowly, *Chewbacca* crept forward allowing the anchor chain to slacken and Bruce started the steady process of pulling up the 100 feet of chain that laid on the sandy bottom. Bringing up that much chain hand-over-hand was a slow and laborious process and I wondered if Bruce was contemplating why an electrical windlass didn't make it on the wish list.

I watched carefully as he directed me on the engine speed and direction he needed to go. I knew that once the anchor was free of the bottom, *Chewbacca* would be adrift in the wind and I would have to power her forward at full throttle to remain in control. If I couldn't gain enough speed to steer *Chewbacca* clear of the fleet it would spell certain disaster. Even in the sharp winds, my palms were drenched in sweat.

Bruce signaled the moment the anchor broke free from the bottom and pointed to starboard. Too late. I could already feel *Chewbacca* being bullied backwards in the harsh winds. I pushed the throttle to the max and waited for the propeller blades to bite into the water. Our rearward descent into an uncontrollable spiral stopped, but the nose of *Chewbacca* had already been caught by the gusts and fell off to the port. Shit, we were pointing the wrong way!

I had no time to think, just act. I couldn't outpower the wind, so I let it take me. I pulled the tiller in tight and aimed smack for the center of a sleek 70-foot ocean racer anchored to our left. Kendall was pointing out my assumed error, but I used the wind on *Chewbacca's* beam to push us sideways just skirting between the racer and a 30-foot wooden ketch with feet to spare. Once clear of our neighbors I took several deep breaths. Crap, that was close… I might have peed my pants a little, but I did it!

Our plan was for me to motor *Chewbacca* around the edge of the fleet and make a circuit of the bay while Bruce changed over to the larger storm anchor. Kendall scrambled on deck and clipped in next to him. Playing surgeon's assistant, she handed him pliers and vice grips to unshackle the smaller anchor. Careful not to drop any tools through the trampoline netting, they worked over the *Blaster* strapped down on the foredeck. The constant movement and saltwater spray only added challenge to their already difficult task. With the CQR disconnected, the bigger storm anchor was wrestled into place. Kendall handed over the tools in reverse order as Bruce shackled it to the anchor chain and the transplant was completed.

Bruce took his place back on the bow as the human windlass and signaled me to bring *Chewbacca* back to our spot toward the front of the pack. My concentration was complete but still in the back recesses of my mind lurked the ugly doubt; *Can I do this?* With Quincy in the salon to monitor the radio, Kendall returned to the cockpit and called out the depths as the anchoring dance began its final act.

I motored slowly forward and held *Chewbacca* into the wind until Bruce set the anchor onto the bow roller and flashed me an OK sign. I felt he wasn't only telling me he was ready but signaling that he also had confidence in me. I slowly motored forward and when Kendall called out 15 feet I held up a clenched fist and waited for Bruce to return the gesture with a nod. I dropped the engine into neutral and our forward movement was instantly stopped as the unsympathetic wind took over and began to push *Chewbacca* backwards. With a final look around, Bruce lowered the anchor and began paying out the chain. It ran swiftly through his gloved hands as he tried to keep control, but the wind was driving us back too fast. *Chewbacca* was dangerously gaining momentum towards the nearest sailboat behind us. Out of options, Bruce whipped the runaway chain onto the bow cleat, which had the same effect as pulling the emergency brake on the freeway. The anchor's oversized aluminum flukes dug deep into the sand and *Chewbacca* stopped dead in her tracks with a jolt.

OK, I wasn't expecting that, and I grabbed hold of the edge of my seat and pulled Kendall to me to keep us both from tumbling overboard. Recovering my balance, I saw Bruce picking himself up off the tramp. He shook his hands from the friction burn he had gotten through the thick leather gloves then carefully paid out the last 50 feet of chain which landed us squarely in our intended spot. OK, not a picture-perfect bit of anchoring but *Chewbacca* wasn't going anywhere. Now I could sleep.

CHAPTER 14

HOMESCHOOL DAZE

"Education is the kindling of a flame, not the filling of a vessel."

-Socrates, Philosopher

AFTER ONLY NINE MONTHS OF HOMESCHOOLING KENDALL AND QUINCY WERE staging an all-out revolt. We were almost to the bottom of Mexico's Gold Coast and I was at my wit's end. There's gotta be a better way, I thought. My students were uncooperative, and they didn't complete their assignments with the gusto I had envisioned. Somehow the girls just weren't excited about me in the role of teacher. Worries about my homeschooling skills or lack-there-of were resurfacing and keeping me awake at night. *What if Kendall and Quincy were grade levels behind when we returned to the United States? What if they couldn't make friends and were known as "those super-weird boat kids?"* We'd do them a huge disservice if we didn't give them a proper education. Self-doubt crept into my consciousness and ate away at the dreams I had of being an exemplary teacher with two enthusiastic scholars.

Sailing down the Mexican coast I had heard of a popular destination for "kid boats" where I hoped to meet other homeschooling moms and learn how they mastered their teaching afloat. At last we had arrived. I took *Chewbacca* for a spin around the crowded anchorage looking for a good spot and counted 45 boats. Most looked as comfortable as a well-worn pair of jeans, complete with patched dinghies, faded sun awnings, and thinning bottom paint. Maybe we had stumbled upon a den of sailors balancing the challenges of cruising and raising kids. *Perhaps I'll find a few kindred spirits here to help pull me out of my fugue.* Not long after Bruce set the anchor, the radio chirped to life.

"Chewbacca, Chewbacca, Chewbacca, this is *Rebel,* over," hailed a friendly female voice from the VHF. *"Rebel* let's go seven-two" I

replied and switched channels. "Hello *Chewbacca*, this is Kimberly, welcome to our little slice of paradise! We've heard you are a kid boat and so are we. School's out at 2 o'clock, come join us on the beach." "Kimberly, April here. Sounds great and I look forward to meeting you. See you then, *Chewbacca* switching back to one-six," and with that I excitedly signed off. Little did I know we had just put down roots in Homeschooling Central.

Sure enough, at 2:00 p.m. sharp, the tranquil anchorage burst to life with the sounds of dinghies zooming to shore, followed closely by surfboards, boogie boards, kayaks and row boats. We piled into the *Blaster* and trailed the surge. It was a cruising kid's fantasyland. There were children of all ages frolicking along the shore and at the river's mouth. Two dozen little people and a few older teenagers commandeered the beach. Some sat cross legged building moats around sandcastles. Others congregated at the river's edge and delighted in making mini avalanches that slowly slid into the shallow water. The more energetic youngsters rode boogie boards through the ocean surf while others ran along the beach pulling homemade kites. Before Bruce and I had our beach gear out of the dinghy, the girls raced off to make new friends.

We merged with the group of parents to introduce ourselves. Kendall joined in on a game of tag along the hard-packed sand and Quincy dragged the boogie board into the surf. I was anxious to discuss the subject of school with other boat moms and was relieved to hear over the course of the afternoon that EVERYONE had rocky patches, and I was not alone in doubting my capabilities as a teacher. Just like us, none of these parents had homeschooled their kids before cruising.

New cruisers had to ingest a tremendous amount of knowledge quickly. There was the long-distance sailing component, the cruising life element coupled with traveling in a foreign land and learning the roles of captain and first mate. It was sink or swim. The scope of the changes in our new lives had most of us overwhelmed. When children were added to the mix, it upped the ante to the stratosphere. Each one of us gathered on the beach had a healthy level of concern about our kid's education and it turned out we had all asked ourselves the same question at some point. Was it fair to take our kids on this adventure?

Some critics back home went so far as to declare that taking our children away from our culture and formal education would result in them not being able to compete in our modern society. They would be stunted intellectually and socially if we carted them off outside their conventional norms. Would they be proved right? When our adventure ended, would Kendall and Quincy be able to keep up with their peers who had traditional schooling? Sometimes in my darker moments, I felt as though the naysayers who embraced the mainstream thinking secretly wanted to see us fail in our children's education as a weird way of validating the well-worn path they had chosen.

Of course, I wanted to make our new life a success story and see our children become productive members of society. Deep down, I hoped our kids would excel beyond our wildest dreams, changing lives for the better and inspiring others. I felt an intense need to set our children up for success and meeting new friends in the same situation proved we were not alone in our schooling quandary. All the homeschooling cruising parents seemed to agree that with a little creativity and consistency, success was achievable.

Sitting in low-slung beach chairs, we traded schooling experiences while my bare feet were caressed by the warm sand and occasionally cooled by a rogue wave racing up past my ankles. This wasn't how I imagined my first PTA meeting would be. We batted around solutions to our thorniest problems of keeping our kids:

1) *on track, and*

2) *excited about their studies*

This was no easy feat when enticing new countries and cultures lay just outside the classroom walls where it would be so easy to forget school for one day… and then another day and another rather than buckling down and staying on target.

As the sun set, it was clear we had exhausted the topic of schooling for one day. Our little band broke up and we dispersed back to our floating homes. The girls were equally exhausted from racing around with their new-found friends. Armed with fresh knowledge and new strategies, Bruce and I set to work planning the next week of school adding some new twists to our lessons. We adopted guidelines for school hours, daily reading, writing and math work. Afterwards I retired to our bunk feeling satisfied that we were on the right path. We had a plan and I was feeling empowered.

Bright and early the next day, Kendall and Quincy were chatting animatedly about playing with their friends. They were shocked when I told them it was a school day and we had lessons planned. I guess the other kids forgot to tell them how school worked in this anchorage. Until 2:00 p.m., all the boat kids had school. Only after school was completed could they come out and play on the beach to their heart's content. So, for the next 12 weeks, *Chewbacca's* crew came to terms with a new format of schooling while afloat and we hit upon a comfortable groove. Hallelujah! From that day forward, we adhered to a few cardinal rules:

- *School was consistent; five days a week.*
- *If we were exploring somewhere new, history, science, English, social studies and math lessons were tailored to take in account our new surroundings.*
- *If we were passage making we studied sailing, nature, weather and the world around us, not bookwork.*
- *The first day in a new country was spent completing official business and getting our bearings, then we resumed the school routine.*
- *The "school year" was finished when the subject lessons were completed. That might take six months, nine months or a year.*

With these guidelines set in motion, I had at last found peace with my role as mother and teacher. Bruce acquired the title of Professor of Mathematics and Music while I commanded English, History and Social Studies. We became a team. With the girls' input, we designed a flag to raise from the spreader when school was in session aboard *Chewbacca*. Much like a DO NOT DISTURB sign on a hotel door knob, it signaled to our non-kid boat friends that we were busy with school.

This also became a chance for Bruce and me to "get schooled" and refine our anchoring skills. We had been anchoring somewhat successfully up and down the Mexican coast, but we were doing it blind, in murky water. With the clearer water, we couldn't pass up this opportunity to practice our anchoring skills in this virtual classroom and we repeatedly honed the routine until it became second nature.

Better than any armchair seminar, we laid out our anchor chain at different speeds and noted how it fell on the bottom and if the anchor dug into the sand or skipped along the bottom refusing to dig in. We observed how in certain conditions the chain wrapped around the flukes of the anchor causing it to pull loose. Bruce and the girls even jumped overboard and evaluated how things looked from underwater. Was the chain laid out straight? Did it have the proper angle or cantilever as it came to the surface for optimum holding power? I could now comprehend and appreciate how a properly set up anchoring system and routine meant the difference between losing or keeping our boat safe. We made an important rule then and there: If any one of us felt the anchor wasn't set firm, even if it was an inkling, we'd do it again. I quickly determined that the best recipe for a good night's sleep was a well-set anchor.

We also refined our communications routine between Bruce on the bow and me in the cockpit. Rather than shouting directions over the wind and engine noise we settled on a few hand signals. I learned that a fist held high meant "stop here" and when he pointed astern and pinched his fingers together that meant "slow reverse" and the index finger twirled meant "rev up." A thumbs-up meant we were "secure" and a finger across throat was the signal to "cut the engine." Only once did I receive the middle finger when I jokingly suggested Bruce pull up 100 feet of anchor chain so we could pick another spot.

Cruising kids have the potential of taking on a lot of responsibility and working as part of a team at an early age. Kendall and Quincy learned first-hand that consequences of actions or lack thereof, could be immediate. For land kids, if they didn't lock their bicycle it could get stolen and they might have to call mom or dad for a ride home. The parents went to a bike shop, bought a new bike and the kid was back in business. For "boat kids," if they didn't tie up the dinghy properly it could float away…out to sea, never to be seen again. It might be a long swim back to the boat without it and unlike a bicycle that could easily be replaced, finding a new dinghy so far off the beaten path would be near impossible and when one was found, very expensive. Tying your shoelaces may be an important skill but making a proper bowline, half-hitch or square knot to secure a sail or a piece of equipment aboard while out at sea could mean the difference between a pleasant day sail or a catastrophic ending.

During our time anchored in "Homeschooling Central" I saw many of the attributes our girls were developing as cruising kids displayed daily with their friends. They were flexible, resourceful, creative and uninhibited. It was our challenge to support their growth and incorporate our new bag of tools into homeschooling aboard *Chewbacca*.

Before then I had never heard the term "third culture kids" but it described cruising kids to a tee. This term is bestowed on children raised in a culture other than their parents for a significant part of their early development years. Wikipedia states:

> *"Third Culture Kids move between cultures before they have had the opportunity to fully develop their personal and cultural identity. The first culture of such individuals refers to the culture of the country from which the parents originated, the second culture refers to the culture in which the family currently resides, and the third culture refers to the amalgamation of these two cultures."*

Many years later Kendall and Quincy described their experience as, "having one foot in America and another in Latin America, yet not firmly rooted in either place."

It had been a magical few months spent in an anchorage full of cruising families, but the seasons were changing, and it was time to move on. I reluctantly waved a tearful goodbye to the thinning herd left in the anchorage.

CHAPTER 15

IN THE NICK OF TIME

"Sometimes the simplest decision can twist your fate, from a favorable path to one of tragedy… and sometimes it simply isn't your time to die."

-Anonymous

BRUCE AND I KEPT WATCH FROM OUR COCKPIT CHAIRS AS THE RUGGED COASTLINE passed by, while the girls contentedly stretched out on the cabin top reading. The sight of their heads in a book always brought a surge of pleasure into my heart. A bookworm myself, I knew a book, like a magic carpet could whisk one away to new worlds. Kendall had almost finished the last book of the *Little House on the Prairie* series. The covers of all 15 books were lovingly worn and creased. Not only did they bring a historical perspective to the way of life in early America, but I marveled how Laura's life paralleled our own self-sufficient lifestyle. These books also held a special place in my heart because somewhere within the pages of *Farmer Boy* the letters and their corresponding sounds made perfect sense to Quincy and she put it all together and started reading.

Unlike Bruce, I always liked to have a plan in the works well before we arrived at our destination. "The guide book shows two places to anchor. The main anchorage here in the larger bay and a smaller one in this cove." Bruce looked up from his paperback as I pointed out our options from the guidebook. "I like the bigger bay away from all the rocks," I added tracing my finger around the longer route. Bruce nodded his head, "OK, good call. Let's play it safe and go around the outside instead of cutting between the islands, even though it shows a narrow passage."

While we settled on our route, friends on the two boats ahead of us radioed back that they were going to stop in the rocky smaller cove for an afternoon snorkel. "We'll join you guys later in the big bay, and if we spear any fish, we promise to share," was Chris's playful response over the radio. The thought of a cool dip and a group snorkel was enticing, and the day was still young. What could possibly happen? And so, we changed our plans.

The scenery grew more and more beautiful the closer we drew to the islands. Red pinnacles jutted up from the turquoise sea, while the crashing waves cast white foam high into the air. It was a lovely, dramatic view from the deck of *Chewbacca*. We were a half mile from our agreed upon rendezvous point when Bruce disengaged *Han* and I took control of the tiller. Hearing the engine change pitch brought the girls up on deck. They oohed and aahed at the beauty surrounding us which took the words right out of my mouth. We puttered along giving Sam on the lead boat plenty of room to choose a spot and drop anchor. The island's burnt cocoa cliffs made for a rich, mesmerizing backdrop yet I remained clueless that the next few minutes would be the most terrifying in my life.

"I'll get the anchor ready," Bruce said as he stepped out of the cockpit. He walked nimbly along the cabin top to the front tramp while pulling on his faded gloves. We had done this drill countless times and it was comfortably rote. Now we had to claim that perfect anchoring spot, just the right water depth AND far enough from the surrounding reef.

"Let's drop at 20 feet," relayed Bruce as I maneuvered *Chewbacca* and called out the numbers flashing across the screen. "We are at 30 feet...the bottom looks flat and sandy," I responded. From practice, I could interpret a good holding sandy bottom from a poor holding one covered in grass or gravel by the pattern displayed on the depth sounder.

I made a pass and Bruce pointed me away from the rocky outcropping and signaled for me to throttle back and coast. He glanced back at me and shook his head. I recognized that uncomfortable look which meant he was feeling hemmed in by the surrounding rocks. I continued to rattle off the numbers as the strong waves squeezing through the jagged gaps between the islands surged under *Chewbacca*. "YOU KNOW IF YOU DON'T LIKE THIS, WE CAN ALWAYS MOVE OVER TO THE OTHER ANCHORAGE," I shouted above the engine noise as

I noticed his deepening frown. "LET'S CIRCLE BACK AROUND. THIS DOESN'T FEEL RIGHT. WE'RE BACKED UP TOO CLOSE TO THAT REEF." Bruce responded. I bent down, clicked the engine into gear and gave it half throttle.

The engine revved and then my ears were struck with a loud BANG and a jolt from the engine compartment below my feet. *Chewbacca* stopped moving forward. I listened intently but couldn't hear the engine over the sound of crashing waves. Something was wrong. A lightning bolt of shock struck my body and ricocheted inside me. Instantly, Bruce was beside me. The girls sat up, books forgotten and intuitively they knew this was a time for them to remain silent. Bruce lifted the cockpit floor exposing the motor and I immediately glimpsed the problem. The engine was twisted out of position and forced out of the water. I wasn't sure how it happened... I just knew that the engine was useless now.

Chewbacca was being pushed backwards by a combination of headwinds and a surging current towards the reef directly behind us. I was momentarily frozen in place as if I was standing on some railroad tracks with the light of an oncoming freight train bearing down on me. Then the adrenaline kicked in. I grabbed the bread knife taped inches from me and handed it to Bruce. I had learned to keep it close for just such an emergency. I seized the radio mic and informed Sam that we were in BIG trouble. *Chewbacca* was lifted with every swell and our home and our lives were being propelled closer to the ominous rocks with every beat of my heart. I realized there was no way Sam could get here in time to save us.

Bruce hung upside down in the engine compartment attempting to find the obstruction to slice through and free the engine. He needed to ensure there was nothing around the propeller shaft and called out for his snorkel gear. I sprinted for the front locker while thinking; *Is he really going to jump in the water and leave us alone here?* I threw open a locker and was confronted with a wall of sail bags, life jackets, boogie boards, sun awnings and a 100 foot of tangled garden hose. *Where in the HELL is the snorkel gear?* I had to dig to the very back of the locker, throwing everything out of the way to locate the family snorkel bag. We had packed carelessly, and I cursed our disorganization. I dumped out everything and finally uncovered Bruce's mask, fins, and dive gloves and flew back to the cockpit. Bruce grabbed only the dive mask and jumped overboard. I handed him the knife and he dove under the surging boat to survey the engine. He surfaced with nothing in his hand but the knife and sputtered, "It's not a rope caught in the propeller. THE ENGINE BRACKET IS GONE!"

Bruce climbed back onboard and desperately tried to force the engine into position, but it wouldn't catch without the missing bracket. Any attempt to restart it caused the motor to swing up wildly. Without the motor, we were adrift. I feared for our lives for the first time since setting out on this adventure. Sensing the danger, the girls started to cry and Bruce calmly, but firmly, directed them to go below and get their life jackets on. They did.

The oppressive weight of doom pressed upon me as *Chewbacca* surged towards a destiny I had never dreamed of. *What would happen to us? "LOCAL FAMILY DIES IN PARADISE" would be the headline in our local town's paper. I hoped our friends and family knew how much I loved them. How selfish of me to risk our girls' lives on my own wish for adventure.* All these thoughts raced through my shock numbed brain at Mach speed.

My eyes followed the girls as they ducked below and moments later stepped into the cockpit donning life vests and surf shoes. As they moved on deck, my focus shifted to a flash of movement about 100 yards away. In my mind, I thought it was a panga...or was it only the ripple of a playful dolphin breaking the surface. Just a fraction of a glimpse and the image disappeared like a desert mirage. Gone. Was it ever there or just my wishful thinking? I strained my eyes to the patch of water where seconds before held the apparition. It seemed like hours... but then a small fishing boat popped up riding the crest of a wave.

Bruce followed my outstretched arm into the open ocean seeing nothing. Damn, was I imagining all this? I wanted to say, "Wait for it," but I knew we had no time to wait, no time to spare. Then he saw it too. Jumping from the cockpit as if stung by a hornet, Bruce sprinted to the bow, but the fisherman disappeared once again into the trough of a wave. We both couldn't be hallucinating. We waved our hands wildly, fruitlessly calling into the wind. The girls sat at the base of the mast holding each other, their small bodies quivering with fright.

Bruce whistled, and I yelled with all my strength, but to no avail. Trying to focus through the gathering tears in my eyes, I stared at the stern of the fisherman's panga as he steered away from us. *DAMN YOU, please turn around*, I mentally flung my pleading thoughts his way. Instead of turning our way, I watched as the fisherman moved purposefully towards the open sea, slamming the door shut for our rescue, our salvation. The further he got from us, the chances evaporated of hearing our screams for help.

I bowed my head in sorrow until my chin hit my chest. I was despondent, our dreams would be crushed along with *Chewbacca*, dashed violently against the rocks. I ran to the girls to hold them and wait for the impending impact.

I had to look up one last time. Movement caught my eye. I strained my head and clutched the girls tighter as I saw the panga begin to circle back towards us. There was no language barrier as the fisherman surmised the desperate situation on our faces. Bruce flung open a locker and grabbed a dock line. He hastily tied it around our bow cleat as the fisherman approached. I looked behind and saw jagged black rocks and swirling surf snapping at our heels. This throw had to be perfect.

The fisherman expertly maneuvered within 10 feet of *Chewbacca* and held out his brown, calloused hand to catch our line. Five pair of eyes gawked at the rope as it flew air born and squarely hit its mark. He quickly wrapped the rope around his cleat and powered forward. The rope snapped taut and *Chewbacca* followed with a harsh jerk. The pangas propeller grabbed traction in the water and began pulling us away from eminent danger. HALLELUJAH! He towed us to the middle of the small cove and Bruce gave him a thumbs-up. Our savior released our line and offered up a salute before he was swallowed by the next incoming swell and disappeared into the open ocean like a hero riding into the sunset.

Relief washed over me, but I realized we were not out of the woods just yet. Bruce hastily let the anchor fly. It slipped faster than usual through his ungloved hands bringing fresh nicks and bloody smears to his palms, but the need to anchor *Chewbacca* was urgent. Seconds later I felt the familiar pull of the anchor burrowing deep into the sandy bottom and I let out a cry of relief as the four of us regrouped in the cockpit. A shroud of silence enveloped us as we sat stunned, rooted in place, paralyzed by the thought of what could have happened. Still in their life jackets, the girls sobbed unconsolably and entwined their limbs in mine. Embracing Bruce, we sank into a communal heap on the cockpit floor. I shook uncontrollably, and I was sure I was suffering from shock. Facing the stern, I took in the water breaking over the reef in the distance. I couldn't tear my eyes from the spot where we would have crashed if not for the intuitive fisherman.

I was awoken from my stupor by the roar of two dinghies charging towards us at break neck speed. The two inflatables encircled *Chewbacca* and settled, one on our starboard side the other to port... a group hug when we needed it most.

I started to breathe again. We were safe, at least safe for now. I welcomed our concerned friends aboard and broke out a Cadbury chocolate bar from my secret stash. I had squirreled away a few as rewards for surviving a stressful situation and today more than qualified. With a deep exhale of gratitude, we washed down the rich chocolate with a finger of dark rum.

Once everyone left I sent Kendall and Quincy to the galley and soon smelled the familiar aroma of Dinty Moore Stew drifting through the hatch. At any moment I expected Quincy to burst into the cockpit with her solo repertoire of crunchy peanut butter on Ritz crackers. Until then Bruce and I entwined our hands and held each other very still. I broke the moment by asking Bruce if he had feared losing *Chewbacca* on the reef. He didn't show it, but was he as frightened as I was? He laid his head in my lap and closed his eyes. I gave him a pass on this one. I reflected on our agreement that we would continue to cruise "as long as we were having fun." The next family meeting would be an interesting one. Everyone got an equal vote on whether we moved on or called it quits. I honestly didn't know how I would vote.

CHAPTER 16

CARRY ON

"Courage doesn't always roar. Sometimes courage is the little voice at the end of the day that says I'll try again tomorrow."

-Mary Anne Radmacher, Author

WE SAT AROUND THE TABLE IN THE SHADOWS OF THE HARSH FLORESCENT light above the galley. I couldn't discern the thoughts etched on Bruce's face, but the lack of bantering at meal time revealed deep contemplation. The responsibilities of captain no doubt weighed heavy. The girls broke the somber mood by clearing the table, which consisted solely of four bowls, four spoons and the now empty pot of stew. They returned with the game box and we ended the evening with several hands of Rummy Cube. Never end any day on a bad note was our philosophy.

Bruce laid down, closed his eyes and was out. I knew this because I laid down, fidgeted, tossed and turned and was envious of his peaceful even breathing. We were hundreds of miles from civilization with a broken boat, yet there he laid, resting peacefully next to me. Ten seconds before he closed his eyes Bruce muttered, "We'll fix this in the morning." Looking back, I realized it was instinct to rejuvenate the body, so the mind could find a solution... but at that moment all I wanted was to choke him in his sleep.

On a boat, the rising sun is a natural alarm clock. That next day I beat it up by a mile! The kettle whistled and signaled that it was ready to make coffee; like I needed any caffeine to jump start my rattled nerves.

The sun broke through the marine haze and once its rays hit the decks, sleep was next to impossible, except for kids. Kids could blessedly sleep through anything and this morning I saw no reason to stir them.

Bruce shuffled into the galley, poured a bowl of granola then revealed his plan. "First," he began between chews, "Let's figure out what happened," another scoop into his mouth, "and then we'll fix the problem." "REALLY? THAT'S OUR PLAN?" *Had I known that, I'm sure I would have slept like a babe in her mother's arms.* And to think all this time I was so worried.

So, now that we had a plan it was time to call the girls and have a family meeting. Daylight was burning bright now, and I didn't know what lay ahead. With all eyes on him, Bruce unfolded the whole plan step by step. *I guess I only got the abbreviated plan.* First, we have to pull the broken engine out of the nacelle to see what the problem is. But even before the cockpit floor can be removed it has to be cleared of all ropes and gear. The girls had their first assignment. What we were about to do was equivalent to raising the hood of our car and pulling the engine out in the parking lot at the grocery store. That is, if your grocery store was hundreds of miles from nowhere and the parking lot was an undulating ocean. No problem, WE GOT THIS.

While the girls worked, Bruce and I gathered tools, ropes and pulleys that we needed to extract the motor.

By now our friends were up and our radio jumped to life. "*Chewbacca*, *Chewbacca*, *Chewbacca*, you guys need a hand?" came the reassuring voice of Sam. *Orion* held every tool under the sun below the decks of her sleek 47 feet. If we needed something unusual *Orion* would have it. *Good Medicine* was also available, and Chris checked in to see how our night was and what help we needed. As everyone signed off, I felt immense relief that we were not alone.

The girls worked well in tandem, and soon we were ready. With the floor board raised Bruce was straddling a hole about the size of the engine compartment of a small truck. Lift the hood of your car and you would see pavement below the engine. Here only the deep blue ocean stared menacingly back at us. And there in the middle sat our broken engine. I played assistant while Bruce disconnected the control cables, electrical connections and brackets holding everything in place. After an hour of working upside-down, we were ready for the lift. With a chorus of "One! Two! Three!" we hoisted the engine out of its lair while the girls helped guide it to the cockpit bench for closer examination. Bruce immediately saw the problem. "Yup, the mounting brackets are gone." He picked at the white powdery residue left where the brackets once were. "Looks like the brackets dissolved completely into aluminum oxide by galvanic corrosion." he stated, reverting to the metallurgist lingo of his working years. "In English, please Daddy," said Kendall.

"Right. So, the engine bracket that holds the motor to the boat was nibbled away," he said while making little biting signs with his hands. "Chomp. Chomp. Chomp." Bruce touched what little was left of the motor bracket and it disintegrated into tiny spongy pieces that drifted down onto the cockpit seat. I broke the teachable moment and interjected "How exactly did this happen?" Bruce sat back on the deck, figuratively scratching the back of his head in frustration "You know, we don't really have any dissimilar metals on *Chewie* that could cause this much galvanic corrosion." He sat for a minute pondering the matter and I could almost hear the gears turning in his mind. Then it dawned on him, "Damn, do you remember those open electrical wires strung under the docks in the water at the marina? Besides being a horrible safety hazard, I think the stray electrical current in the saltwater attacked our brackets." Trying to lift this somber thought, Bruce turned to the girls and said, "During all that time at the marina our bracket must have looked like an irresistible chocolate bar to those sneaky electrical currents," and he smacked his lips. But underneath the clowning, I could hear the seriousness in his voice and I blurted out what must have been going through his mind on another level. "But how do we fix it?" That was met with a stony silence which scared me even more. After a few minutes, the girls lost interest in our plight and went off in search of a snack. Oh, the freedom of childhood, not a care in the world, I thought enviously.

Soon the sound of dinghies converging on *Chewbacca* reached my ears. The collective stared down at the injured motor and like watching a car wreck, none were able to look away. Even with their backs to me I could hear murmurs of, "Wow," "Man-o-Man" and even a "Holy Shit." Fortunately, our adult friends from the other boats weren't tempted to bow out for the siren song of chunky peanut butter on Ritz crackers and politely put on their game faces to mask their apprehension.

Cruisers love to come together and although it was usually for food and socializing, analyzing problems and finding solutions was passionately embraced. Our friends knew this situation could easily had been theirs. I held my breath and awaited their opinions. The reality was we had no spare part and we were a hard two-day sail from civilization. The landscape was void of any sizable town until Puerto Vallarta, over 200 miles away so we may as well have been on the far side of the moon.

Looking concerned Sam shared with us what he learned via the morning radio net. The weather report called for a tropical storm and we could expect strong winds within 24 hours. Shit. In a short while our situation would become at best uncomfortable and at worst untenable. "OK, let's concentrate on fixing this and moving to the safer anchorage," said Bruce calmly, like we were fixing a flat tire on the side of the freeway. *WHAT THE HELL?* I was two steps beyond frazzled and starting to miss home. I hated feeling vulnerable and not being in control of a situation. I was about ready to turn over the keys to *Chewbacca* and head for dry land.

Everyone hunkered down and examined what was left of the brackets. *OK, let's focus on the positive,* I thought to myself, *there are some pretty smart people here, and we'll figure this out.* My fingers were crossed. I held various sizes of screw drivers in my hand while Bruce carefully scraped what was left of the bracket, which was pretty much nothing. I handed him the smallest screw driver and slapped it into his palm, feeling like a dental assistant helping Dr. Bruce remove a filling from a patient. Sam pulled out a set of calipers from his bag of tools and carefully measured the diameter of the remaining bracket holes and the length. I passed out scratch paper and the guys sketched what they thought might work. The part of the bracket that held the engine in place was long gone, but if they could find a bolt or rod just the right size, they felt they could cobble together a makeshift bracket. As quickly as the dinghies arrived, they took off on a serious scavenger hunt. I tried to think happy thoughts but, if we came up empty, *WE WERE SCREWED.*

Time was ticking. Bruce spilled out jars of spare nuts and bolts and directed the girls to search for anything we could substitute for our missing piece. He drew what they should be looking for so that precious time wasn't wasted. It was a helpful task for their little hands, but I also suspected that Bruce was trying to keep them calm with a distraction. Sometimes our nervous energy spilled onto them even when we tried hard to conceal our anxiety…and that morning I had more than enough anxiety to spare.

As the last jar's contents rattled onto the Formica table top, I wished we had brought more spare bits of this and that. Meanwhile, as the pile on the table was whittling down, in desperation, I examined our supply of welding rods, dowels and pieces of thin steel cable. In a moment of sheer serendipity, the girls grabbed a couple of eye-bolts that looked promising. It wasn't exactly like Bruce's drawing, but it was pretty close. Put them in the "maybe" pile.

The sound of dinghies once again invaded my thoughts and I looked up to see our friends zipping our way. As I glanced around, I noted the clear morning sky was now streaked with cirrus clouds or mare's tails. Windy weather was brewing, and the sky frowned. We were running out of time.

Everyone stepped aboard and laid their finds on the cockpit bench seat. One by one Bruce tested each bolt. "Almost, but not quite" was said 8 times until he picked up the last piece of hope. Time slipped into slow motion and the seconds ticked by at an agonizingly slow pace as Bruce carefully slid the last eye bolt into place. It fit perfectly… well close enough to temporarily hold the engine in place at least. Beggars can't be choosers. We all stood there for a few seconds mesmerized by our luck until Sam broke the silence with high fives all around. Now we only needed a matching nut and washer to secure everything into place. Once again dinghies fled the scene and with a little imagination I could hear the tinkle of nuts and washers tumbling onto table tops.

We were sorting through piles of fasteners when our radio sprang to life with the report of a delivery coming our way. Worth its weight in gold didn't even come close to describing the happiness I felt upon receiving the prize. It was like fitting the last piece into place in a 1,000-piece puzzle. All eyes were riveted on Bruce's adrenalin laced hands as they shakily threaded the bolt through the bracket, stacked on the washers and finally threaded the nut in place. A FIT! Not factory perfect, but hopefully close enough so the engine wouldn't come loose.

After a final inspection, the guys carefully helped lower the engine back into its home. Bruce guided it into place and spun the attachment clamps closed with a wrench. Upside down once again, he plugged in electrical lines and strung the transmission cables to complete the process. "OK, April start the engine" he said, mopping his sweaty brow with the bottom of his dirty T-shirt. Turning the key, the engine jumped to life with a satisfying purr. Cooling water poured out in a steady stream; our first sign that the engine was working, and we hadn't messed anything up. "OK, now for the real test."

As the girls sat in their places above the cockpit, I noticed their hair flying wildly around them, and gooseflesh had risen on their brown skin. The temperature was falling, and the sky was taking on a menacing purplish hue. Bruce lowered his head back in the engine compartment while I gently shifted into forward. I felt the gears engage and the motor slipped into gear. Bruce reached his arm back and gave me a pat. I shifted into reverse.

I added some RPMs and the engine didn't budge, the improvised bracket held fast. SUCCESS!

CHAPTER 17

A MUTINY BREWING

"Only those who will risk going too far can possibly find out how far one can go."

-T. S. Eliot, Poet

"WE NEVER LEAVE A MAN BEHIND," SAID SAM WITH A SERIOUS NOTE IN HIS DEEP voice as he leaned against *Chewbacca's* hull. The water was already getting choppy bouncing him up and down in his dinghy as he held firmly onto the lifeline. I scanned the sea around us just as a telltale white cap popped up and brushed the surface. There would be more of them soon. "We need to skedaddle to the bigger bay if we are going to ride out the coming storm. I'll get Chris and we'll escort you guys over to make sure you get your anchor set and then we'll follow." He was right, this small bay would become as inviting as a sprung bear trap very soon.

I started the engine and Bruce retrieved the chain. Once the anchor broke the surface Sam and Chris kept pace with us in their dinghies as I steered around the tiny islands and into a spacious bay a half mile away. I held my breath as I brought *Chewbacca's* nose into the wind in 15 feet of water just outside the growing surf and Bruce lowered the anchor. I was thankful we had designated the Big Boy as our everyday anchor and it quickly grabbed hold of the sandy bottom while Bruce paid out all 100 feet of chain. So far, so good I said under my breath as I gave the engine full throttle digging the anchor deeper. Both Sam and Chris stood by in their dinghies just in case… but the fix held and with a thumbs-up from Bruce they sped away to ready their own boats for the move.

Deep into the night and still I couldn't sleep. Once again, my life mate snored softly beside me while I laid eyes wide open, staring into the darkness. We had successfully cheated death from the reef, completed our makeshift engine bracket repair and now we were anchored securely in a beautifully spacious bay. I guess it doesn't get any better than this at least according to Bruce who reasoned "Everything is going according to plan." *OK, whose plan?* I tossed and turned until the daylight broke bringing more bad news. While hopeful we could move on that day, one look out the porthole at the mounting waves made me doubt it. Yesterday's forecast was proving correct. Sighing, I remembered a popular cruiser mantra: *The sailor with the most time, gets the best weather.* It didn't pay to be hasty where weather was concerned. The bay was wide and open like a loving mother's outstretched arms, but the warm comparison ended there. With no protection from land, the unbridled wind grew and with it, the ocean swells. Like a child with a burning fever, *Chewbacca* tossed and turned in the building seas.

The weather seemed to have no intention of quitting. We listened to the forecast, hoping for good news, but the prediction of strong winds lasting a week stood. Even after the storm abated, it would take a few days for the seas to lay down enough for us to leave. Day after day, we watched *Orion* and *Good Medicine* crest the monstrous waves only to sink back into the trough. All I saw was a mast dropping down and then resurfacing as it rose with the next roller. The wicked wind made it impossible to even take a stroll above decks. We were truly cabin bound!

We were running low on food and water, but there was no way we could get to shore for fresh supplies even if there were a village beyond the sand dunes. Besides the dangers of breaching the mountainous surf, it wouldn't be safe to leave *Chewbacca* unattended in such volatile weather. We concentrated instead on cultivating our patience and finding work to do. Reading, schoolwork, games and boat projects sustained us. Bruce spent an afternoon rebuilding a spare foot pump and emptying the settee storage seat to rearrange his spare parts. He whittled away hours organizing and categorizing his entire collection of boat paraphernalia. The girls turned a math assignment into a sorting game, reorganizing his jars of nuts, bolts and screws. I inventoried the cabinets in the galley, taking stock of our dwindling supplies.

Sleep did not come easy on this week-long roller coaster ride so none of us were well-rested when good news arrived over the radio.

A disembodied voice told us that the wind would fizzle out over the next couple days. "It's about time," was my only come back to the digital display.

As the weather window started to crack open a bit and the storm front began to destabilize. Everyone was antsy to leave but who would be the sacrificial goat to head out first? Each boat in the anchorage had a different tactic for sailing out of this weather hell hole.

Orion was the biggest boat and Sam decided to make his getaway just before dark. He theorized that the wind died at night, (which is mostly true) and the reduced wind would bring flatter seas (which is also mostly true). Unfortunately, the ocean doesn't always play fair and *Orion* was thoroughly pummeled as she made her getaway north. We listened throughout the night to their radio reports of slow progress as they pounded into the still roiling seas with green water pouring over their bow. We decided it wouldn't hurt to let another day pass before we left. Thanks *Orion*.

The next morning *Good Medicine* stuck her nose out but soon radioed back that they were experiencing a very bumpy, uncomfortable and difficult slog. They too got hammered... but not as soundly as *Orion*. "Looks like the conditions are improving, but not by much," said Bruce, exasperated. Looking out at the pounding surf breaking over the reef, he asked, "Who's in for waiting another day?"

Two days later, D-day dawned for us. Calm seas barely washed over the reef at first light and sent us into a frenzy of preparation. "OK, let's go for it!" We rallied and pulled anchor. Worry lines creased my forehead as we skirted the reef guarding our bay and set *Chewbacca* on a course due north. I wondered if we had made the right decision, but only time would tell. We couldn't be 100% sure of what lay ahead until we rounded the headland and faced open water.

Hallelujah. The morning sea conditions proved favorable, and IF *Chewbacca* kept plowing along at six knots we would be at our destination in a couple days, easy. That was the plan anyway.

Everything was going so smoothly… until just after lunch. I glimpsed white caps on the horizon and they were marching our way. At first there were just a few, but soon the once smooth water was turned into a frothy chop. *Uh-oh*, I thought to myself. I scanned the skies and sure enough, the blue was streaked with mare's tails, those wispy clouds that signal high winds. They trotted across the sky, forcing the wind to settle right on our nose. I'll confess that when it comes to sailing I'm a smooth water, gentle breeze kind of gal. While some sailors get a rush out of seeing white water and mare's tails, I cringe.

The horizon ahead of us was turning darker by the minute. Nobody had to tell me, this was going to get ugly. We needed to make a decision. Do we turn back now or head further out to sea? I couldn't see going back, but the direct path to our next anchorage was cut off. "WE'LL HAVE TO TACK OUT INTO OPEN WATER IF WE WANT TO MAKE ANY HEADWAY," shouted Bruce over the escalating wind. Reading my fears, Bruce looked at me and mouthed "It'll be okay." My lip quivered, and I gave my best pout, like a toddler given a time-out.

Sometimes sailing requires grit…. and I made an effort to muster mine. I pulled on my weathered sailing gloves, foul weather jacket and shimmied into my safety harness. I probably looked more prepared than I felt. We met on deck and tied a reef in the mainsail and switched over to our smaller jib.

I asked the girls to make sure everything below was stowed in the lockers, not left out to rattle around or fly off the shelves. Even though *Chewbacca* did not heel over, I was still cautious about flying objects and the damage they could do to human flesh. After they double checked that everything was secure, they headed to their bunks. The looks on their faces told me they were both excited and a little scared as they anticipated a bumpy, wild ride. I flashed my most confident smile as Bruce winched the sails in tighter and hunkered down for battle… a beat to windward.

I equate sailing into the wind to clawing my way up a steep icy ski run. There's a reason sailor's call this "beating to windward." It's going against the grain sailing and sometimes impossible if the wind and seas are fierce enough. Given the same condition, sailing with the wind is like coming down the powdery ski slope in a quick and smooth sleigh ride. But that wasn't in the cards for us that day. Four hours later we were reducing the mainsail to its last reef point and changing our small jib out for an even tinier storm jib.

I was wet, tired and miserable, but had enough strength to conjure up my worst beat to windward. It was a do or die 12-hour nightmare back in our crewing days aboard *Raven*...

We were three days out of Tahiti in the middle of the Pacific bashing to windward and getting doused in a wall of frigid salt water every 20 seconds but that wasn't the worst thing. The bilge alarm sounded continuously indicating we were taking on water… we were sinking.

Desperate to find the water leak, Bruce pulled up floorboards hoping to discover a hole. He found nothing but seawater…too much seawater. Staring into the growing pool, it occurred to me that at this rate we wouldn't survive the three-day trip back to Tahiti. Raven would be lost if we didn't do something NOW.

Our once safe and dry cocoon was quickly turning into a watery coffin. One by one the electric bilge pumps failed under the strain of the rising water prompting Bruce to steal unused bilge pumps from other areas of the boat. I had watched Bruce methodically install electric components in the past but not that day. He hastily snipped and stripped wires with a pair of nearby scissors, then roughly twisted the wires together with a wrap of black electrician's tape. The temporary fix was good, but only temporary. Within an hour our last two electric bilge pumps burned up.

Time to implement Plan B. Raven contained a back-up manual bilge pump with a three-foot handle resembling a small oar. We each took a 10-minute shift on the pump but on my third round the aged rubber diaphragm split and the pump became useless.

I needed a panic button to push. To cut the tension, the captain reminded us that we were only two miles from land… unfortunately that land was directly below us. We needed a Plan C to implement, but I wasn't ready for it.

Plan C involved preventing Raven from sinking in the deep blue ocean by running her up on land… or given our current location, beach her on an atoll. Up until now we had been zig-zagging our way north purposefully missing the islands, and all of a sudden here we were looking for one to run up on. Forty miles to our east lay our minuscule target about 10 city blocks long and only four feet above sea level. Bruce turned the wheel.

Meanwhile, I was below on my hands and knees bailing the rising water from the bilge with a small bucket trying to keep the inevitable at bay, or at least delay it. I couldn't stand upright because the boat was heeled over like a carnival fun house teetering in the heavy seas. I frantically dipped the bucket into the swirling oily bilge water and then scrambled up the companionway ladder to dump the contents down the cockpit drains. I repeated this process hundreds of times, just barely keeping up with the rising water now percolating at the floorboards of the cabin. There is a saying, "The best bilge pump is a scared sailor and a bucket." And it's true!

The starboard side of the diesel engine was half-submerged, and seawater was lapping menacingly at the alternator. BANG, POOF and a wisp of smoke signaled that the alternator was kaput…and the amp meter slammed to zero. Bruce yelled down "CUT THE POWER" and I scrambled for the electrical panel. I hoped we had enough power left in the batteries to send a last-ditch Mayday distress call. Maybe we should have made the call earlier?

With the sun setting on our backs, we raced on against imminent darkness. The sky was black with storm clouds making navigation near impossible. I knew we had little choice but to press on. Failure was not an option; especially when the penalty for failure was sinking in the middle of the Pacific Ocean.

We knew the island was somewhere out there and we needed a miracle to find it. Ted was scanning the horizon ahead and caught the glint of the sun's reddening rays reflecting off something in the distance. Keeping the binoculars pressed to his eyes he told Bruce to come to starboard 10°. Where was he taking us? Then Bruce saw it too and honed-in on the beacon. But it wasn't a lighthouse *or navigation aid that saved us. Luckily an inter-island freighter running from the same storm happened to be approaching the same island from the opposite direction. The sinking sun was almost kissing the horizon as the first palm trees came into view. With no time to spare, we followed the freighter into the protected lagoon just as the last rays were extinguished. Maybe we weren't going to die tonight after all!*

At last the seas and Raven were still. In the fading dusk, the captain scanned the tiny bay for a beach to run the boat up on or a shallow spot of sand to scuttle Raven. Exhausted, I filled the bucket and bailed one last time, while Bruce gathered all our valuables and readied the dinghy to launch. Passing by the open floorboards, I peered into the dry bilge and did a double take. Wait a minute, a DRY bilge?

Could this be some sort of trick or wishful thinking? Half giddy from dodging a very bad situation, I retraced my steps and once again peered into the empty hole. After a thorough search of the boat Bruce discovered the source of our distress… a broken thru hull fitting that was submerged under water in the stormy seas while heeled over on a port tack. Once the boat sat upright in the tranquil waters of the bay, the ocean stopped pouring in.

Luckily, *Chewbacca* wasn't in anywhere near that kind of trouble but still it was going to be a rough ride for all aboard. Hour after hour, fiberglass slammed into standing waves. Slashing wind bit into my face and frigid salt water spray doused me every chance it got but thankfully the bilge alarm never sounded and the comparison to my first beat to windward ended there. I grabbed my seat and hung on.

Sometimes you just can't go straight up a steep mountainside and you are forced to zig then zag your way up the switchbacks to reach the peak. The wind was smack on our nose, so the only forward progress we could make was to bare off to one side then the other. It took twice the distance to cover the same ground, but it was the only way forward. In sailor lingo, it's called a tack and that was our only route forward now. It took energy, concentration, care and patience to execute a proper tack. A finger caught between the winch and the line because of sloppy seamanship could mean a lost finger. A jibe of the boom could deal a mortal blow to the head if it swung uncontrolled across the cockpit. It took timing and teamwork to release the headsail sheet in unison with a course change then winch in the sheet again on the opposite tack. We had spent months practicing this maneuver in all weather conditions on our home turf in the San Francisco Bay and now that practice would hopefully pay off.

All afternoon *Chewbacca* faithfully labored back and forth as the wind increased…20, 25 then 30 knots. She bashed on a port tack and then bashed on the starboard tack, clawing her way towards our destination.

We slogged our way all day and night making as much forward progress as possible. A grey dawn revealed no relief from the winds standing between us and our destination, but at least through the haze I could see the waves bashing into us. We accepted the pummeling for another 24 hours. Somewhere along the beating I must have dozed off because at the first kiss of dawn, I woke to find Bruce changing out the tiny storm jib for the larger working jib. "Come help me shake the reefs out of the main" Bruce called recognizing that fair weather was finally upon us.

"Good teamwork yesterday," Bruce announced as he joined the crew back in the cockpit. "Who'd have thought we could have pulled that off a couple of years ago?" I gave *Chewbacca* a few affectionate pats on her cabin top. "She sure proved she could do what we asked of her." We all shared renewed confidence in our boat and ourselves.

The soft breath of a 15-knot breeze ruffled my hair and Neptune's apology for the rigors of the previous two days and nights granted us with a glorious sail carrying *Chewbacca* deeper into Banderas Bay. In anticipation of a short stay at the local five-star marina, Bruce tasked the girls with prepping the dock lines and scrubbing our dock fenders which were spotted in black mold from months of storage.

The radio jumped to life. Our friends had been calling us for the past three days and we were finally within VHF range. They were curious of our jaunt up the coast, but they also had some bad news to share. Because of the foul weather, no one had left the marina and boats with reservations had to anchor up the coast in a holding pattern waiting for slots to open. The news was deflating.

Bruce glanced around the cockpit and was met with three bedraggled faces. We were a dirty and wretched lot. The girls looked like street urchins from 18th century London and I didn't even want to think how I appeared after a week without proper sleep. My hair felt salt incrusted and stood on end. My new worry lines had progressed into deep furrows and I couldn't bring myself to reach down into the almost bare food lockers to present another GOK canned food surprise for dinner. The GOK, or "God Only Knows" pile were cans that had lost their labels along the way and opening one was culinary Russian Roulette.

A naval insurrection was forming.

Bruce reached for the radio mic. "Paradise Village, Paradise Village, Paradise Village, this is sailing vessel *Chewbacca*, come in please." "*Chewbacca*, this is Paradise Village Marina, Dick speaking, let's move to seven-two, over," returned the familiar, warm voice of the Marina Manager. "Hi Dick, Bruce here.... I have a little favor to ask..."

I awoke the next morning after a blessed 14-hours of sleep. Dick had somehow squeezed us in and saved the day!

Mutiny averted.

CHAPTER 18

A WHALE OF A TALE

"What is life without a little risk?"

-Sirius Black, Harry Potter and the Order of the Phoenix

IT WAS TIME TO GIVE THE KITTY A REST. OUR STAY AT THE MARINA WAS OVER the top, but a single week of dock fees ate away an entire month's worth of cruising funds. By unanimous vote we decided to continue north and cross over to explore the Baja Peninsula and sail up into the Sea of Cortez.

But sailors are a superstitious lot. Upon hearing of our pending Friday departure, we were warned not to leave. I thought it was because I was breaking up our Friday night Rummy Cube tournament, but according to Wikipedia:

> *"The origins of many superstitions are based in the inherent risks of sailing. Friday is an unlucky day in some cultures and perhaps the most enduring sailing superstition is that it's unlucky to begin a voyage on a Friday."*

OK, this was serious business. We let Friday pass.

The next day we reluctantly said our farewells to our friends and turned towards the open ocean. It was a tearful parting for all sides, with promises to "See you down the line." Being the only children in the marina, the girls had made fast friends with several surrogate aunts and uncles as well as a couple of four-legged friends. The girls were beginning to learn that the wandering life was full of hellos and goodbyes, but mostly "Hasta luego," see you later.

Next stop, a gentle curve of beach at 24° North and 110° West. Our destination was Ensenada De Los Muertos, otherwise known as Bay of the Dead. The name piqued the girls' interest as they wove fantastic if not gruesome stories to explain the naming of this mysterious bay.

The sun was an hour from setting and the girls listened in as Bruce and I discussed that night's route. The area was notorious for partially submerged unlit fishing nets that could stretch for miles, so Bruce and I agreed to spend our first watch together, until we got further offshore, reasoning that two set of eyes were better than one. After the girls retired to bed, we took turns scanning the horizon with binoculars, adjusting the sails, correcting the autopilot or jotting notes in our log. I was beginning to take on the responsibilities of plotting our hourly position and making course corrections on my own but tonight it was good to have a watch partner.

The night was warm, and I relished standing night watch barefoot. The weather looked ideal for the four-day passage perfectly timed to be escorted by a full moon. The moon's glow splashed across the deck invitingly and I set our beach chairs on the cabin top where we surveyed the bright-as-day panorama. In between watch duties we swapped dreams and ideas on how to improve our spartan home afloat. A huge bowl of fresh popcorn sat between us as we talked on into the night, guided by the light of a silvery moon.

The girls inhaled a breakfast of fresh papaya atop homemade granola and we settled into our daytime routines. I read them the sad conclusion to *Where the Red Fern Grows* which left both girls teary-eyed. I thought now that they were getting older, we'd select more mature novels where not everything ended happily ever after. My bad. Quincy sniffled and pleaded "Mama, the next book we read needs to have a happy ending." "Yeah," Kendall piped up.

"Find us a happy book then," Bruce called out from his perch on the front tramp. At this challenge both girls dashed below, elbowing each other out of the way to find a brand-new adventure. A few minutes later Kendall surfaced clutching a new paperback. On the cover was an illustration of a spectacled boy straddling a kitchen broom. "Let's see what this story is about," I said and scooped Quincy up in my lap. Cracking open *Harry Potter and the Sorcerer's Stone*, I read the first line; "Mr. and Mrs. Dursley, of number four, Privet Drive, were proud to say they were perfectly normal..." The story of a magical boy's journey of self-discovery as he grew into a young man would eventually parallel our own girls' journeys from childhood to young adulthood. I handed the book to Kendall and as her words drifted on the wind, Bruce joined us, and we lounged in the cockpit listening.

"Looks like a great day to sail," grinned Bruce. We had motored on glassy seas all night, but with sunrise the wind once again filled the sails. I let its cooling breath wash over my body. Mimicking me, the girls stood and turned their faces into the breeze to take measure of the strength and direction of the wind. It's not that I didn't trust the digital wind instrument perched atop the mast, I just felt more in tune with the wind dancing on my cheek.

Bruce scanned the surrounding skies and seeing no sign of thunderstorms or other worrisome weather, declared it the perfect time to bring out "The Monster." "That means we'll go really really fast, doesn't it?" asked Kendall, our budding eight-year-old sailor. "Yeah, really really fast," mimicked Bruce with a broad smile. "Come help me hoist this beast and maybe we can cover some big miles today." Kendall lent a hand unfolding our prized headsail. At nearly twice the size of our working jib, Bruce appreciated her help. The sail cloth had the weight and feel of a giant white nylon windbreaker as it laid crumpled on the front deck like a collapsed parachute. In the cockpit, Quincy broke from playing with her stuffed animal and grabbed a line to help hoist the sail. Once aloft the sail filled and took on the shape of the wind and the entire blue sky in front of *Chewbacca* disappeared behind a gossamer veil. Instantaneously I felt the pull and *Chewbacca* sprinted forward like a racer leaving the starting block. With the headsail set and moving us nicely, I reached down and shut the motor off. Ahhh... peaceful silence.

"Warp speed!" shouted Bruce from the helm as we surged forward he tweaked and trimmed the sails to maximize our speed. We scrunched happily together in the cockpit as *Chewie* rushed along. Sometimes sailing was an agonizingly slow affair and one could stare at a landmark for what felt like hours before it finally passed. "There's a big difference between traveling at 4.5 and 10.5 knots" I remarked, my hair flying in the breeze. The sensation of speed was exhilarating, and

Chewbacca was in her element. I turned my face to the sun and drank in the rays, immersed in the fresh ocean air and rhythmic sound of the sea at our stern. Bruce saw *Chewie* as an intricate well-oiled machine while I viewed her as a dear friend, an entity with a soul. Differences between the sexes are sometimes highlighted at sea.

I loved to sneak in a little homeschooling whenever I could and as a bedtime story, I read about the Sea of Cortez (also called Gulf of California or Baja Peninsula) quoting from one of the guidebooks:

> *"The Sea has been described as "ferocious with life" by John Steinbeck and as "the aquarium of the world" by Jacques-Yves Cousteau. The name is in honor of Hernan Cortes, the conqueror of the Aztec Empire, who sent Francisco de Ulloa to map the area in 1539."*

They were still hanging in there, so I continued:

> *"Baja California is one of the longest peninsulas in the world, second only to the Malay Peninsula in Southeast Asia. There are 37 islands in the sea and it is considered to have some of the highest biodiversity on the planet."*

With this last tidbit of information, they were both asleep and I joined Bruce on deck. We shared the watch and talked into the night, enjoying the solitude and rhythm of a gentle ocean under the smile of a bright moon.

Morning came fast and while I was below preparing breakfast Quincy took over the helmsman chair and in less than two minutes gave out a squeal of delight. Off in the distance she spotted some faint water spouts announcing the possibility of a whale crossing our path. Breakfast would have to wait. It was "all hands-on deck" as Bruce altered course just a bit and I throttled back the engine to quietly approach whatever it was. I was both nervous and a little excited. Our friends on *Atlantis* told us of the time they had hit a sleeping whale at night and the story resurfaced in my brain as we crept closer. *Chewbacca* was built for speed not impact and I didn't want to think about what a whale could do to our fragile home. Through the binoculars, I spied more than one spout spewing mist. I handed the binoculars to Kendall and went to retrieve our *Whales and Dolphin Species Guide*. I leafed to the page depicting various water spouts, pointed to the description and asked Quincy to start reading. "Unlike most whales where the spout shoots straight up high into the air, the spout of the Sperm whale is aimed to the left and forward," she read. But then her reading tapered off as she was drawn to the incredible sight unfolding before us. If only one kind of whale blows their water spout off to one side, we were about to encounter a pod of Sperm whales (*Physeter microcephalus*)!

Laying the book down, Quincy stood at the lifelines, enthralled. I was a bit apprehensive approaching a pod of whales with teeth the size of a T-Rex, but the opportunity was too good to pass up.

Whales in general might be big, but they aren't all that easy to spot in the middle of the ocean. Like bird watching, you need to know just what to look for, those telltale signs unique to each species. The elusive Sperm whale is harder to find than other whale species because they don't stand out of the water very much and their distinctive blow doesn't spray up more than six or eight feet, making them hard to spot from a distance. Unlike California Greys or Humpbacks, we rarely saw Sperm whales because they spend so much time underwater. Sperm whales are deep divers, holding their breath and diving thousands of feet to feed on deep sea squid and fish. Only rarely do these energetic animals take a break and rest on the surface. But this is what they seemed to be doing; resting or maybe even sleeping.

Because of the whale's keen sense of hearing, I suggested we shut off the engine and ghost along using only the mainsail to tug us in their direction. Another reason for shutting down the engine was that I didn't want to spook a whale, and have it hit our spinning propeller. Let's not make them angry. Who hasn't read *Moby Dick*?

I tried to calm my own excitement by quietly reading to the girls out of the guidebook:

> *"The Sperm Whale is the largest of all toothed whales, and many people immediately think of the story of Moby Dick when they see one. In Herman Melville's classic novel, a Sperm whale called Moby Dick is portrayed as an evil monster which sinks ships and kills*

sailors. This is the reputation these whales have gotten throughout the years, perhaps because of their large size and huge teeth."

Oh great, they had to mention the huge teeth. We drifted closer and I read on:

"Many people think that the Sperm Whale is very lazy. They are sometimes seen engaging in a behavior called logging. This is a position where they remain just below the surface of the water. They simply float in this position and are very calm. While floating motionless, part of the head, the dorsal fin or parts of the back are exposed at the surface. Sperm whales seen logging are relatively easy to approach in this state."

And there they were, floating on the surface like partially submerged sequoia logs. I half expected their skin to be black, shiny and smooth, like a wet inner tube ready to pop, but it was greyish and wrinkly like a shriveled prune. What stood out the most was their massive blunt heads with all the grace of a concrete cinder block.

I lowered my reading voice even further so as not to disturb the dozen sleeping logs floating by:

"Sperm Whales are one of the deepest-diving mammals in the world. They are believed to be able to dive up to 10,000 meters in depth and two hours in duration to the ocean floor. These toothed whales eat thousands of pounds of fish and squid per day. They feed on several species of squid, octopuses, and rays. The white scars often seen on the bodies of Sperm Whales are believed to be caused by life and death struggles with giant squid."

That got a collective hushed "WOW" out of both girls.

Not wanting to break the spell, we observed the sleeping pod as we drifted past each other in total silence. I gripped the life lines just because it seemed like something one did when passing by sleeping whales. All too soon the group was astern, and Bruce set *Chewbacca* back on course.

The next three days passed uneventfully and on the 4th afternoon the air heated up noticeably as we approached the Baja coast. The rugged land spread out before my eyes and like the Siren's song, its unique beauty lured me. The landscape continued to change before my very eyes. The few green hillsides faded like a passing cloud to be replaced by the high desert mountains tumbling to the sea. At first glance, the landscape looked barren, but upon closer inspection it was highly textured, like an old tweed coat. It looked scrappy, and full of character as if to live here required grit and fortitude. Indeed, I noticed an absence of civilization, even along this spectacular stretch of coastline which I deemed as prime real estate.

Bruce disengaged *Han* and I steered towards an area the guidebook had marked with an anchor. The water became a brilliant turquoise and the land turned a russet brown. A palate of new hues shimmered before my eyes and I was greeted with every shade of earth tone imaginable from deep gold, light amber, browns and ochre reds. Contrasted against the striking blue water, the colors were breath taking. We had left the humid, green jungle behind and the dry, stark desert landscape was spread out before us.

Once anchored I could see the girls were chomping at the bit to go ashore. This gave me some quiet time to tidy up *Chewbacca* while Bruce and the girls piled into the dinghy to explore this new deserted paradise. They were anxious to run and stretch their legs. The alluring white sand beach called, and I watched from the galley window as they ran wild, arms and legs flying about celebrating life.

I had just set my flour out to begin making a batch of bread dough when I heard the distinct roar of the returning dinghy motor going at full tilt. Too fast. But it was the screaming above the sound of the motor's whine that had my heart pounding. I rushed on deck to see Bruce steering the dinghy with one hand, while the other was wrapped tightly around Kendall trying to control her convulsive crying. Quincy was trying to console her sister yet at the same time using her weight to hold the bow down on the racing dinghy. What had happened?

Bruce bounced the *Blaster* against *Chewbacca's* hull and literally tossed Kendall up on deck. I immediately saw the angry red welts rising across her calves. Red stripes puffed up on her legs where the tentacles of a Portuguese man-of-war (*Physalia utriculus*) had wrapped themselves around her as she played along the surf line. Without a word, I dashed below to get our medical kit. First, I uncapped the bottle of antihistamine and had her swallow one. My mind raced back several years to Bruce's spider bite in the South Pacific and I was thankful we had learned from the experience to keep prescription strength Benadryl in our medical kit. Next, I doused her tortured legs in vinegar and sprinkled on meat tenderizer to neutralize the poison. Then Bruce pulled out his pocket knife and told Kendall to hold very still. Visions of medieval bloodletting filled my mind but quickly passed as I saw Bruce scraping the blade down her legs like a razor attempting to remove any remaining stingers from her skin. Quincy pulled out a cold can of Coke from the icebox and rolled it over Kendall's welts tracing the wounds with its icy cooling powers. This seemed to offer her the most relief as she settled on the cockpit floor in a heap.

With the emergency stabilized, I sat down to read from our medical journal about administering further to her jellyfish stings. We had been lucky aboard *Chewbacca* that nothing stronger than Tylenol or antibiotic cream had been called for so far. Thankfully we carried an extensive medical kit. "Maybe we should keep something in the dinghy" suggested Quincy. Together we listed what we needed to incorporate into the smaller dinghy first aid kit to address a coral cut or scrape or a jelly fish encounter and one for day hikes to treat blisters or even a desert scorpion sting to keep in our day pack. We were surrounded by a new environment that would surely bring with it new challenges.

CHAPTER 19

MONTEZUMA'S REVENGE

"Survival is triumph enough."

-Harry Crews, Author

AFTER A COUPLE WEEKS OF EXPLORING OUR ISOLATED ANCHORAGE WE WERE running low on provisions and were reluctantly driven towards civilization. It was a morning rich with both sun and frothy clouds as Bruce pulled anchor and I took a victory lap around the tiny bay before heading towards open water. Bruce set a course further north into the Sea of Cortez to La Paz; a town with the promise of supplies for us and ice cream for the girls. Our plan was to stop at the marina dock, check in with the Port Captain, replenish our food lockers and grab an ice cream cone. A brief stop. Nothing more.

After an easy overnight sail, I stepped off *Chewbacca* and was instantly mesmerized by the incredible clarity of the water and assortment of rainbow colored fish cavorting around the dock. The girls followed and laid on the splintered boards peering into their very own personal aquarium. Suddenly a sea horse wheeled into view and the girls gave out a squeal of delight. The encounter with this four-inch mystical creature was too hard to resist and soon there were four bodies lying in a row as Bruce and I joined the girls. I was bewitched. The four became six, then eight, as word spread up and down the dock that a sea horse had been spotted. It didn't take long for a huddle of prone adults to become fully engrossed in this whimsical denizen of the sea. "It's like discovering a unicorn," Kendall said, her eyes still focused on her new friend as he propelled himself seemingly willy-nilly from one wooden piling to the next. When he disappeared under the dock and emerged on the other side everyone shifted in unison to the new vantage point. No one wanted the show to end. This little guy was creating quite a stir and it was a half hour before the press of boat responsibilities pulled us away.

We caught a bus to town and trying to meld in I noticed that picking a cruiser out of the crowd was easy.

All cruisers wore wide brimmed canvas hats from dawn to dusk along with sunglasses on tethers, Teva sandals, and carrying a canvas shopping bag or knapsack completed the stereotypical profile. I had acquired an appreciation and admiration for the Himalayan Sherpa who carry everything on their backs and sometimes felt our lifestyle shared many similarities. I could also pick out our fellow cruisers in town, not only by their dress, but because they always walked with purpose, as if on a mission, rather than sauntering along with nowhere to go and no list to complete. Hmmm... ChapStick with a high SPF replaced my coral colored lip gloss, zinc oxide replaced blush and SPF 45 sun screen replaced my body lotion. My perfume was whatever scent came out of the Right Guard deodorant stick and a pony tail was my hairstyle of choice. For me, I always thought my hands gave me away because they were transforming to a weathered deep brown and my short unpainted nails reflected the practical lifestyle I now led. Bruce had become the official family hairdresser and once every few months we lined up and our hair was lopped off somewhat straight at the shoulders. He buzzed his own hair with all the skill of a blind gardener mowing a lawn. No one seemed to particularly care.

We had no mirror onboard *Chewie* so, it was quite a shock when I looked at myself in the full-length mirror in the marina's bathroom. I jumped back at the sight of myself. A strong, lean country girl who had seen a lot of the outdoors stared back at me. The girls, on the other hand, were mesmerized by their reflections. After appraising their looks, they smiled, stuck out tongues, flipped their hair and ran their fingers over their freckled noses and cheeks. They simply had no practice looking at themselves to see what others saw. They saw themselves from the inside out. Our reflection didn't reveal tourists on an extended vacation, but rather our newly adopted lifestyle. And what would this fantastic life bring next?

"Daddy doesn't sound so good," Kendall said as she nudged me from sleep. She was standing at the side of our bunk and I reached across the void that earlier held my husband. "What's wrong?" I mumbled as my mind surfaced from wherever it had been wandering and I opened my eyes. "I don't know but…" Before she could finish I heard the unmistakable sound of vomit hitting water. "Eww" was all I could say when I flashbacked to Kendall upchucking birthday cake all over the side of our cabin wall last week. The faint smell of the sickly-sweet icing still lingered and what was happening out on the back tramp made me pause.

Uh-oh. *Didn't we both eat the same thing from that little street taco stand?* My mind raced to recall how many hours ago that was. Now I wasn't feeling so hot. *Was this just sympathy pains from hearing my husband violently puking out his guts?* Not moments later, like a dutiful wife I knelt beside him and joined the party. As dawn shed its first ray of light, we were still sprawled on the back deck, spent and well… ready to die. Death would be a relief, but we had kids to take care of so dying would have to wait.

For the next five days we were too weak to get out of bed, but at least we had stopped heaving up stomach acid and our volcanic fevers had at last broken. I couldn't smell myself and wasn't sure if that was a good thing or a bad thing. My mouth tasted awful and my eyes felt as crusty as a dry river bed. Just moving my head was painful. I wondered if I looked as bad as I felt. Maybe worse.

Somehow the girls survived. I crawled my way to the galley and saw the remnants of the cans and packages they had lived off while Bruce and I were delirious. Thank goodness, the girl's natural survival skills included how to lift the pull tab on a can of Spam and how to use a can opener for fruit cocktail. Two empty jars of peanut butter were on the counter, each with a spoon still sticking out.

We were still moving a bit slow from our brush with death as we walked gingerly through the market restocking *Chewbacca's* food lockers. "I think it's time to Get out of Dodge" declared Bruce, once everything was stowed and our water jugs were full. This little detour had added an unexpected week to our marina bill and I knew we would have to spend many weeks on the hook to make up for this surprise expenditure. We unfolded our charts and looked for a little get-away deeper in the heart of the Sea of Cortez.

The sea, with its ever-changing shades of blue met the mountains head-on in an explosion of contrast that left the beholder spellbound. I was beginning to feel better and read from the guidebook, "These mountains are the Sierra de la Giganta," pointing to the giant mountain range seemingly reclined alongside *Chewbacca*. At first, I couldn't take my eyes away from this barren ruggedness. From my vantage point it looked like the moon, but I suspected it held a hidden life we had yet to discover.

Our days passed in perfect harmony and by the time the girls had read about Harry Potter confronting his deepest fears by conquering a Boggart, and the Hippogriff named Buckbeak had rescued Sirius, we were preparing to anchor. We had pulled down the jib, flaked the mainsail into the lazy jacks and fired up *Chewbacca's* engine as Kendall read the last sentence of the book. I smiled thinking about *Chewbacca* laying all alone under a brilliant blanket of stars. This seemed like a perfect resting spot for the night.

As the sun hit the hills behind our little cove and darkness overtook *Chewbacca*, we were plunged into the silence of night. "Dad can we listen to some music?" Kendall asked. She got her pick of CD's, which I had no complaints about since they were essentially all mine. *Dan Fogelberg it is.* We were constantly aware of our power resources but tonight our batteries were full, and life was good.

Bruce flipped on the light above the salon table and the girls began to clear the dishes as *The Leader of the Band* played. They had just set the plates on the galley counter when I heard a long exhale coming from outside. Bruce heard it too and opened the door to the cockpit. *Is somebody out there?* The sound grew steadily to a howl and then escalated into a roar as warm wind swooped across the water and brought *Chewbacca* to attention. She swung into the wind hard and I was nearly thrown to the floor by the sudden lurch and wondered if we had been hit by another vessel or a breaching whale. Kendall shut off the music as I raced outside to stand by Bruce in the pitch-black cockpit. My hair was pulled back by the fierce wind. "IT SOUNDS LIKE A TRAIN IS PASSING THROUGH," shouted Bruce, his voice barely heard over the roar. The canyon walls of the island amplified the wind. Although we felt confident that our anchor was set firm, we were taken off guard by the fierceness of these sudden gusts. I could feel my heart pounding through my skin. The girls passed our battery powered spotlight up into the cockpit and I made a sweep of the empty anchorage. Satisfied we were well away from the shoreline, I returned below to retrieve the trusty guidebook. "Ah, here it is in the next chapter… they are called Coromuels." Everyone gathered closer to hear above the howl as I read:

"The winds are created when cool marine air from the Pacific side of the peninsula is drawn over the desert to the relatively warmer side of the Gulf of California. The winds received their name after Samuel Cromwell, a sailor from the 19th century, believed to be a pirate. He visited La Paz very often and legend says, hid one of his biggest treasures on the beach that carries his name. Because the natives could not pronounce his last name, they called him "Coromuel.""

Nothing like a little impromptu night school. I hoped reading aloud calmed their nerves better than mine. But the girls were unconcerned about the screeching wind outside and intrigued by the possibility of finding buried pirate treasure on the beach. They reluctantly headed to bed while weaving whimsical tales of pirate adventures.

For us adults, bed was not an option. We hunkered down at the salon table for a night of anchor watch and unlimited hands of Gin Rummy. By three in the morning I was up 300 points and looking for an excuse to put the final kibosh on Bruce when suddenly the buffeting winds stopped. They didn't slowly abate but shut off as if someone had flipped a big switch in the sky. Bruce took advantage of the situation, made a final sweep of the horizon with the spotlight and declared the game a draw. I was too weary to argue and dragged myself to bed.

I awoke with blinding sunlight streaming through the porthole at my feet. Squinting past my toes, I could see the deceivingly placid water. Having been bitten once by this wind, I hastily paged ahead in the guidebook to determine where we might take better shelter from the brunt of the ferocious Coromuel. Maybe there was a reason why this attractive little cove was all ours.

This pretty anchorage was as alluring as a Venus fly trap looking for a hapless victim… and we just happened to be buzzing by.

CHAPTER 20

SOME LIKE IT HOT!

"The biggest adventure you can take is to live the life of your dreams."

-Oprah Winfrey, Actress

WE GOTTA GET OUT OF HERE. THE GUIDEBOOK SUGGESTED AN ISLAND A little further offshore where an anchor symbol marked a small bay on the leeward side, promising good protection from the Coromuel winds.

Breakfast was underway and after a ten hour sail, we rounded the point and wandered into the anchorage of our dreams. At least my dreams. The ribbons of dark blue, lighter aqua and turquoise water were the clearest I'd seen yet. Red cliffs tumbled down to a narrow strip of white sand beach, framing this postcard perfect setting. "What a cool hidey hole," Bruce grinned after our anchor was firmly set.

"Let's get in the water," shouted Kendall already in her blue polka dot Lycra suit as she pulled out her snorkel gear ready to beat her sister into nature's swimming pool. The race was on as Quincy wiggled into her matching pink polka dot ensemble. Both girls had inherited the one-piece zip up suits made from stretchy Lycra material from fellow boat-kids. They were the perfect protection from the sun's harmful rays and from stinging jelly fish and coral scrapes.

As promised in the guidebooks, there was no surf crashing onto the beach and Bruce motored the *Blaster* until it glided to a gentle stop. I stepped into warm ankle-deep water as easily as climbing out of a parked car. At first the sand was coarse but as I walked out of the water's reach, it softened into fine white powder that squeaked underfoot with each step.

Bruce decided this was the perfect place and time to give the girls their first Drivers Ed lessons piloting the *Blaster*. They were just as excited as any 16 year old about to hop behind the wheel of the family car for the first time, even though they weren't anywhere near their teen years. I heard Bruce reviewing the basics of the outboard motor operation. His patient voice drifted through the port hole above me as I prepared a batch of bread. By the time I had punched down the dough after its second kneading, each of the girls had lapped *Chewbacca* 100 times. I could see the concentration plastered across their nervous faces from the porthole in the galley but within a half hour they were taking solo trips puttering around the small bay.

School continued, but many days it was "beach school." Between lessons we would take recess and comb the pristine shoreline seeking Mother Nature's treasures. I was on the lookout for the elusive pukka shells and perfect sand dollars scattered along the sensual curve of beach while the girls kept their eyes open and their small plastic shovels at the ready to unearth any pirate treasure. Unfortunately, the girls found no pirate treasure, but that didn't keep them from digging and their unbridled imaginations continued the quest. With each plunge of their plastic shovels they listened intently, hoping to strike upon the metal of an old chest filled with ancient coins. When my back needed a break, I plopped down and rested my eyes on the distant mountains watching over us bathed in assorted shades of gold and red, seemingly touching the blue sky. I drank in the desert landscape and soon forgot the color green.

From *Chewbacca's* deck I could distinguish individual grains of sand 15 feet below. For Kendall and Quincy, the bay was their playground and personal aquarium. There was so much sea life that brushing food scraps over board invited a feeding frenzy as hundreds of fish boiled up in the normally placid waters. Trigger fish, eagle rays, parrotfish and schools of squid, eyed us as they passed by. Each evening at sun set, we had front row seats as dozens and dozens of manta rays sprang out of the water, summersaulted and landed back in the water with a loud slap. Whether to remove annoying parasites, or just fun, I never knew but their show was awesome entertainment.

As quartermaster, I took daily stock of our food and water supply, gauging how long we could remain in our private paradise. If it continued to rain every few days, our 30 gallons of water would last indefinitely, but food was another matter. Bruce seized the opportunity to turn the inventory into a math lesson and directed the girls to sort the cans into meal groups figuring out approximately how many meals we had left.

We typically waited until the bitter end to leave an anchorage and would inevitably find ourselves feasting on a "little bit of this" and "a little bit of that" before we finally admitted that indeed it was time to leave. "I think it's time to go" Bruce declared shaking his head, when I opened a jar of pickles and spilled a box of crackers onto a paper plate then selected a can out of the GOK pile that had the size and heft of a can of fruit cocktail. "Peaches. Hey, I was pretty close. Could have been peas." I said with a smile. Perhaps once again we had strayed too long in paradise.

As Bruce was pulling up the anchor I felt as though we were being cast out of the Garden of Eden… but we'd be back.

For the next six months a regular path of travel emerged whenever the ice in the icebox was gone, the water jugs neared empty and the cupboards thinned out. While the ice wasn't as important as water, it meant we could have fresh vegetables, meats, cold drinks and preserve our fresh catches from the sea. We made our provisioning run about every two weeks and sailed *Chewbacca* the five hours to a small settlement on the mainland. "We've repeated this trek so many times, I feel as though we've worn a groove in the sea," I remarked to Bruce as we set sail once again towards civilization.

It took us a day to shop and a few trips in the dinghy to ferry it all out to *Chewbacca*. First, we would transport a 50-lb. block of ice the size of a carry-on suitcase out to *Chewbacca* and hoist it three feet up and out of the *Blaster*. Countless times it could easily have ended up as a baby iceberg bobbing off into the sunset and fantasies of owning a real freezer danced before my eyes. The icebox aboard *Chewbacca* was cavernous and large enough to hide a small child, (don't ask me how I know this), and easily swallowed up the large block of ice but didn't leave a whole lot of room for food. On top of the ice went cheeses, hot dogs, lunch meat and a couple of cold beers and any fresh produce piled on top. Last, we stashed 30 gallons of water, 5 gallons of fuel for the dinghy and enough staples and canned goods to last two weeks before retracing the route back from our island retreat to civilization.

We had to find a way to supplement and extend our food stores or we'd be forced back to civilization all too soon. Lucky for us, one morning before even a hint of offshore breeze stirred through *Chewbacca's* portholes, the radio chirped to life and an invitation was extended for dinner that evening, followed by, "Do you all like clams?" For cruisers in the Sea, an invite to dinner usually included helping catch said dinner. Our green crew had no clue how to find a clam, much less how to catch one. While Lee and Debbie were in their mid-60's, they exuded a youthful playfulness that struck a chord with us all. Debbie, a fiery Italian had a vibrant personality that propelled her well beyond her 4' 10" stature. The galley was the hub of *Escape* and delicious aromas wafting from her open hatches teased the anchorage both day and night. True to form, Lee pulled up in his dinghy and quickly offered to teach the girls how to find the elusive Chacolate or chocolate clams (*Tivela planulata*) that hid just a few inches under the sand…but only if you knew just where to look.

It took awhile to get the knack of locating the tell-tale signs of a clam's hiding spot, but the two clear "soda straw" looking air tubes poking through the sand gave them away to the trained eye. Once spying them was accomplished it took some stealthy hovering in place to successfully sneak up on your prey, all the while never allowing your shadow to fall on their hiding place to tip your hand. With a powerful kick, you had to dive down and scoop through the sand to capture this delicacy, but you had to be fast. Sometimes they put up a formidable fight, frantically digging deeper while your fingers tried to get a grip on the fleeing hors d'oeuvre. The desire to bag your quarry fought with the need to surface and breathe. This balancing act was a contest of wills between predator and prey; sometimes you won and sometimes they won. It was all part of the fun and obsession of underwater clam digging and I never looked at the sandy bottom again without conjuring up a new clam recipe.

Summer was in full swing and the water temperatures rose to a bath-like 83° causing the blanket of sea grass to die. This natural deforestation exposed previously hidden coral reefs and gardens increasing our snorkeling sites. Each morning we stepped down the swim ladder and sunk beneath the water looking for our next meal. It felt vaguely primal armed with spear guns kicking along the water's surface side by side scanning the sandy bottom left and right scouting out prey, diving down to check out a rock ledge or peeking into a dark cave. Bruce and Quincy each had a large dive knife strapped to their legs and Kendall carried a large mesh bag for any bounty caught along the way. Our lifestyle had evolved from a city-based life to a rural life tied closely to nature. We reverted to the hunter gatherers of times long past.

I'm not sure how formidable our hunting party looked. Bruce worked out a method to rig our hot pink beach umbrella in the dinghy to protect us from the merciless sun. While we puttered over to another rock outcropping that promised good hunting, the girls shimmied into their indispensable one-piece zip up polka dot lycra suits. I smeared white zinc on their ear tips and noses like war paint, which only added to the warrior illusion.

We anchored the *Blaster* and one by one slipped over the side and dipped below the water's surface. The water became a sanctuary from the oppressive heat and I found myself spending more and more time immersed in its cooling depths. Laying on the surface I felt like I was floating in a tepid bath but a short dive to the bottom quickly raised goosebumps.

Visions of tribal hunting parties crossing the savannas in search of a meal came to mind as Kendall signaled she'd found her first victim. Her closed fist signaled "stop" and then she pointed a finger to a patch of sand. We all stopped kicking and lay still on the surface like floating clouds as Kendall took a breath, kicked her flippers and swiftly dove down 15 feet and like a hawk deftly pounced upon her prey. A puff of bottom sand momentarily obscured our view and then she was back opening her bag to show off her first clam of the morning. In less than an hour, her bag was full of 18 fist-size milk chocolate colored shells. Over time we came to discover that different water depths yielded different sized clams. The shallower the water, the smaller the clams, and depending how hungry we were, we shopped accordingly.

It became a family ritual to slip extra clams to our friends the octopuses before heading home. Bruce refused to say "octopi" and as an English major it was painfully sad to take English lessons from an engineer. We could easily recognize the octopi, or octopuses' (*Octopus bimaculatus*) lairs as they were littered with the empty shells from past meals. We set our gifts in front of the rocky grotto and backed away. "Pizza delivery!" Within minutes an inquisitive tentacle would reach out and expertly snag the tempting treat. Once the show was over, we swam back to *Chewie* and hung our mesh bag on the swim ladder giving the clams time to purge the beach sand from their systems. By evening, the aroma of BBQed clams, topped with a sprinkling of chopped garlic and a dollop of Worchester sauce was carried on the soft breeze.

As the sun's rays attacked our skin from above, the reflection coming off the water attacked from below and we did everything we could to keep from getting roasted. We covered up with long sleeve baggy cotton shirts and our ever-present wide brimmed canvas hats. These accessories were crucial armament when it came to the fight against wrinkled, leathery skin and melanoma.

The midday desert heat rippled and reached out to grip *Chewbacca* in her fiery embrace. Bruce looked over at me sprawled out in the cockpit like a sun baked lizard and I had the urge to flick my tongue in his direction like a contented iguana… but I couldn't muster the energy. *I wonder if this is what a dry martini feels like?*

The temperature inside our home teased into the triple digits creating an environment ripe for shortened tempers and irritability. To lessen instances of contention within our 33-foot capsule we each found our own bubble of time and space to stretch out and be alone. The girls liked to hide out under a sun shade on the front tramp playing with their toys and whispering stories out of ear shot of their parents. I found solace at dawn catching the cool morning breeze generated by the rising sun and I planned the day sipping my morning coffee on the bow while my family slept. Watching the stars pop out each night was Bruce's escape from the heat and a time for problem solving where some of his best solutions came to him as he laid on the cabin top and gazed into the Heavens.

People often asked; *Why in the world would you venture to the desert during the hottest time of year?* Cruisers in Mexico faced a dilemma each year when hurricane season approached. The choices were simple to get out of the hurricane zone. You had to move either north or south. South would force us all the way into Central America while north took us up into Baja and the Sea of Cortez.

The Sea is a fairly protected body of water and its upper regions are protected from the full fury of the Pacific by the Baja Peninsula. Although the bottom portion of the Baja tends to get whacked every few years by a major storm, it also contains some of the most breathtaking anchorages. And with a roll of the dice, that was where we chose to seek sanctuary from the greatest storms on earth.

CHAPTER 21

A TANGO WITH JULIETTE

"Life isn't about waiting for the storm to pass…it's learning to dance in the rain."

-Vivian Greene, Author

"HURRICANE COMING!"

All ears were tuned to the morning weather report coming over the radio. Silence invaded *Chewbacca* as the foreboding message was digested. Hurricane Juliette[1] was creeping up the Pacific side of the Baja Peninsula. There was a slight possibility that she could veer due east, cross over the peninsula and pounce upon us in the Sea of Cortez where we were hiding, so we listened intently to the updates.

"Right now, she is moving along the Pacific coast," Bruce stated. He had a chart spread out with a pencil dot on Juliette's last known position. "Typically, these hurricanes keep going right up the outside of Baja then turn left out into the open ocean and fizzle out. We are protected by the Baja Peninsula between us and the Pacific." He continued in a steady, even voice, showing no hint of concern. "OK, let's think about our options. We were smart to come this far north." He moved the chart closer to the girls on the other side of the table. "We are here at Isla Carmen and there is Escondido only a half days sail away." His finger traced the course to the harbor. Kendall asked, "Is that the safest place to be in a hurricane?" Bruce reiterated our plan "If Juliet moves closer, we'll pack up quick and skedaddle over there to hunker down." I added in a reassuring tone, "Remember how that bay was almost totally enclosed

---

1   Hurricane Juliette ranked as the 5th strongest Pacific hurricane on record and caused twelve deaths and $400 million in damage when it hit Baja, California.

by the mountains and sheltered from the waves? We'll be safe there."
I had to speak those words aloud as much for myself as for the girls.

The next morning Bruce's ear was tuned to the radio again. "Shit.
Juliette jumped over the peninsula. She's coming our way!" Before the
details of the morning weather update were finished, Bruce was pulling
on his gloves and I was warming up the engine. Without a word, the
girls stowed the breakfast dishes in the galley sink and helped prepare
Chewbacca for sail. They instinctively realized we had two routines for
up-anchoring. One was leisurely and the other was NOW. By the time
I shifted the motor in gear, both girls emerged from below, took their
positions and harnessed in. Kendall called out numbers from the depth
sounder while Quincy acted as lookout. In less than 10 minutes we
were underway and moving through the anchorage. All around us we
could hear the rattle of chain from nearby boats also preparing to get
underway. We were in a race with Juliette.

We could expect that cruisers from the nearby islands would be
converging in droves on Puerto Escondido during the following days.
When we arrived five hours later, the protected inner bay was already
filling up fast and the once spacious sanctuary looked dangerously full.
Bruce and I discussed our options and decided that if we could find a
good spot in the far less crowded outer harbor we would be safer. The
downside of anchoring outside would be our exposure to the full brunt
of Mother Nature, but I trusted our own anchoring skills more than
I trusted others. It was settled.

Already the skies were changing. Juliette had grown to a Category
4 hurricane and we had 48 hours to prepare for impact. With the
inevitable collision imminent, we stripped and streamlined *Chewbacca*
of anything that could fly off or catch the wind. Bruce wound rope
around our main sail cover to secure it from unwrapping while the
girls unstrung our canvas awning leaving only the stainless-steel frame
as naked as a Halloween skeleton. We debated whether to leave the
Blaster tied on deck, ready to deploy in an emergency but decided it
would be more prudent to store it folded and tied down along the port
hull. It would present the smallest target for the destructive winds to
grab and blow overboard, but it also left us vulnerable with no escape
vehicle in case things turned dicey. As Juliette brought her dance card

ever closer, more and more boats streamed past us and continued into the inner harbor. It was bursting at the seams and potentially the recipe for disaster.

We were boat bound now. To keep the girls' minds off the ever-strengthening wind, homeschool was in full session. They crossed the line between reality and fantasy each day as they charted Juliette's progress towards us and colored in tightly wound swirls on construction paper. Bruce used the opportunity to throw in a few word problems and they practiced with the dividers and geometry tools of the trade. They wrote daring stories of survival for their figurines to live out. We read aloud stories of courage from the Brian Jacques novels of Mossflower Country. As the storm raged outside we were cozy inside the imaginary walls of our Redwall Abbey. To occupy my time, I turned to the galley and the aroma of fresh baked breads, soups and stews filled the cabin nourishing our souls as if we were safely snowed in at a mountain retreat rather than bracing for the punch of a hurricane.

And suddenly Juliette was upon us. Her winds screeched through the rigging at a steady 40 knots with gusts reaching over 55 knots. We were catching just a taste of what she could bring. I couldn't stand on the cabin top for the strength of the wind would bowl me over. I could only sneak a quick peek to survey our surroundings before being blown back to seek cover. The rain didn't fall from the sky but came horizontal across the bow like stinging bullets. The slap, slap, slap of white caps could be heard hitting the hulls as the increased wind built up steep waves that smacked into *Chewbacca* and tugged angrily at her anchor chain.

We had picked our anchoring location well. *Chewbacca* was partially protected from the full fetch of the sea and brunt of the wind by the tiny spit of land standing guard at the mouth of the bay. However fierce Mother Nature was, she didn't pose the greatest danger to *Chewbacca*; it was the unmanned boats moored on the fringes of the bay that I most worried about. If any one of them were to cut loose, we could be crushed or carried out to sea with them. Neither a pleasant option.

The winds continued to strengthen throughout the day. Over the radio, I heard drama playing out in the inner harbor as boats chaffed through their mooring lines and broke loose or dragged anchor and rammed into other boats like carnival bumper cars. The unlucky ones were wrecked upon the shore. The ferocious winds overhead had now reached 70 knots... hurricane strength. No one slept.

"MAYDAY, MAYDAY, MAYDAY" burst from the radio and the panicked voice grew shriller by the second, "My boat is dragging anchor and the engine won't start." He added that he was a single hander and alone on his boat. "This is sailing vessel *Pegasus*, can anyone assist?"

"*PEGASUS*... OH, MY GOD, *Pegasus* is anchored right in front of us!" I yelled to myself as much as to anyone listening. *Pegasus* was 70-feet of heavy steel and a massive sailboat, even for a full crew to handle. My mind racing, I searched for options. It would be foolish to up anchor in this storm and physically impossible for Bruce to pull up all the chain in these pitching seas. We could cut the anchor loose and make a run for it before we were mowed down by this oncoming freight train, but visibility was zero and we'd probably end up on the rocks. We were out of options.

I swung open the cockpit door and was instantly seized by the maelstrom of strong winds and piercing cold rain. Bruce pushed past me and started the engine, thrusting it into gear with just a little forward throttle. His plan was to ease some of the strain on our anchor to be sure we held tight, yet not move forward into any danger. He directed me to stand guard near the tiller with the hope that I could maybe maneuver *Chewie* out of harm's way if *Pegasus* broke loose.

Thunder crashed so loudly that even standing shoulder to shoulder we had to shout to be heard. Any hope of light shed by the pale moon was snubbed out by a thick blanket of clouds overhead. The only light came from the lightning casting a supernatural glow upon the water for a split second. Like camera flash bulbs going off in my face, I was temporarily blinded with each strike. I imagined Zeus up in the heavens raining thunder bolts on us. We were caught in a battle and that was exactly what the storm felt like, a battlefield.

Feeling helpless, I reached under the cockpit seat for the spotlight, but I was shaking so hard it took both hands to hold it steady. I vigilantly scanned the area around *Chewbacca* and in front of us was the stern of *Pegasus*, looming larger than life only a few yards away. My eyes were frozen on her stern. *Was she slipping closer?* I thought so because before, her name was just scribbling, but now I could clearly make out the fancy script lettering on the stern.

Bruce took the spotlight from me and dashed to the bow waving it about as if the beam of light could stave off a collision. Mama bear instincts kicked in and I launched myself below, waking the girls. I shepherded them to the salon and roughly shoved their groggy bodies into their life vests in case we had to abandon ship. Besides being crushed, my other fear was that *Pegasus* would catch our anchor chain and drag us both to an uncertain fate. Our boats were in a dicey situation as *Pegasus* rolled from gunnel to gunnel dragging ever closer. The owner looked up from his frantic effort to start his engine and I swear he was close enough to Bruce to shake hands, but we had nowhere to run.

Suddenly I saw a cloud of blue black smoke rise from the stern as her engine coughed to life and slowly, the seconds dragged into minutes as she began to pull away from us.

Pegasus hovered a safe distance away for over an hour as we were pummeled by the storm but for now the madness ended. I carefully unsnapped the girls' life jackets and slipped them from their bodies as they slumbered on. Bruce shut down the engine, flipped off the instruments and put the spotlight away. I returned to the cockpit and hunkered down with Bruce as the storm continued to rage around us, but for us this was a win. Tonight, there was one less boat on the reef.

CHAPTER 22

CABRITO ANYONE?

"Great friends are hard to find, difficult to leave, impossible to forget."

-Anonymous

FALL DESCENDED ON THE SEA OF CORTEZ LIKE A RUDE SLAP IN THE FACE. WE had made this our home for nearly six months and I could feel the seasons changing. Temperatures quickly cooled and like migratory birds, the time had come to retrace our steps south towards warmer cruising grounds. It seemed like the whole flock was about to scatter and plans were brewing for one last party before our tribe disbanded.

The fleet had all left for the Thanksgiving rendezvous spot, leaving *Chewbacca* alone in the anchorage when I heard Lee from *Escape* place an urgent radio call. I caught the word EMERGENCY and turned up the volume. I called Bruce over and we leaned closer listening intently to the broadcast. "Could anyone find and bring the vital missing ingredient for Debbie's family ravioli recipe?" What, no MAYDAY? I understood the seriousness of an Italian food calamity and accepted the challenge. After a slight detour to the local mercado, we hoisted our largest sails to make our best time on the overnight sail towards the gathering. Packed on ice inside our cooler was the special delivery; dark green Swiss Chard.

By mid-morning the next day we spied a cluster of masts hidden in the aquamarine water of the shallow bay. Red rock hillsides surrounded the anchorage and standing sentinel at the entrance was a rock pillar crowned with an Osprey nest. I was slowly circling the knot of boats when Bruce abruptly signaled for me to power down. Not sure what was happening, I slipped the engine into neutral and we glided in silence. Then I heard it. The gentle sound of bells coming from somewhere. I wondered if the girls were playing a prank on us or if they had just discovered a hidden toy. Bruce scanned the scenery and followed the sounds to a small herd of goats (cabrito) climbing the nearby hill and he pointed them out to me. The small brass bells tied around their necks tinkled as they pranced nimbly up steep paths that crisscrossed the rocky crevasses. Both girls came topsides to see what the quiet was about. "Is one of those sweet goats going to be our Thanksgiving dinner?" asked Kendall. "Well, our turkey may have hooves this year," replied Bruce. "That sounds good because I'm tired of canned tuna," added Quincy shading her eyes to get a better view of the barren cliffs that made up her ever-changing back yard. I pushed the throttle back into gear and by the time *Chewbacca's* anchor hit the pristine water, the goats had trotted over the ridgeline and out of sight.

The late afternoon sun turned a deep marigold as the cruising fleet united on the beach to coordinate Thanksgiving festivities. With the girl's newly minted driving permits, Bruce and I were ferried like royalty to the water's edge. We discussed who was bringing what and rallied volunteers to be a part of the ravioli assembly line, which turned out to be everyone. Everybody wanted to be "Italian" for a day. The real question was how many people could fit aboard *Escape* before she dipped below the gunnels?

The topic soon turned to the main course. More than *Chewbacca's* crew had noticed the grazing goats. Bruce floated the idea that since there wasn't turkey…maybe a goat would suffice. Heads nodded and soon a small contingent of cruisers hiked to the nearby settlement to meet with the local goat herder in hopes of placing an order. As luck would have it, the farmer agreed and even gave us the pick of the litter. No one stepped up to decide which goat would be the guest of honor, so they voted to let the farmer choose. Cowards!

The sense of togetherness and comradery was palpable. These new friends had become family and we'd shared many a potluck with each other up and down Mexico's shores for more than a year. We had weathered chubasco's and surf landings. Hell, we had even survived a hurricane. Together we had solved mechanical and electrical dilemmas and patched up more than a few cuts and scrapes. Some of our friends were leaving Mexico to explore further south and one couple was even heading to New Zealand. A few were going back to California leaving cruising life behind while others were opting to make the sea their permanent stomping grounds. This would be the last time together for many of us.

When we arrived for ravioli duty bright and early the next morning with the all-important chard, *Escape* was already sitting low in the water from the weight of so many bodies onboard. Debbie assigned some of us to run the freshly made dough through her hand cranked pasta machine while others cut, shaped and stuffed. We became one large, boisterous famiglia Italiana and the sounds of laughter and merry making drifted across the water. A few hours and 300 raviolis later, our bounty was carefully packed into Ziploc bags and distributed throughout the fleet's dorm sized refrigerators. Anticipation was high as we piled into the *Blaster* after *Escape's* galley had been cleaned and all the remnants of our ravioli making party were washed and put away. "Oh, I'm super excited about eating the ravs tomorrow. They looked so yummy," exclaimed Kendall as she steered us towards home.

"Your dad and I have had our share of memorable meals" I said as she docked us gently against *Chewie's* stern and we scampered onboard and filed into the salon."

I'm thinking of our first invitation to a Polynesian luau and our gourmet contribution." Bruce winked at me and we were on the same page. Instantly I was whisked back to our crewing days in the South Pacific when we coasted into the dramatic bay and dropped anchor beside two other sailboats. One of the cruisers called over to say that the chief of the village had invited everyone for a traditional Polynesian luau. However, the newly elected chief had an unusual request and he asked if each boat could bring a native dish to share with his people. No problem. I didn't have time to bake a cake, so I decided to make my favorite all-American snack… and I made enough to feed an invading army and still have left overs. But what could I carry it in?

We rowed ashore and the chief introduced us in his Marquesan tongue and we communicated with a lot of head nods and smiles. Soon we were shown a spot inside a large communal bamboo hut and plopped down on a woven mat blanketing the entire floor. Set upon it were an assortment of native dishes. Surveying the tempting array of food, I felt a bit embarrassed about the meager offering we had brought but I was even more embarrassed because the only container I had was a shiny black Lawn-N-Leaf bag. I still can't believe I brought food to my first real luau in a garbage bag.

In traditional Polynesian fashion, the guest is served first from the native delicacies as they are passed around while everyone else looked on. Since we were the guests, the most favored food began its rounds and I felt it was only polite to accept a little taste of everything passing my way. I nodded to the meat from the cheeks of a grouper and next the eyes plucked from another fish were placed on my banana leaf plate. Even Fafaru, or "stinky fish" eventually found its way around the circle to me. These fermented pieces of white fish meat were served directly out of the pot in which it had been fermenting in for several days. Unlike the Korean jars of kimchi, which are buried with fermenting cabbage, these pots and their fishy contents are set out in the hot tropical sun to stew and ripen. The stench was enough to drive even the most courageous taster away, but with everyone's eyes resting squarely on my face I brought a piece to my mouth. I swallowed it with only hint of a cringe and chased it down with the next prized dish handed to me proudly displayed on a bed of orchid petals. I instantly recognized the thinly sliced pink rectangular slabs of canned Spam.

While I took in the beautiful spread of food, I was astonished that our meager contribution had migrated to the place of honor at a raised dais directly in front of the chief. While we feasted on island delicacies, the islanders heaped their plates with this strange new offering from the New World... Jolly Time Popcorn!

The entire crew of *Chewbacca* was excited for Thanksgiving to arrive and as an added bonus, a surprise came chugging into the anchorage. The splash of an anchor and clattering of chain broke the silence where my eyes rested on a beat-up shrimp boat parked on the outskirts of the fleet. "My mouth starts to water every time I see one of those rust buckets," I said to Bruce as he joined me in the cockpit. "I'll go see what they have," and before he could even turn around the girls were already in the dinghy, each declaring it was her turn to drive. "Some things never change, even if you live on a sailboat," Bruce remarked as he grabbed my largest mixing bowl and climbed into the passenger seat.

"OK, Quincy you drive us there and Kendall you drive us back," were Bruce's words as my family drove away to negotiate for fresh shrimp.

They returned with the bowl brimming over with jumbo shrimp each twice the size of my thumb. We set the girls to work deveining and cleaning our catch in clean salt water. It was a time-consuming messy job, but the rewards promised to be delicious, so they worked without complaint. After the girls completed their first task, I got them busy chopping scallions, cilantro and crushing garlic while I went looking for my heavy skillet and butter. With my galley helpers, preparation went quickly and just as I finished arranging the sautéed shrimp on a platter, I glanced outside and noticed that the main course had arrived on the beach. A large bundle wrapped in aluminum foil was carefully lifted out of a fisherman's panga and laid on one of several tables set up on shore. A call over the radio announced the "turkey" had arrived and steaming al dente raviolis, shrimp and a multitude of side dishes were packed up and ferried to shore. Waves rippled through the anchorage as a dozen dinghies converged on the beach ready to celebrate.

"It's about the size of a German Shepherd" remarked Bruce as he peaked at the bundle of steaming goat just off the spit. "Let me check to be sure those are hooves and not toe nails on our little buddy." This was met with a collective groan, but strangely I was salivating like a Pavlovian dog hearing the dinner bell.

The scene was harmonious. We celebrated our bounty from land and sea and the labor of our hands. I knew I would have to pace myself as I chose between a little goat, garlic shrimp, ravioli, yams, slaw, homemade bread, mashed potatoes and gravy, corn bread stuffing and for dessert pecan pie.

Someone brought an American flag mounted on a bamboo pole and pitched it alongside the tables. Not to be left out, soon a Canadian flag and the Republic of Texas flag stood on either side of the stars and stripes. Before I could question Owen on why he brought his Texas flag he exclaimed to the crowd: "There are only two types of people in the world; those that are Texans, and those that want to be Texans." How could I argue with that? We bowed our heads, as one by one we gave thanks for our abundant blessings. It was exactly the Thanksgiving I had hoped for.

CHAPTER 23

PARTY LINE

"Believe only half of what you see and nothing that you hear."

-Edgar Allan Poe, Poet

CRUISING LIFE IS FUNNY. DESPITE BEING SURROUNDED BY CHEWBACCA'S 21ST century electronics like radar and GPS, our main line of communication with other cruisers was the party line... or VHF radio as some call it.

The VHF marine radio became our indispensable tool for line of sight communication with the cruising community. Turn to channel 16 and put out a distress call, and many will respond. All you have to do is dial to channel 22 for local weather updates or meet up on other open channels to share news of events, recipes or where the lobsters are hiding that day. It's all there.

While writing lists helped prioritize and kept me on task, so did listening to the cruiser's VHF net. Tuning into the daily net was my equivalent of reading the morning newspaper while sipping my first cup of Joe back home and it became an anticipated and savored ritual.

Forget Google; just float a question over the airwaves like:

• *How many drops of chlorine bleach do I put in five gallons of drinking water?*

• *Are the fish biting on red or blue feathers today?*

• *Anyone have a spare sparkplug for a five horsepower Yamaha?*

The net covered used items for sale or trade (e.g. guidebooks, charts, books, outboard motors and even food) weather and info covering cruisers' needs from A to Z. Need to find a dentist or get your shoes repaired? Need a haircut or anchor chain, just ask. The cruiser's net had the answers. Before you could count to five... the radio would crackle to life.

The radio net was a forum of information but don't think that it was a free flow of chaotic chatter. There was a proper format to follow.

Strict radio procedures establish hailing channels, emergency channels, weather channels and talking channels. Never chat on a hailing channel once you make connection to your party or the immediate response from somewhere on the other side of the airwaves will be; "PLEASE, MOVE YOUR CONVERSATION TO ANOTHER CHANNEL!" "Roger that, moving to channel 12, we're clear." Protocol requires you to say channel one-two and not channel twelve, because that could be confused with something that sounds like twelve, or rhymes with twelve. I'm really not sure what. Radio etiquette among some cruisers is severe and when caught in some minor indiscretion, the radio novice will be made to feel humiliated as if slapped on the wrist, which is what the VHF Net Nazis live for. For a few, radio is their life, and in this somewhat loose cruiser lifestyle, there needs to be structure, rules and luckily for *Chewbacca*... some very gullible people.

Of course, if it's a slow fishing day, too hot to play on the beach or one is bored, you can always hail your secret friend over the party line. Toss in some juicy gossip and you can almost feel the "lurkers" being drawn in like proverbial moths to a flame. Things said in confidence over the open radio airwaves seem to take on a life of their own; especially when a secret clandestine meeting is discovered... and that is where the fun comes in:

"*Fant-A-Sea Too, Fant-A-Sea Too*, this is *Sally Girl*, over"

"*Sally Girl*, this is *Fant-A-Sea Too*, How you doin' Girl, over"

"Just fine after last night. I think I forgot a little something on your boat."

"Is you know who still there?"

"BREAK, BREAK! THIS IS A HAILING CHANNEL,

PLEASE MOVE TO ANOTHER CHANNEL!"

"Oh, so sorry, we forgot. Hey girl, let's move over to Bravo channel."

"Rodger-dodger that. Moving to Bravo."

OK, the fact that there is no Bravo channel only turned up the heat as the lurkers frantically punch the scan button to follow the roving soap opera. This Payton Place on the water could get the better of even the most cynical cruisers. The other fact that this conversation was taking place on *Chewbacca* between Bruce on the radio below decks and me on a handheld in the cockpit was irrelevant. After all, entertainment is entertainment!

Imagine only having access to one TV channel. Deplorable. And that's why on any given sultry tropical day it wouldn't be difficult to follow several soaps being performed right on the radio for all to enjoy. Falsetto voices of lonely mermaids were often joined by the worst foreign accents imaginable. At times, the plays involved several sailboats all vying to see how far they could push the gullibility envelope. And the answer was pretty far.

Who wouldn't want to have a free brunch on the Holland America cruise ship that just dropped anchor outside the harbor? I shook my head at Bruce as a general hail went out over the VHF to the entire cruising fleet by the "Captain" of the glorious *Oosterdam*. A thick German accent came forth, "It would be the pleasure of Captain Von Stubing to welcome all cruisers in the anchorage to enjoy the hospitality of our beautiful cruise ship. Our champagne brunch will be served from eleven-hundred hours to thirteen-hundred hours and we hope to see you all there, auf wiedersehen." Even I was tempted to jump in the dinghy for a glimpse of the ornate innards of this floating palace with its 1,848 passengers and 800 crew. Only after several cruisers in their dinghies were turned away at the gang plank did the fleet despair that it may have been a hoax.

CHAPTER 24

WHISPERS IN THE NIGHT

"At night, everything is more intense, more true."

-Elie Wiesel, Author

I T'S JUST TOO DARN COLD FOR ME. THE DECEMBER WINDS INTENSIFIED, AND I donned a long sleeve shirt and pants, yet another sign that it was time to leave the Sea in our wake. Maybe it was time we said good-bye to Mexico altogether. Perhaps it was time to sail further off the beaten path and on into Central American waters. I needed some time to dwell on that idea and maybe I'd bring it up at the next family meeting. In the meantime, I allowed myself to soak in the rich and beautiful desert landscape because in a few days, our view would be drastically different.

We all gathered in the cockpit to discuss our game plan and watched as Bruce traced our intended path on the chart. Before us stretched our longest route thus far with the girls. Our five-day passage would take us across the Sea of Cortez and south into the heart of Mexico's Gold Coast. For the girls, these were like any other days, but for the grown-ups, this was a serious change of pace and routine with brutally disturbed sleep patterns.

It was obvious we were preparing to get underway as we stood on deck and tucked a reef in the mainsail and hanked on our working jib. Friends dinghied over to wish us a safe passage and exchanged hopes to reconnect "down the road." Uncle Max and Aunt Stella of *Dream Catcher* were going stateside for a few months and it was a tearful farewell as we exchanged strong and lingering hugs. We promised we would meet again. Other friends were headed to La Paz to celebrate Christmas and some were headed just across the Sea to enjoy the holidays there. We would be making the longer solo jump all the way to the central coast of Mexico for Christmas.

With the sun set, Bruce and I suited up for the night while the girls headed below decks and climbed into their bunk. I took the first watch and tethered myself into the captain's chair. Within easy reach were binoculars, air horn, spotlight, egg timer and flashlight hung securely around my neck. I had brewed a thermos of tea and the girls had set out a basket of snacks, so I was all set. The green and red navigation lights glowed bright on the masthead as we sailed on with the full moon our only companion.

I love the tranquility of my night watch… except when I hear things in the dark. I mean, hear things besides the creaks and groans of the fiberglass hull moving with the ocean or the unmistakable clicks through the hull when the dolphins come calling. I tried to reason that the water rushing alongside *Chewbacca* made the eerie noises that sounded like people calling to me as it swirled around the transom and swished away. But tonight, the voices became louder and more ominous the further into the night I got.

Then suddenly the whispers disappeared. Brilliant streaks of phosphorescence illuminated the water like trailing rocket plumes crisscrossing in front of our path. Beacons of explosive light dashed everywhere. Dolphins were welcome any time, but in the dead of night when everything is intensified, they carried away the weight of responsibility and lightened my mood. My fugue evaporated with their congenial company. Their squeals silenced the voices and brought me comfort. Sadly, all too soon, they tired of *Chewbacca's* ponderous progress and charged off to play with something more exciting. I missed them the moment they left.

Three hours later, Bruce and I switched places. It was now my turn to doze in the cockpit while he watched and listened to the sounds of the night. I fell into a light sleep and I imagined the yellow moon keeping him company as the hours and miles passed beneath *Chewbacca*. All too soon, I felt a tug at my leg and it was my turn back in the saddle.

Alone again, in the quiet of the witching hour I heard them. Distinctive voices, yet I couldn't make out the words. *Were they calling each other? Were they calling me?* A chill raised goosebumps along the nape of my neck and I shivered. I heard them. *Was someone down below conversing? Were the girls up? Were they playing a prank on me?* I carefully moved around Bruce and down into the salon. I checked on the girls and they were both sound asleep. The radio display glowed a dim lime green, but it too was silent. I looked around the cabin half expecting to see someone. A stowaway or a ghost. Sometimes it was a single voice. Other times two, maybe more. When I first heard them, Bruce told me he heard them too. *Thank God, it's not just me.*

I resumed my solo watch and took in my surroundings. I could only make out the horizon where the black empty ocean met the star filled sky. No one was out here. We were all alone, *Chewbacca* and me. I almost welcomed the vague whispering that came back to keep me company throughout the rest of my watch and just as the stars gave way to the first blush of day, the voices evaporated.

I turned my face to soak in the warming rays. I gently kicked Bruce's leg as a subtle signal to relieve me. I found it impossible to sleep below in our bunk while Bruce was in the cockpit alone on night watch, so I needed some day light hours to catch up on some real sleep in my bunk. Kendall was up and carrying two bowls of granola into the cockpit, accompanied by an open can of peaches packed in heavy syrup. I buried my head in my pillow before witnessing the father-daughter ritual of passing the can back and forth as they slurped up all the motor oil-thick, honey colored treat. Glug, glug, glug.

After my required naptime, it was Bruce's turn to recharge his batteries. He first filled the sun shower with freshly caught rain water and laid it on the front tramp to heat up for our evening bath. This was his favorite spot on the boat. He stretched out in the open air and dozed in the sun while I took my place in the cockpit to enjoy a late breakfast and keep watch. It was heaven with the steady breeze coming off the stern pushing us towards our destination. The miles ticked quickly by under *Chewbacca's* rudders and happily I plotted our hourly progress on the paper chart. To me the chart was like a roadmap, except that a chart has lines marking latitude and longitude but more importantly for sailors it had fathom markers revealing the water depths. It was satisfying to physically pencil the little X on the chart and the ritual connected me to our journey more than by watching the soulless digital display of the GPS.

It was hardly late morning and my arms and legs were already glistening with sweat. It was painfully obvious that we had re-entered the tropical sauna as the day lengthened and the humidity gripped me.

We all gathered in the cooling breeze on the front tramp as I read aloud from a James Harriot novel. Laughter rolled across the ocean as James and Tristen made mischief at the veterinary practice and the story was only interrupted when we took turns doing a full scan of our surroundings every seven minutes. Like clockwork throughout the day one of us would walk back to the cockpit to make sure we were still "on the road" as the girls called the GPS track. I scanned the flat horizon surrounding us for any signs of life. Nothing. We were all alone. The waves undulated under my bare feet and we were carried upon it like Aladdin's magic carpet.

Another night-shift. The girls had turned in and I reviewed the chart, studying the stretch of sea we would be traversing during the night, looking for any dangers: shallows, shoals, sea mounts or anything unusual. Once again, I stared out into the darkness, signaling another round of solitary night watches ahead.

I opted for the first watch and hunkered down for round two with a steady breeze coaxing *Chewbacca* along. I felt refreshed and looked forward to a monotonous three-hour watch. The full moon greeted me right on schedule and it wasn't until my third hour that the voices returned to keep me company. Bruce and I cycled through the watches, but I didn't mention that night's nocturnal visitors to him. No sense scaring the both of us.

We finished the watch together bundled in a quilt against the chill night air. At daybreak, I heard Quincy rummaging down below as she scooped homemade granola into bowls and splashed a little powdered milk over it. Next, she passed out a can of fruit cocktail and the can opener. I averted the girls' anticipated tussle over the lone red cherry half by popping it in my mouth.

After scanning the morning skies for any threat of thunderstorms we shook out the reef in the mainsail and hoisted the larger jib. I could feel *Chewbacca* lurch forward as the wind filled the canvas and our speed jumped a knot and a half. The day warmed up quickly and we set about our routines. I kneaded a fresh batch of bread dough, covered it with a dish towel and handed it out to Kendall to place in a sunny spot on the deck to rise. She was perched in a folding chair on the cabin top reading another James Harriot story. We'd read all three of his books this passage, laughing and crying, very often on the same page, as his life experiences with animals and humans unfolded.

Quincy was sitting in Bruce's arms in the helmsman's chair while he reviewed a lesson on the finer points of sail trim. "Now your mother doesn't care if she hears a little flapping on the trailing edge of the sail, but I like a nice quiet sail…curved just so." Bruce winked at me as he continued. "See, like this" he demonstrated tightening the outhaul and the tell-tails on the sail streamed back nicely. "Nice and quiet. Now watch how that little adjustment increases our speed." I looked over and saw the knot meter rise from 6.2 to 6.3 knots. *Really? A tenth of a knot?*

We enjoyed the day, riding high on the excellent weather and feeling fortunate to have so much time on our hands. When passage making, I allowed the concerns of the world to slip away. I was locked away in my little space ship, apart from the earth. These days with time unto ourselves was an aspect of the cruising life that I cherished the most.

As Bruce plotted our intended course on the chart he went over the plan out loud. "Tonight's passage will take us past the Tres Marias, the Alcatraz island of Mexico. Our route will keep us three miles away from her shores and in the early morning hours, we should clear them on our starboard side." He added with a wink, "Let's hope the prisoners haven't planned a water escape tonight." "Not funny," was my solemn rely.

By sunset we had all bathed with the hot water from the sun shower. The girls helped me prepare grilled cheese sandwiches and soup for dinner as the sun cast its final warm red glow over our little ship. The mainsail was reefed, the smaller jib was flying, and I was ready to get on with my night's work. As soon as the moon peeped over the horizon I was the only one awake.

Later as lights of the prison island slipped by, I shivered, not sure if it was from the nighttime temperature or the possibility of catching a deserter swimming in the silvery moonlight. On the horizon the lighthouse atop Isla Isabela winked as I went below and plotted our position on the paper chart. With satisfaction, I noted how our marks now stretched across the sea. We were almost there.

It was always comforting to hear the whistles and clicks of dolphins through our fiberglass hull, especially at night. It not only broke the monotony of a solo night watch, but their chirping raised my spirits. But these were different. The voices were back. They came as murmurs, whispers and undertones of a language I recognized, yet couldn't decipher. Were they actual words or just the creaking of the rigging as the wind passed through? Could it be the rushing sounds of the water against the hulls, or the working, twisting of fiberglass moaning like an old man getting up from his chair?

Bruce was dozing restlessly up in the cockpit and I reached out and shook his leg. Did he hear it too? I shook him again and he reluctantly sat up rubbing his eyes. I knew he heard it by the way he cocked his head. If he heard it too, that meant I wasn't hallucinating. I wasn't crazy. But if it was real, what was it? Bruce stuck his head down the companionway and held up a finger. "Shush." He stayed still for the longest time and then turned back to me and smiled. "The whales are back."

"Whales!" Damn him. All this time he was telling me it was the souls of drowned sailors. I willed him to lay back down so I could choke him in his sleep.

Morning finally arrived and with every breath I inhaled the pungent fragrance of earth and jungle vegetation. Landfall was near. By noon the land revealed a kaleidoscope of colors, and the patchwork exploded in every hue of green before my eyes. "Wow, I have been looking at browns and reds for so long, this is bizarre," I said squinting as I turned to Bruce. He shaded his eyes as well and said with a wince,

"Whoa, my eyes actually ache." Could it be that after being deprived of the green part of the color spectrum for so many months, our eyes had to readjust? The girls stood up and I noticed that, they too, hid their eyes and looked as if their senses were also being assaulted by the sudden appearance of green.

We had left the desert behind.

CHAPTER 25

SIMPLE PLEASURES

"Simplicity is the ultimate sophistication."

-Leonardo Da Vinci, Renaissance Genius

AFTER THREE YEARS OF CRUISING, I DECIDED THAT LIFE COULDN'T GET ANY better. No way, no how. As a family, we'd struck it rich with the tremendous amounts of time together. As husband and wife, we'd added a whole new fulfilling dimension to our relationship.

As a family, we had reached a consensus that the cruising life was just too good to give up, yet others in our cruising community reached this fork in the road and decided the opposite, choosing to swallow the anchor and return to a life on land. The reasons varied but for some it included:

• *Life aboard a sailboat was too harsh, too stressful and the physical demands were too extreme.*

• *Personal tastes and wants outpaced their financial reality.*

• *Marina life was expensive and drained the cruising kitty in no time.*

• *Maintaining the systems on a large boat was expensive, especially in third world countries, where labor may be cheap, but expertise and parts were not.*

• *Caring for aging parents factored in for some.*

• *The mental and psychological demands, (especially in a third world cruising environment), zapped the initial enthusiasm for travel by sailboat, if not tempered by humor, flexibility and patience.*

One gift sailing life had given me was the joy I found in the simplest of pleasures. Some of my most cherished memories were sailing under the glow of a full moon, being barefoot, poking around a tide pool, a new book and pizza Fridays.

We began to think this cruising life we had chosen was normal. At least the girls did, because they remembered no other. *Didn't all dads stay home? Aren't all kids homeschooled? The seasons are changing, it's time to move on.* But every now and then, I realized, how unusual our adventure was and how privileged we were to be living our dream.

Of course, I could dream up luxuries that would escalate my happy life to an even more perfect plane. I fantasized about sleeping in a real bed. Not a bunk where I had to climb over my significant other to get in or out. I would be thrilled to work in a galley without foot pumps that jutted into the corridor waiting silently to rip off a toenail if I stepped out of line. Oh, the joy of sleeping through the night during a good tropical downpour without having to get up and collect fresh water. The girls asked about having a real bedroom door instead of a curtain and oh yes, they were getting tired of sharing a bunk! Well, as often happens, we met someone along the way who put all these fantasies into perspective.

Life was just about perfect, yet I'll admit I felt a little twinge of envy when a BIG powerboat dropped its humungous anchor in our little cove and the wake sent *Chewbacca* rocking. Our cabin temperature was hovering just north of 100° when I muttered. "I am certain those people have an air conditioner," as sweat dripped off the end of my nose. "I bet they also have a real fridge and probably a freezer," I continued as I mopped my forehead once more for dramatic effect. Bruce kept his head lowered but I could swear I heard him say, "Oh, don't forget their washer and dryer."

It had been a challenging morning aboard our little home. Bruce was buried in yet another boat project while Kendall and Quincy were rebelling over their schoolwork. "It's not me that's asking you to do this exercise, SEE IT'S THE CURRICULUM." I reiterated. "It says to do the odd problems 21-49," I continued punctuating each word as I spoke. *Just how did Mary Poppins do it?* I imagined the heat had something to do with my deteriorating mood and the shadow cast by our new neighbors wasn't helping.

Bruce unscrewed the little peephole on the sewage holding tank trying to assess why the little red light wasn't working. The indicator light was important because it signaled when it was time to empty the contents. He was wedged in a tight space on his belly stretched out across the tank opening. This was a stinky job and no one was jumping to volunteer for this duty.

"If I find one more Barbie doll shoe in here...," Bruce trailed off as he worked the wrench. The girls peaked around the corner to see what all the grumbling was about. "I imagine that big boat actually has plenty of room to work in and they probably have an electric macerator pump that squishes up all the poop and even pink Barbie shoes," he added making squishy sounds. "Ewwww, how gross Dad" chorused the girls. They were excited to forget about math for the moment and engage in this bizarre topic that only cruisers talked about, like others talked about the weather.

Beads of sweat rolled off Bruce's bare back as he muttered on, tracing the electrical wires looking for a short. Becoming blue water cruisers required we knew every system onboard right down to the toilet valves.

The next morning, I heard the clank, clank, clanking of an anchor being raised, (by a motorized windlass no doubt) and looked out the companionway door to wave as the big boat motored out of the bay. Bruce was finishing screwing in the last bolts on the inspection plate and his ugly job with the holding tank was complete. No Barbie shoe discovered. Only the wires needed replacing, so the girls lived yet another day. He came up to join me on deck watching the motor yacht head for the horizon. "They probably cruise at 20 knots and will be in Puerto Vallarta for brunch," Bruce observed. That trip was a couple days sail for us, but I pressed that thought out of my head.

After three quiet months on the hook it was time we moved on. We unanimously agreed to indulge ourselves in a rare stint of marina life in Puerto Vallarta...and all that it entailed: long hot showers, laundromats, swimming pools and ice cream. Two days later, when I looped the line around the cleat on the dock, I'll admit I was grinning ear to ear. No need to catch water here, it came from the spigot...

right at the dock… as much as I wanted. *Was I really getting excited about drinking water out of an old garden hose?*

Because of our wide beam, we were instructed to tie up in the slips reserved for the big boats. As we pulled into our slot I noticed the yacht tied next to us cast a familiar shadow across our whole boat. I craned my neck up three stories and gave a wave to the mistress. To my surprise this was the same mega yacht we had seen on an especially hot and sweaty day while at anchor a few months back. Their family had just returned from a stateside visit and she called down wanting to know if we would like to come over for dinner later? Curiosity got the cat, and I replied, "Love to. What can we bring?"

We arrived at the appointed hour, homemade peanut brittle in hand wearing our spiffiest clothes. We climbed up what seemed like a complete flight of stairs just to reach the deck. Stepping onto the freshly polished teak, I ignored the "Boat Shoes Only" sign since I was already barefoot. There was no need to bend over and climb down the companionway because a full-size sliding glass door marked the entry to the living room. Cases and cases of water, juices, sodas and beer lined the wall. "Don't mind the mess, we went shopping today and still have to stow this stuff in the lockers," said John, waving us in. Looking around he continued, "The second load should be delivered tomorrow."

We sat politely on one brocade covered couch facing our hosts sitting on another. I noticed they had curtains; real window curtains hung on decorative curtain rods. A colorful Persian rug that ran almost the length and width of the room covered the polished teak and holly floor. There were lamps on tables, artwork gracing the walls and even electrical outlets. I imagined a vacuum cleaner sitting in a closet somewhere. It was as if we were in a house, except we were floating 15 feet above the concrete docks. In spite of myself I could feel the envy monster come alive within me as a blender whirled to life. Viola! Margaritas were served.

Our hostess was wearing a short cocktail dress while I was wearing my best Bermuda style cargo shorts that were beginning to show a little fray around the hem. Bruce wore his only button up shirt which depicted Hula dancers and palm trees swaying somewhere in the tropics. The whimsical theme framed his deeply tanned neck and forearms but looking at it made me wish I owned an iron.

Suddenly, a pack of kids including ours clamored up the spiral staircase and instinctively homed in on the fridge. My mouth fell open. Had it really been that long since I'd seen a real stand up refrigerator? As it swung open I spied a variety of gourmet food. I am not usually an envious type but sometimes the contents of another's refrigerator were cause for jealously, especially when my galley only had a top loading camp style icebox. Cheeses, ready-made dips, salamis, prosciutto, rounds of Brie and Gouda burst forth. I also caught a glimpse of white wine bottles stacked neatly and chilling on their sides. No room temperature boxed wine here. My imagination went free-flow conjuring up what delicacies were behind freezer door #2.

While our hostess was throwing together a cornucopia of delights, my mouth started to water at the thought of sampling thinly sliced pepper laced salami atop a stone-ground sesame cracker with a garlic stuffed green olive crowning it all off. Bruce nudged me. Maybe he was poking me because my mouth was open and I had drool running down my chin, or maybe he was as flabbergasted as me. Anyway, I needed to pull myself together quick.

Somewhere in the background I heard our host inquire about our yacht club affiliation in California. What was our favorite marina so far? When did we plan to head north? And about half a dozen other questions all delivered in rapid succession. Bruce revealed that we'd only been away a few years and we planned to continue as long as we were having fun. John chuckled at Bruce, "Fun? You calculate fun into the equation?" He admitted that they planned to be out cruising for 12 months, but it had been more expensive than they had dreamed so they might be cutting their trip short.

Our hostess returned, and I restrained myself from pouncing on the offerings. Instead, I let someone else be the first to snap up a gorgeous morsel from the tray. I pushed aside our paper plate of homemade peanut brittle like a red-headed stepchild at a family reunion, so I could concentrate on the "real" food. Aboard *Chewbacca*, I wasn't above using a genuine Tupperware brand lid to present a feast, but Caroline served us from a sterling silver tray set down on an embroidered table runner! One of us had so much to learn about cruising!

As she joined us at the table, she asked something that Bruce and I could hardly believe. We were so astonished that we replied in a perfectly synchronized "Pardon?" She asked again, "If I may be so bold, how can your family afford to cruise full time? You've been gone for over three years. How is this possible?" By the look on her face she was dead serious. I thought back to my first golden rule regarding boat ownership; the bigger the boat, the more systems to maintain, the costlier to keep which equaled less time cruising even if you were a millionaire. *Was this seemingly wealthy woman envious of US?*

I rose and moved to the curtained picture window and pulled back the thick, heavy fabric. *Chewbacca* looked even smaller from this vantage point. John followed and said, "Ah, you're on a little sailboat. Splendid. Bet you save on fuel costs." "Yes, we've only used two gallons of gasoline to get from the Sea to here," stated Bruce. "Wow," chuckled John, "Our engine burns ten times that in diesel every hour and we have two of them." While he was gazing out the window, Bruce whispered in my ear. "You know, John probably spends as much on fuel in a year as we spent on purchasing *Chewbacca*."

We all retired from the salon to the dining table where Caroline had already set out a wonderful tossed salad. I noticed that there were two forks set to the left of my place mat and a spoon and knife was on the right. Sheepishly, it made me think again about how many times I served my family an open can of fruit cocktail to pass around with a community spoon sticking out.

Sometime between the courses of our grown-up gourmet meal, the girls had their fill of microwaved pizza rolls and Hot Pockets and headed back to *Chewbacca*. From my window seat, I caught the yellow glow of a light emanating through the hatch above their bunk.

After finishing a delicious gourmet meal accompanied by an excellent California Cabernet, desert and coffee, it was time we returned to our beloved *Chewbacca*. We took an extra stroll along the docks walking silently hand in hand into the balmy night and finally returned stepping into our tiny cockpit. Bruce went below while I stopped to take it all in. *Is this my life?*

I ducked into our cramped living space, lit by a single 12-volt bulb. My galley was the size of a phone booth, my ceiling was four feet high and our kitchen table could hold four dinner plates... if they were all touching. I stood silent for a while then heard Bruce and the girls giggling in their shared berth. I gazed around at our humble little abode. YES, this IS my life. My momentary envy instantly evaporated and I realized that I was never more in love with our little boat and our cruising life than at that moment. I felt we were the most fortunate family in the world, even after spending an evening aboard a luxury yacht ironically named... *Simple Pleasures.*

CHAPTER 26

AMONGST THE MAYA

"Extraordinary things are always hiding in places people never think to look."

-Jodi Picoult, *My Sister's Keeper*

WE HAD ARRIVED AT ANOTHER FORK IN THE ROAD OF OUR JOURNEY. SHOULD we retrace our steps back north or venture into new territory? Show of hands. The decision was three-to-one. For Bruce, hovering closer to the unknown was the essence of the cruising life while I tended to lean towards a tamer one, packed with routine and familiarity. I'm not always the adventurous one, but majority ruled. Adios Mexico.

I sat on deck for hours watching the rugged Guatemalan coastline pass slowly by. I was mesmerized by the deep forests that lay like a plush wooly blanket, cascading headlong into the ocean. There were no beaches...just green meeting blue. Between the pristine serenity and the dolphin encounters, lunchtime was quickly upon us and I spread out thickly sliced spam and homemade bread. The miles ticked away peacefully, but as the day waned, the coastline changed. Where had the uninterrupted carpet gone? Evidence of clear-cut logging where pristine forest once graced the landscape sobered me. As if a line had been drawn, the wreckage stood out like an ugly scar. The hillsides lay barren...raped. I wondered who would win this battle?

After two days at sea I turned *Chewbacca* into the small, well protected bay and we prepared to set our hook.

The usual questions ran through my mind upon arriving anywhere new:

- *Where do we check into the country?*

- *Is Chewbacca anchored here safe from weather and thieves?*

- *Where do we tie the dinghy up?*

- *Where can we fill our water jugs? Is the water potable (drinkable) or do we need to buy bottled water?*

- *Is there a big enough town nearby to have a bank so we can get some local currency?*

- *Is there a local market to buy fresh produce?*

- *Where is the local pay phone so we can call home?*

Puerto Quetzal is a busy commercial and industrial port but tucked all the way back in the basin was a Guatemalan military base. According to the cruising scuttlebutt, the commander welcomed cruising boats to anchor in "his" harbor and only asked for a slight fee as a token of appreciation.

We had barely set the anchor when a small launch pulled up. The Port Captain and Base Commander stood in starched, crisp dress white uniforms and asked permission to come aboard. They briefly checked our boat documents, passports and immigration paperwork. Bruce gladly handed over a crisp $100 bill to the captain as an "anchoring fee" and in exchange we were granted use of the harbor, access to the Officers Club restaurant, bar and swimming pool. I was reassured by the officials that it was safe to leave *Chewbacca* unattended in the anchorage. This statement was confirmed by the 24-hour presence of a serious looking sailor carrying a machine gun at the small wooden dinghy dock not far away. His sole job was to stand guard and watch the foreign sailboats at anchor.

After we tidied up *Chewbacca*, Kendall ferried us to shore where we indulged in a swim at the Officers Club. I cast my eyes about and was struck by the classic Mayan features that were etched distinctly in the profiles of those around us. Thumbing through the pages of the guidebook, towns with mysterious names such as Quetzaltenango, Mazatenango, Huehuetenango and Totonicapán graced the pages. We were definitely in a new land now.

After a few days of R & R we buttoned up *Chewbacca*, hitched on our knapsacks and headed for the hills. Guatemala is a colorful, culturally rich country and I was eager to explore it again, this time with our kids. A stone's throw away from the base entrance was a bus stop with connections to the Guatemalan highlands. Although I still harbored a deep apprehension for chicken buses, these were the cheapest and most abundant form of transportation. I was excited to do some inland exploration, and this was the only game in town.

"Hey girls, did mom ever tell you about our first bus ride to Tikal?" "No dad, but I feel a story coming on," Kendall replied with a knowing grin. "Well, we were here 15 years ago, and back then the guidebooks advised against taking the "chicken bus" through what it described as "... *the treacherous highlands of the Petén region.*" Instead, it suggested we fly to Tikal, but we couldn't afford it, so we took the bus. And we both thought; how bad could a bus ride be?"

"You can read all about our bus ride in this letter," I said as I searched the bookshelf. "A teacher friend had asked me to retell an adventure she could share with her class and so after it was over, I wrote about the journey. She saved all my letters and returned them to me just in case I wanted to share them with you someday. I hope things have changed" I mused as I handed Kendall the envelope. She pulled out the thick bundle of folded, ragged edged paper torn from a binder and began to read:

The dilapidated school bus squealed to a halt and to avoid being hit I took several steps back. It's not like I didn't have plenty of warning. I heard it coming from half a mile away and now I could see why. The muffler was missing just past the engine block, leaving a foot-long stub of rotted pipe looking like Satan's flute. The bus sat directly on the rear tar covered axle and the shocks or what was left of them were visible through the rusted-out quarter panel.

Bruce and I huddled together in the pre-dawn darkness with the Guatemalan campesinos and formed a cluster just outside the door waiting for the crumbled sheet metal to open. Like garlic cloves going through a press we somehow squeezed into the bus and began filling the tiny seats originally designed for 3rd graders.

I found it odd that the aisle seats were filled first. My lucky day. My first choice is always the window seat. Anticipating my glee, Bruce whispered, "The reason no one wants to sit by the window is because those are the first people to get shot." "Oh, real funny," was all the response I could muster. But I didn't see Bruce laughing. The northern part of Guatemala was embroiled in a civil war and we had to cross that zone to get to where we wanted to go.

Smiles flashed my way as I trundled down the aisle, my eyes scanning for an open seat. In a sea of black hair, my blond ponytail and light skin stood out and I was conscious of my companion's stares, but they were looks of curiosity and warmth.

I had to climb over an apron clad matron to claim my space as there weren't any aisle seats left. I summoned my best "Buenos dias" and asked if we could take the two empty seats next to her. Bruce squeezed in next to me as the fresh morning breeze wafted through our window which was frozen in place two inches from closing. We were sentenced near the back of the bus over the tire well that reduced our miniscule leg room even more. Straw baskets and cloth bundles joined the swaddled babies and tethered chickens inside this claustrophobic tin box. The bus seats were all taken, yet the passengers continued filing through the doorway. Back home, two elementary school kids would share a seat but here three to a seat is typical so we were already squashed six across a row. Small wooden stools were pulled from the overhead racks and wedged into the aisle, allowing two more to shoulder into each row.

My seat had long ago given up any pretense of padding. The worn black vinyl coverings had spider cracks that pinched into my skin with every movement. I could hear the roof wince as the thin sheet metal was loaded with more bodies, a cargo of cardboard boxes and 50-pound nets full of oranges, avocados and peppers. The air became thick with the odor of so many tightly packed bodies. It wasn't an altogether unpleasant smell, but I was inclined to face the meager window opening for the next rustle of breeze as I settled in and waited for the show to begin.

Topping out at 5' 2" I am no giant, but I had no difficulty looking over my companions' heads to the windshield covered in stickers, holding the cracked glass in place. Just in front of the welded rebar acting as the gearshift lever was the only clean area on the bus. This place of honor was reserved for a miniature Mother Mary statue. Bigger than a shoebox and circled with blinking Christmas lights, our saintly copilot silently watched over us.

The bus coughed to life and the gears protested as they groaned forward. For the first 200 miles of the trip we bounced along pockmarked asphalt stopping at every village or bend in the road to pick up a passenger or drop off a bag of goods from the rooftop. A whistle or bang on the loose sheet metal siding signaled a stop. Often it was much easier just to climb out the rear emergency exit or slip out an open window than to try and push through the solid pack of humanity clogging the aisle of this moving scrap pile which averaged 18 miles per hour.

Bathroom breaks came about every three hours and gave me a chance to uncoil from my cocoon and shake the blood back into my legs. Twenty-five centavos got me a few squares of abrasive toilet paper and an open stall. Three cents well spent. But was I the only person who missed a toilet seat? Surely the locals must have wondered what those two holes in the back of the porcelain bowl were for. Meanwhile, the men wandered off to the side of the road or behind whatever local eatery the driver parked at. We returned to stand by the bus like prisoners not wanting to go back into the cell. But all too soon our pardon was over. Like cordwood we were restacked into the bus.

Along the way, we crossed countless roadway speed bumps which locals lovingly refer to as "sleeping policemen." These speed bumps on steroids caused the driver to down shift into low gear and rev the engine just to scale over them and I was soon convinced these barriers were placed as opportunities for enterprising locals.

They heard us coming. Before the driver could even grind the transmission into first gear, vendors circled the bus selling weary travelers a variety of food, drink and snacks held high overhead. Tortillas wrapped in newspaper, cooked chicken parts and the local favorite, ears of roasted corn speared on a stick slathered in mayonnaise and sprinkled with red chili powder all competed for a buyer. Waved aloft in the humid air, different colored fruit drinks in baggies with the straw sticking out rounded out the menu. This was retail at two miles per hour and items were thrust through the windows and money exchanged. I opted for a bag of plantain chips and a canned soda. Bruce was more adventurous and bought an ear of corn minus the mayo and a stack of homemade tortillas. By the time the rear wheels passed over the sleeping policeman all the transactions were completed, the bus shifted gears and we rumbled down the road once again.

I had finished my snack and sat back with the remnants in my hands just gazing at the scenery as it crawled by. The lady sitting next to me tapped my arm, plucked the trash from my lap, added it to her basketball size bundle of rubbish and deftly tossed it all out the opposite window. She flashed me a smile and a nod like she had just passed me the winning lottery ticket. My jaw dropped as the litter bounced into the lush jungle. On the bright side, if I ever got separated from the bus, I only had to follow the trail of garbage strewn in our wake.

For a couple more hours, we limped along over potholes connected by broken pavement. Each time we came to a blind curve the bus driver would automatically cross himself and pass whatever car, donkey cart or bicycle that was somehow moving slower than us. I wasn't nervous until I noticed that on some especially twisty curves, half the passengers were crossing themselves in unison and fingering their rosaries as the horn got a riotous workout to the tempo of HAIL MARY, FULL OF GRACE. I swear.

By late afternoon, the pavement gave way to a mixture of mud and gravel and not long after, just mud. We had entered the Petén region. As the bus shimmied up a slippery incline, the back wheels continuously swerved off the trail and into the rutted margin. It felt like I was on an amusement park ride being thrown back and forth, meanwhile above my head, I imagined the rooftop attendees were riding quite a thriller. Struggling up the incline we ground to a stop and it was clear that the bus was overloaded. The driver signaled for everyone to get out and the empty bus struggled its way to the summit while everyone trudged behind. Spewing a geyser of steam from under the hood our chariot awaited us. We piled in and continued along the rutted tract for another hour until we came to a row of orange safety cones marking a Guatemalan Army checkpoint. A dozen armed soldiers in camouflaged fatigues carrying US M16 rifles were waiting for us. Everyone out.

I stood with my rucksack at my muddy feet and watched in silence as several young men were segregated from the group. When the soldiers approached me, I held out my U.S. passport. The officer in charge crisply stepped forward and snatched it from my hand. He seemed to be studying the golden eagle embossed on the blue front cover. He didn't even open it. He motioned for Bruce's and repeated the process. My antiperspirant was failing as the Captain looked up with a forced smile, handed back our passports and with a slight nod moved down the line to the next anxious passenger. A half hour later almost everyone was back on the bus bumping down the road.

Two dozen bends and three steep climbs later we came to another checkpoint. Something was different. Instead of orange safety cones, a fallen tree covered half the roadway. Everyone out. This time we were met by young boys with an assortment of weapons and indistinguishable, mismatched uniforms. Guerillas. Again, we were asked to line up alongside the bus. I was frozen in place yet could hear my heart pounding in my chest. It was hot, so maybe they wouldn't notice the extra trickle of sweat running down the inside of my arm and dripping off my elbow. First, I felt his presence as he went down the line drawing ever closer to me, then the tug of my passport from my hand. A young man casually thumbed through the pages pausing to decipher a few of the colorful immigration stamps I had accumulated. He asked for my bag. At least I think he did. It was as if he was calling from the bottom of a well and all my freshly acquired Spanish was nowhere to be found. Finally, the boy soldier standing to one side tapped my shoulder with the barrel of his gun. "OK, I'm guessing he wants your bag" said Bruce in a barely audible voice. I slung my knapsack off my shoulders and placed it on the ground in front of me. The man in charge took a stub of white chalk from his pocket and marked an X across the front of it.

My mind flashed back to one of our guidebooks, where in the appendix were translations for common phrases:

¿Donde está el baño? - Where is the bathroom?

¿Comó está usted? - How are you?

¡Por favor, parada me atormentando! - Please stop torturing me!

At the time, Bruce and I had a big laugh when we read that last phrase. Now I was trying in vain to reboot that phrase from my data bank but before I had time to reach panic mode the young man picked up my bag and gently placed it back on the bus. I concluded that yet again, recognition of the U.S. eagle on the blue *cover gave us safe passage. It seemed neither side wanted to mess with Uncle Sam.*

The next person in line wasn't so lucky and he was taken away for questioning. Once more, we left with a few less men."

The girls were game for an adventure and once again, I stood on a dusty shoulder of a Guatemalan road and waited for our ride. I heard it coming from half a mile away. Déjà vu. *How could the same dilapidated school bus that transported us to Tikal 15 years ago still live? Could it be possessed?*

Just to prove that times change, Kendall pointed out a new fact; passengers were not allowed to ride on the roof like our previous ride. Darn. With the child seating closed above, our family shuffled like a shackled chain gang through the grimy, halfcocked doors to find a seat.

I climbed the worn step and nodded to the driver declaring "Yo Soy Caliente." It was hot outside, but by the puzzled look on the driver's face I think he missed my meaning. Bruce poked me from behind and whispered, "Yes, you are sexy hot, but I think you should have told him "Hoy hace calor" if you mean it's hot today." OK, now my face was crimson red, and not from the heat.

Everyone still called these chicken buses, which from previous experience I took to mean you were constantly scared witless the whole time the bus was in motion. Silly me, the term comes from all the campasinos (farmers), carrying their fowl to the market. If this is truly the case, our bus was the baby cow bus because taking up the whole rear seat was a little black and white calf. A little disappointed about having to ride inside the bus and not on the roof, the girls at least had a good tale to write the grandparents about. They just about stroked the fur off the poor animal by the time its stop came, and the farmer led little Bessie down the aisle and off the bus.

We used this opportunity to shift further forward in the bus so we could see out the driver's windshield as he rattled up the road. Quickly I discovered that perhaps it was better in the back. From our new perch, I could tell whenever the driver was planning to pass the slow-moving traffic by one of two clues: 1) we were approaching a blind curve usually along a steep grade, or 2) the driver crossed himself before he reached to downshift the gear lever. OK, so some things never change. Hail Mary!

A new and sophisticated addition to the bus was the services of the driver's assistant. His duty was to continually reach over and honk the horn whenever the driver sped around blind corners, passed ox driven carts or other slower traffic. Besides being the chief bus horn honker, I believed his real duty was to hold the driver's arm to keep him from tumbling out of his seat when making hair pin turns in the steep winding terrain. Sort of like a human seatbelt. He was also responsible for setting the Virgin Mary back up on the makeshift altar whenever she toppled over. Kendall leaned over to me and giggled, "And all this time I thought you and dad were making this stuff up."

All too quickly the months rolled by. With the passing days, the rains came a little earlier and stayed a little longer. We worried about *Chewbacca* left at anchor and held a family meeting to talk about moving south once again. We explored the Guatemala highlands and neighboring Honduras and rediscovered the natural, archeological and cultural riches of these countries without the scourge of war. This had been a magical interlude, but the start of the hurricane season was upon us and it was time to continue south and deeper into the unknown. And this time… the vote was unanimous.

CHAPTER 27

CUT AND RUN!

"Maybe everyone can live beyond what they're capable of."

-Markus Zusak, I am the messenger

I T WAS OPPRESSIVELY HOT, AND A THIN LAYER OF DUST COATED MY SWEATY limbs, but I was undeterred in my search for a pay phone. We'd been in El Salvador for over a year. Our visas had run out and I wanted to let my parents know we were moving on.

I pictured my mom answering the telephone in her bright yellow kitchen, the cool tile floor under her bare feet. She would have spent the afternoon in her garden, tenderly trimming, weeding or adding mulch to her tidy rose bed bursting with color. My dad would be sitting at the kitchen table, air conditioner whirling, working on the *New York Times* crossword puzzle, their West Highland Terrier, curled up, sound asleep in his dog bed tucked into the corner. A scene worthy of Norman Rockwell's talents. It had been over four years since I'd seen my parents, and when the phone was picked up I was instantly enveloped in a group hug. As the first words tumbled from my mouth I realized our realities were worlds apart and suddenly homesickness overwhelmed me.

It was time to move on and my sights were set on Costa Rica.

Our homeschooling revealed that Costa Rica provided habitat for over 10,000 flowering plants, 850 bird species, 3,000 species of butterfly and 209 species of mammals. I wanted to see them all. Volcanoes, rain forests, cloud forests and lowland jungles were waiting for us to explore. Starting at the northern most bay of Bahia Santa Elena we experienced a rich wonderland over the next month as we wove our way southward. Giant Scarlet Macaws screeched overhead as we puttered the *Blaster* up countless rivers looking for spider monkeys in the dense jungle foliage. At Tamarindo and Playa Grande we walked the beaches and the girls dared us to body surf the biggest waves I'd ever seen. Further south, we rendezvoused with Max and Stella from *Dream Catcher* and traded boat sitting. We hopped a bus and ventured inland to Monteverde Cloud Forest Reserve, where bromeliads of every specie hugged the nooks and crannies of trees and orchids in every shape and color seemed to sprout from out of nowhere as we hiked the soggy trails. Bird life abounded and after craning my neck for days on end, I was finally rewarded on our last morning hike with a flash of cobalt and iridescent green. A pair of elusive quetzals flew by, the male's magnificent foot-long tail feathers shimmering only a few feet above our heads. A finale to remember as we said good-bye to the cool mountains and returned to the coast.

Back aboard *Chewbacca* the radio chatter all week had centered around Christmas which was right around the corner and the girls were excited. Okay, we were all excited. I was ready for Santa and had our nine-inch plastic tree already set up in the salon. While underway, Kendall had designed a fireplace out of construction paper and both girls colored it in and taped it to the salon wall. To make the illusion complete they had also cut out cardboard logs and added red and orange crape paper flames. I caught them sitting on their knees, leaning forward and rubbing their hands together in front of the fireplace on more than one occasion. It was a tropical 85° in the cabin, but somewhere in the world it was a frosty Christmas.

Someone knew of a little anchorage in the Gulf of Nicoya that boasted a cruiser-friendly resort complete with a volleyball court and swimming pool… and that was our destination. Bruce's voice broke my revelry as he left the cockpit and walked to the bow. "I hear this isn't the most secure of anchorages in a blow, so we need to keep alert." Not wanting to break my festive mood, I countered, "Party pooper."

OK, he was right. I looked across the bay to the distant mountains towering over the sprawling town below. "Remember the cruising guide warns that if you ever see clouds spilling over that mountain, it means trouble" I said, making eye contact with each of the girls, then added "OK, let's get our chores done quick and then we can take the dinghy and go have a look see at the resort." The girls sprang into action tidying up *Chewbacca*.

They had learned that many hands made light work and the sooner they completed their chores, the sooner they could explore.

The anchorage was no more than a nook and offered no protection from the north, which was where the guidebook noted the "bad wind comes from." Bruce was careful to choose a spot with plenty of water beneath our rudders to compensate for the huge tidal range. He signaled me to stop in 15 feet of water and I heard *Chewbacca's* anchor chain clatter overboard. I surveyed our place among the field of boats and with one last look around I was satisfied that we were secure.

Nature had somehow become an integral part of my life. Before cruising I don't recall ever scanning and studying the horizon. I only looked up to the clouds to comment on how pretty they were or checked the weather report to see if I needed my umbrella. But now we didn't do anything before consulting the weather and taking in our surroundings. We had become attuned to wind strength and direction, the phases of the moon, tidal ranges, ocean currents and sea surface conditions.

We followed our fellow cruiser's lead and spent the first day resupplying and then the next few days brazenly relaxing. A long cool dip in the pool, a picnic lunch and then a rousing game of Mexican Train Dominoes took center stage until darkness descended and we headed back to our boats only to renew the contest the following day.

But laundry awaited. It didn't seem like we wore a lot of clothes but there always seemed to be an abundance of dirty laundry aboard *Chewbacca*. I filled a sail bag and dinghied the load to shore where Bruce then lugged it up the hill and dropped it in front of an outdoor sink with a million-dollar view. The huge concrete tub sat under a thatched roofed shelter with a clear view of the sailboats nestled below and the mountains across the wide bay.

While the girls played in the pool, Bruce and I set to work sorting, soaking and scrubbing. The job was monotonous but with the beautiful view I couldn't complain. I scrubbed, I gazed, I rinsed. In a short time, the task was done and our clean clothes snapped in the sea breeze on a line strung between two palm trees. "I'll drag that chair over and watch it dry," I said to Bruce and sent him back down the hill to the pool.

I settled into my position and basked in the generous breeze climbing up the hill. Coupled with the hot afternoon sun, our sheets dried quickly and were soon ready to fold. As was my habit, I looked seaward, scanning the horizon. From my lofty perch, I spied a few lingering clouds on the tops of the distant mountain range. The wispy clouds were beginning to gather like circling buzzards drawn to an updraft. I looked up from folding my third sheet and saw the white clouds had merged into a thickening wall and peered down at the sleepy town below. The mountain range became the dam holding back a lake of clouds from bursting. I played back the warning in my head that I had read. I stopped my work straining my eyes to study the increasing cloud cover. Soon small streaks of mist began to spill over the hilltop, cascading down the mountain like tendrils of silver hair. Within minutes, the mass of clouds descended downward, not like a circling scavenger but swooping like a great bird of prey towards its quarry. The dam had broken.

Goosebumps rose up my spine. I ran down to the pool sounding the alarm when already columns of white caps began marching across the channel. Row after row, the advancing army was moving across the 12-mile stretch of ocean. They were coming for us.

Like deer trying to escape an oncoming forest fire, there was a frenzy of activity as friends packed up quickly and raced down towards the dinghy dock. Bruce rounded up the girls while I returned to unclip our clothes as fast as I could and thrust them into the open sail bag. Bruce came alongside me and untied the rope clothesline, quickly rolling it up, clothes and all, without breaking his stride. We shoved the ball of clothes into the bag, grabbed the girls' hands and rushed down the hill.

I could feel the wind increase on my cheeks and my hair whipped up on end as our feet hit the wooden planks of the jetty. The *Blaster* bobbed wildly on its tether and we had to time our landing into the bucking bronco. Our short ride to *Chewbacca* was wet and wild. The once gentle swell rolling beneath her bows was now a wall of three-foot waves. I imagined *Chewie's* impatient words, *"Hurry up, let's get out of here!"* as she jerked wildly at her chain. If we were to escape the jaws of this closing trap, we had to cut and run to ditch this anchorage...and we had to do it now.

Bruce practically rammed the *Blaster* into the stern as *Chewbacca* pitched violently in the growing seas like a seesaw straddled by two angry kids. We had no time to secure the dinghy properly, so Bruce tied the line and allowed the *Blaster* to trail behind us like a reluctant dog.

I was already in the cockpit flipping on the instruments and turned the key to the engine. The girls were below, closing the hatches and filling the deep galley sink with anything that could take flight during our hasty getaway. They knew we were preparing for battle. Bruce was on the bow hastily pulling on his gloves signaling that he was ready to up anchor. I knew the drill. I powered *Chewbacca* forward, relieving pressure on the anchor chain while Bruce quickly pulled it in, hand over hand. As he neared the last bit of chain, he looked back at me with an exaggerated nod and I pushed the throttle to full. All around us, crews were preparing to bail. Luckily *Chewbacca* needed very little preparation to get underway and we avoided the imminent traffic jam.

I powered ahead between the still anchored boats, as Kendall read off the depths and played lookout. She had a big grin on her face, enjoying the action as much as the motion. I was saving my smile for when we cleared this dangerous windward shore. I quickly steered for open water. Quincy remained below decks already pulling out the chart and setting out the plotting instruments. If it weren't for the girls help we would have been twice as long getting underway. Only six minutes had elapsed from the time we jumped out of the *Blaster* until we cleared the last boat.

I looked back to see several boats pitching dangerously up and down with the growing fetch, tugging angrily at their chains, fenders flying and green water skittering across teak decks. I throttled back and hovered a bit trying to assess if anyone needed assistance. It would be madness to return with *Chewbacca* into the maelstrom, but Bruce was already preparing the *Blaster* to go back.

One by one the boats struggled to break free of the building waves and joined us in calmer water. Once everyone was accounted for, Kendall turned to me and said, "Wow, mom you look like a pro at the tiller." I really appreciated the compliment and some of my tension evaporated. I eased my grip a little and responded with a wink. "I guess practice makes perfect." My job was to steer our little home with my family away from the mayhem of the anchorage in less than ideal conditions and I had succeeded. A smile of profound satisfaction crossed my face. I thought of how much my seamanship skills had grown since casting off that October morning years ago in California.

Bruce reviewed the charts looking for a safe place to land. Our target was a small island that offered good all-around protection in its tiny bay. He plugged the new waypoints into the GPS and read the new compass heading to me. I changed course hoping that it would become our safe refuge.

CHAPTER 28

LOST IN THE BRONZE AGE

"Some beautiful paths can't be discovered without getting lost."

-Dr. Erol Ozan, Writer

OUR COSTA RICAN CHRISTMAS DAY ADVENTURE WAS NOW SIX MONTHS BEHIND us and our visas were once again about to expire. The family vote was "Time to explore a new country." Panama was next in line.

Our guidebooks were sparse with information on the mostly uninhabited northern islands of Panama, but I had heard through the cruiser grapevine that these often passed by islands were definitely worth a stop if you had the time. And to other cruisers it seemed that *Chewbacca* had all the time in the world. When someone inquired about our next destination or schedule, Bruce would often answer; "Schedule? We have no schedule, and by God we're sticking to it." I penciled an X on the chart and set our course. We poked our way down the rugged coastline for the two-day sail with excitement in the air to be raising a new flag in *Chewbacca's* spreaders. Twenty-four watch cycles later a rose-colored dawn ushered us into Panamanian waters.

We consulted the charts and coasted into a well-protected lagoon surrounded by white sand beaches with a line of swaying palm trees holding back the dense jungle beyond. We had barely set the anchor before two young locals in a dugout canoe paddled out to greet us holding up freshly speared fish on sharpened bamboo poles. The fishermen flashed their pearly smiles and pulled alongside *Chewbacca*. One of the boys pointed to a rough grass hut along the shore which I took to be his home, and I had no idea we were about to be invited back in time to the Bronze Age.

Two families inhabited the island beachfront, or more exactly, one family extending over three generations. The patriarch lived at one end of the beach with his wife, while his son's family occupied a bamboo hut on a bluff at the tip of the other end of the beach.

From *Chewbacca's* cockpit this tropical life looked idyllic. I cast my eyes up to the reddish bluffs encompassed by low flowering shrubbery where a garden of colors burst forth. I found solace and contentment hiking up to the bluff and sitting for a time, drinking in the natural beauty of the nearby surf swept islands. I often thought how absolutely complete the moment would be if only I had a glass of Cabernet and a plate of sharp cheddar at my side. No such luck. Still, I was full to brimming with the exquisite beauty surrounding me. If I were John Keats I'd be writing a famous ode, the vistas were that inspiring.

But all too soon, I began to suspect alluring tropical island views were only for the well fed to appreciate, not the hungry. Living hand to mouth, one couldn't afford to sit still and revel in the beautiful. The islanders never had time to even look up from their labors to take in Mother Nature's gift. I was soon exposed to the physical hardships that came with maintaining complete self-sufficiency where every ounce of energy was spent on sustaining life.

The isolated inhabitants lived a simple hunter/gatherer lifestyle mixed in with a seasonal slash and burn style of farming. They cultivated annual crops of corn and rice and there was also an abundance of mango, banana and coconut trees on the island. But for Valentine's family, most of their subsistence came from the sea.

Fishing was their daily ritual. A fact of life. Every day while I was brewing my morning coffee, the locals were hopping into their dugout canoes to fish. A day without coffee only made me grumpy, but for the locals, a day without fishing meant a day without food. Whether hand lining from their canoe or spearing fish in the shallow eddies of the reef, the ocean provided the major protein in their diet. I knew when the fishing wasn't productive because I would see Valentine's three grandkids heading down to the tide pools foraging for cockles, periwinkles and snails for dinner.

The world bustled about its business, but here on this isolated island there were no markets, no schools, no electricity, running water or anything that indicated we were living in the 20th century. This island paradise was visible from the mainland of Panama, yet we may as well have been in the far outer reaches of the universe... except for the Yamaha outboard engine leaning against a palm tree.

Valentine had inherited an old dilapidated 15-horsepower outboard from some passing cruiser and was thrilled to show us his treasure. I thought the rust streaked, battered engine was better suited for an anchor, but nonetheless Valentine was very proud of his acquisition. Using equal parts Spanish and animated gestures, he asked Bruce if we could help get it to work. Bruce circled the rusted hulk and turned to Valentine and said "Es po-see-blay." Yes, anything is possible, but I think a more accurate assessment would have been, "When pigs fly."

The motor made a clunking noise each time the frayed starter rope was pulled. Not good. Bruce went back to *Chewbacca* and returned with a small toolbox, then selected a wrench and removed the mismatched spark plugs. Even I could see that one plug was so long that it hit the top of the piston with each stroke. Probably not the factory recommended plug. Bruce reached into our spare parts bag and found two old spark plugs that might work. A tweak here and a tweak there, the right mixture of two-stroke oil, and somehow, he got the motor sputtering to life on both cylinders. Next, the water pump failed. A little epoxy here, some hose clamps there and presto, a working water pump. Two days later the junked outboard shook to life in a cloud of blue smoke. The old man was ecstatic. Too bad he didn't have a boat to put it on.

When we questioned him about a boat, the 78-year-old patriarch pointed to a mammoth tree beyond his driftwood and bamboo hut. He made a motion with his hands like he was describing the curves of a bodacious mujer. In his eyes, there stood his new dugout canoe. OK, never mind that three of us couldn't hold hands and reach around the tree's circumference.

The only tools on the island were a machete, an old hatchet and an even older adz, not to mention Valentine himself was old enough to be my grandfather. But that didn't stop him. After his breakfast of smoked fish and coconut he had a go at the tree. The wood chips flew. Three days later the giant tree came crashing down shaking the ground beneath our feet. Somewhere imbedded in Valentine's DNA was the blueprint for a canoe and while the new dugout was forming in his mind, a school lesson was materializing in mine.

I was aware that perhaps we were witnessing a lost art. This nearly forgotten skill was passed down through the generations and sadly, the next generation of Panamanians took little interest in such traditions as they preferred to pilot their modern fiberglass pangas powered by flashy new 40-horse power outboard engines rather than paddling a more traditional craft. I feared this would be the end of the line. I ferried the girls to shore every morning to their open-air Anthropology classroom to take notes and draw pictures of the evolution of a real hand-hewn dugout canoe.

The tree lay before us like a sleeping giant. The first canoe was paced off at 27 feet in length. Yes, the FIRST canoe. The son claimed the next 20 feet for his craft. That left eight feet for ours exclaimed Valentine excitedly pointing to the log, then to me and back. Did I mention that this was a BIG tree? I humbly declined the offering but stayed to observe the shaping of his canoe.

Father and son walked along the trunk and slowly began to whittle down the top half. Several days later a gentle arc that would be the gunnels of the dugout appeared. With charcoal and string, they laid out the complex shape of the canoe hull and sat down to the business of hollowing out the immense log.

For the next three weeks, a pile of wood chips the size of two parked Cadillacs gathered on the ground. Chips flew off the ax at an impressive rate as the interior of the tree was hollowed out until it resembled the Log Jam ride at an amusement water park. Next, the outside began to take the shape of a traditional canoe with compound curves and fine lines which only years of practice and skill could accomplish. As Señor Valentine's gnarled fingers worked to the bone, Kendall and Quincy sketched each day's progress. Resting on their haunches amongst the ever-growing pile of wood chips, the girls wrote and observed the birth of a vessel from raw wood. Perhaps, when Michelangelo was chiseling away at David, youngsters gathered at his feet as the marble slab took on the shape of a masterpiece.

Next, four seats were created and held in place with hand-carved wooden dowels. When it came time to attach a support to strengthen the transom and allow for the additional weight of the refurbished outboard motor, Bruce didn't believe the wooden dowels would take the strain. He made a quick trip to *Chewbacca* and came back with a handful of long stainless screws and his drill. Valentine knew of the existence of power tools but had never seen a battery powered one. The drill might as well have been a laser working its magic. Valentine was awed by its speed and power to accomplish what would have taken him hours by hand. Bruce let Valentine wield the tool as he delighted in countersinking holes and driving the screws into the now beefed up transom plate. Modern technology collided with ancient craftsman techniques.

Each evening as the sun dipped into the sea and stained the sky red, I soaked in the beauty that surrounded us and felt privileged to have witnessed not only the ancient art of canoe building but the ritual of life for the islanders of this lost paradise.

After two months of back-breaking work and an infinite amount of time and patience, Valentine's canoe was completed. It was truly a thing of beauty, sporting amazingly fine lines and smooth features. Now we only had to wait another month to let it dry out and cure on the sandy ground.

The burning question was how would Valentine move his new vehicle from where it was felled to the water's edge? The answer came one morning as a few small trees were toppled, stripped of limbs and whittled into small logs to be placed under the canoe. I imagined the Egyptians using this same technique to haul the giant blocks of stone from the quarries that formed the Great Pyramid. Little by little the canoe was rolled down to meet the crest of the high tide and as the waves flowed under the canoe it rode up and was slowly pulled out to sea. We gathered at the water's edge and wondered if there was going to be some fanfare, a christening or coconut bashed against the newly hewn bow. But no, there was no christening, no handshakes or slaps on the back. The vessel was simply paddled through the surf and pressed into immediate service in their ongoing fight for survival.

CHAPTER 29

OUT OF THE PAN AND INTO THE FIRE

"Only one thing that you can see and hear that is beautiful and frightening at the same time, and that is a thunder storm."

-R. K. Cowles, American Poet

I FLIPPED THE CALENDAR TO EXPOSE MAY, AND WITH THAT THE PREVAILING northerly winds slowly started to shift direction. All too soon our once protected nook became wind-swept and choppy as the change in season steadily exposed us to Mother Nature's wrath. By June, cotton ball formations of cumulus clouds invaded the once clear blue skies and each afternoon the distant rumble of thunder alerted us that something sinister was brewing.

I had earplugs in and still the sound was deafening and frightening as it reverberated through *Chewbacca*. I was encased in the ear-splitting staccato as it bellowed overhead followed by a curtain of rain descending in an earsplitting drum beat. I cowered in my bunk, burrowing deeper under the covers. I was petrified. On 33 feet, there wasn't any place to hide and I didn't dare stand close to the 50-foot aluminum lightning rod we called a mast. In contrast to my reaction, Bruce, Kendall and Quincy peered expectantly through the cockpit doorway. They were counting the seconds between the white-hot lightening striking the shore and the following crack. "Eww boy, that one was close," stated Kendall calmly as her hair rose on end from the electrically charged air. The storm was directly over us now forcing the flash of lightening and clap of thunder to fuse together in a single delivery. Flash-BANG!" *Would I ever get used to this rabid display of violence by Mother Nature?*

Over dinner that evening Kendall read from the weather book:

"Lightening is a sudden high-voltage discharge of electricity that occurs within a cloud, between clouds, or between a cloud and the ground. Globally, there are about 40 to 50 flashes of lightening every second, or nearly 1.4 billion flashes per year. These electrical discharges are powerful and deadly."

"OK Mama, here's something to remember:"

"When thunder roars, go indoors. This is the most important rule to obey to avoid death or injury from lightening."

I wasn't convinced that our thin fiberglass boat floating on the water truly counted as indoors.

I knew a lightning strike could sink a boat but even without a direct hit it could destroy any electronics onboard, including our radar, depth sounder, radios and our laptop computer. I didn't need to witness the halo of St. Elmo's Fire to envision a luminous electrical discharge wrapping itself around our mast, engulfing our boat, blowing out our thru hulls and electrocuting us all. This prospect was so serious that some cruisers voyaged as far as Ecuador to escape the lightening. That seemed pretty extreme to me because it's cold enough to wear long pants down there and I'd long since given up the thought of wearing socks. I needed to weigh my options.

Island life on Parida proved a fascinating glimpse into the past, but the ever-violent seasonal storms, coupled with the girls' declaration that SPAM was not a major food group, prompted a family decision to visit civilization for a while. Sadly, the trade winds only blow in one direction and we knew it was unlikely we would ever return.

Bruce had an idea, but prefaced his plan with "You might not go for this." For me crossing an open ocean was not unsettling but Bruce's proposal of snaking our little catamaran 26 miles up a shallow, narrow, current swept river sent shivers down my spine. At the moment the lightning storm didn't seem so bad.

Tales of terror floated around about the unpredictability of sand bars that piled up around every bend, beastly currents that could sweep a boat into the sides of the river or the white-knuckle navigation required to get around the dreaded Boca Brava. "You know that means

Brave Mouth in Spanish," interjected Quincy as she listened to our discussion. I could feel my anxiety level rise another notch.

To help calm my fears Bruce got on the ham radio and put out a query asking if anyone had experience taking their sailboat up the river. A familiar voice came back from our Sea of Cortez days. Jason had made the trip a dozen times. He was planning a resupply run soon and he'd lead the way if we wanted to follow *Osprey*. Bruce and I quickly accepted his offer to rendezvous in a week. *Osprey*, like *Chewbacca*, was a multihull driven by a small outboard, so we'd be well matched for the adventure. Surprisingly, I started to look forward to a guided two-day jungle river excursion.

Jason confided in me that the first leg of the trip was the scariest. As I looked past the smooth ocean to the tumbling surf beyond I was wondering; *What did I get myself into*? I lined up the approach to the mouth of the river and just as I had been forewarned, we were confronted with violent, warring waves converging all around us. OK, Jason wasn't kidding. Legend has it that there are scores of local fishermen buried at the bottom of the entrance and being in the midst of the tempestuous and frenzied surf I believed it. We were within spitting distance of the sand bars when Jason abruptly turned *Osprey* to starboard. "It's as if someone is whispering instructions in his ear" said Bruce as I tailgated *Osprey* and we followed the hidden river channel and scurried away from the graveyard of lost mariners.

I had survived the first test and was feeling pretty good... until we rounded the first bend of the river. Just ahead of us was an electrical cable strung across the gap connecting the island of Boca Brava to the mainland. It looked high, but then so was our aluminum mast! Our 50-foot stick seemed to touch the sky and my imagination went wild with visions of me snagging the wire and all of us being electrocuted.

Jason had a plan to get *Chewbacca's* mast under the wire safely but first we needed to wait for a low tide. The key was enough water under the boat, so we wouldn't run aground, but not so much that our mast would snag the wire. Second, we wanted slack tide, so we wouldn't be battling the current. We sat idly by for two hours snacking and expanding our provisioning list until the tide tables deemed it was time. As proof I threw a cracker overboard and it sat still upon the placid water. It was time. I took a deep breath and cautiously eased *Chewbacca's* engine into forward and followed *Osprey*. It was surreal watching *Osprey's* masthead just miss the sagging wire. From my vantage point it looked like she was going to clip it for sure. Our turn. But *Chewbacca's* mast was taller by several feet and all necks were craned skyward. I felt my face scrunch up as I eased *Chewbacca* forward in *Osprey's* diminishing wake. I forced myself to look straight ahead, and it wasn't until I heard Bruce and the girls let out a loud collective "whew" that the cringe fell from my face and became a smile. We had passed under the wire...just barely.

Jason gave a thumbs-up and shouted, "I really didn't know if you guys were going to make it under the wire." I shook the blood back into my hands and returned Jason's thumbs-up. I stuck on *Osprey's* tail steering *Chewie* around a pile of rocks barely submerged in the middle of the channel and we dropped the hook in front of a small village. We needed to wait here for the incoming tide, otherwise the river would be too shallow to venture further. "This really isn't for the faint of heart," I called over to *Osprey* trying to drain off my nervous energy. Jason shouted back, "The wire was the worst of it, relax and enjoy the scenery." I turned to Bruce and asked "Didn't Jason say the surf was the worst? Now the wire was the worst. How many "worsts" does Jason have in store for us?"

A few hours later we were on the move again. I had a running conversation with Jason over the radio as he moved from one river bend to the other, zig zagging our way towards his favored anchoring spot for the night. Both *Osprey* and *Chewbacca* were snuggled behind a notch of river bend by dusk, just before the skies opened and the rain descended. I listened to the rain as it tapped on *Chewbacca's* deck and was lulled into a sound sleep.

I woke to the aroma of coffee brewing and inhaled deeply. Day two of the jungle trip dawned, along with a rising tide at 5:30 a.m., and we were underway to take advantage of the deep water. In the soft morning light, the river looked beguiling. Then, abruptly it exploded in sound. Parrots, toucans and songbirds all shouted good morning in unison while Howler monkeys loudly protested our crossing into their turf.

We were racing the sun, but today we were also racing the tide. I knew that low tide would return and halt our progress once more unless we pushed on. The jungle canopy abruptly closed in on the river blocking out much of the cloudless blue sky. The trees from each side reached out for the other and I truly thought *Chewbacca's* mast was going to kiss the green foliage. The air was still and heavy as the ocean breeze was choked off. Following Jason's lead, I turned at a particularly tight bend with only inches to spare from the tunnel of vegetation. I focused on Jason's every move precisely, because to step out of his tracks would surely put us aground.

At last we came around the final bend and I took in the rust streaked tin roofs marking civilization. The anchorage was just a small bulge in the river where a couple of ramshackle buildings with a dinghy dock constituted the marina. *Chewbacca* and *Osprey* dropped anchor amongst a handful of small fishing boats and shortly thereafter we were raising our glasses to Jason and toasting to his expertise in guiding us here.

We were now anchored in what I would categorize as prime cockroach country. *Chewbacca* was anchored far enough from shore to catch a slight cooling breeze, but I feared we were still close enough to be an inviting new habitat for roaches and other pesky vermin that lurked amongst the tangle of mangroves.

I had learned early on about cockroach prevention. On *Chewbacca* I had strict rules regarding what could be brought aboard. Cardboard was an absolute NO as cockroaches are attracted to the glue holding the box together. Creepier still, their eggs were often hidden in the corners and creases and I didn't want any surprises weeks later when the eggs hatched. An adult roach was hard enough to run down and kill with a shoe, tiny ones impossible. All cardboard and packaging material were stripped from our purchases before being loaded aboard or in this case before even being loaded into the *Blaster* and ferried out to the boat. Cockroaches also fly so always covering the hatches with a screen, especially in the evening would become law when anchored so close to the jungle.

Some cruiser's cockroach phobia went so far as to remove all the paper labels from their canned goods. I didn't go that far, realizing cruising was full of enough surprises without increasing our canned food GOK pile. Another tactic I practiced was to stash bottle caps filled with powdered Boric Acid in the deepest, darkest recesses of *Chewie's* interior just in case a roach got aboard and escaped our notice. So far, my diligence had paid off and I had no intention of letting my guard down.

The rainy season took firm root and we were bombarded with strong winds whistling down the river, heavy rains and violent thunderstorms. Lightening was now a daily occurrence, so Bruce consulted his notes and caught a bus to town to buy the necessary copper plates and welding cable to rig our "lightening protection." At the first hint of a thunderstorm he lowered the grounding plates to dangle in the water while I raced to unplug our ham radio and radar. Even though we knew neither grounding or isolating the boat were fullproof, Bruce reasoned; "If we did nothing and got struck, then I'd kick myself for doing nothing. But if we do something and then we are struck, at least I can say we did something." Sometimes Bruce's engineering logic escaped me, but I learned to just go with the flow. Some cruisers went to the extreme and put their laptops in the oven which theoretically protects it from the damaging electrical current that lightening emits. In some ways, I was happy *Chewbacca* had no oven because inevitably after a storm we would hear of someone who had forgotten about the laptop and lit their oven for a post storm baking session!

There is an earthy, musty smell that comes with imminent rain; the scent of the jungle undergrowth being whisked and churned up as if in a giant blender. With each approaching storm front the once balmy air was quickly replaced by a cold chill causing gooseflesh to appear on my once warm skin. I learned to anticipate the wind building to a howl as it screeched through the boat's rigging, forcing *Chewbacca's* mast to shudder with each blast like a pulse racing unbridled through swollen veins.

The dance was about to begin. Waves slapped against the hulls, jostling and jerking our home on her tether to the river bottom. Looking outdoors I could see only sheets of water falling from a blackened sky. Visibility remained zero until a crack of lightening flash froze the shoreline and seared the white image into my mind. The furies of Greek mythology had been unleashed, and I was their captive.

I never appreciated the intensity of a torrential tropical downpour until I experienced them firsthand. Living through their onslaught at anchor, sheltered only by a thin fiberglass shell was LOUD. Rock concert loud. Even standing shoulder to shoulder with someone, I had to shout to be heard above the rain drops pummeling the deck. The blinding flash of lightening ripped the sky apart, chased by the deep bellow of thunder compounding the ruckus. The fury raged above and was slung at me like a string of insults.

As all hell broke loose around me I was braced for the end.

CHAPTER 30

A BLUE JOB TURNS PINK

"Life always begins with one step outside of your comfort zone."

-Shannon L. Alder, Author

ABOARD CHEWBACCA THERE WERE SCORES OF CHORES, MANY OF WHICH FELL into either a "Blue" or a "Pink" category. Without being sexist, the pink jobs tended to lean more towards rotating the canned food supply, sorting weevils out of the flour or mopping up the gray-green mystery ooze that collected in the bottom of our icebox. The blue jobs happened when it was time to rebuild the clogged head, fillet a big Dorado, BBQ a rare steak or make popcorn. When we up-anchored, Team Pink drove the boat because only Team Blue was physically strong enough to haul in 200 feet of chain shackled onto a 35-pound anchor. Other tasks, such as laundry, chart plotting or homeschooling, were a blend of colors.

After a year of floating in a river of bionic sludge, a thick layer of crustaceans completely covered the bottom of *Chewbacca's* hulls. No way we were going anywhere fast until that goo was removed. Luckily for me, it was a blue job to slip into the ooze and scrape off that growth of barnacles and slime. Visibility in the brackish water was about an arm's length, tangled with dead branches and decomposing leaves. But that wasn't the worst of it. While Blue Bruce snorkeled in these murky depths, my duties were to faithfully stand crocodile watch on deck. *Really?* Armed with a long aluminum boat hook I tried in vain to make out Bruce's bright yellow fins just below the surface. Just how Pink was to prevent a crocodile from snatching Blue, I wasn't quite sure.

Blindly scraping the boat's bottom paint, Bruce came across an extraordinarily large barnacle. The stubborn bugger was hanging on tight, so he gave it a couple good swipes. The tenacious barnacle fell off into his hand feeling much like the flattened donut of a plastic thru-hull fitting. Thru-hull fittings are just what they sound like, a fitting that goes through the hull underwater to bring in salt water to cool an engine or pump salt water into the galley sink, or in this case to fill the toilet. Take it away and you have an open hole in the boat… underwater. Yikes! Calling to me Bruce calmly inquired, "By chance is there any water flowing into the head where the toilet intake valve is?" Calm is a good thing, but too much calm is scary. From his extra careful tone, I knew we were in deep shit.

I dashed below and saw the thru-hull valve connected to the head wobbling like a drunken sailor. Only a thin layer of sealant held it in place. I hate these freaking thru-hulls. The loss of this $10 part could sink a boat, as we almost found out on *Raven* while crossing the Pacific. For such emergencies, Bruce had bought tapered wooden bungs that could be tapped into a missing thru-hull hole much like tapping a cork back into a bottle of wine. Unsurprisingly, my Eagle Scout husband was prepared and had tied an emergency bung around each of our thru-hull valves. As I gingerly untied the knot from around the wiggling valve, I wondered; 1) Why were my hands shaking and 2) why had Bruce tied such a good knot? With the bung and a mallet in hand I was ready to plug the dike.

I shouted out YOU BETTER GET IN HERE AND LOOK AT THIS."

Bruce appeared over my shoulder dripping wet and without a word headed straight for the spare parts bins. No spare thru-hull. Shit. He left me in charge to monitor the teetering seal that was keeping the river at bay, while he went in search of a thru-hull from the three neighboring boats in the anchorage.

Amazingly Bruce returned in less than a half hour with the exact plastic thru-hull we needed. It seemed another boater had one stuffed in a drawer and didn't even know why he had it since all his boat's thru-hulls were bronze. The Gods were smiling upon us, but we weren't quite ready to do the victory dance yet. Now all we had to do was pull the broken thru-hull out and slide the new one in…all while two feet underwater.

We switched places and this time I donned the snorkel gear and slipped into the coffee colored yucky swamp water. Did I forget to mention the crocodiles? Funny what you'll do to keep your home from sinking. Kendall and Quincy stood guard with the boat hook and a coil of dock line in case they had to wrest mama from the jaws of death. Suddenly I wondered how this became a Pink job.

Meanwhile, safely inside, Bruce methodically gathered his tools for the quick switch. The plan was for me to create a water dam on the outside, so he could extract the broken thru-hull from the inside without sinking the boat. I sank into the mire holding an empty plastic margarine container with some of the girls modeling clay squished around the rim. I pushed the makeshift contraption against the hull sealing off the hole. Now, theoretically the only water that could get inside the boat was the little bit in the margarine container. Theoretically. I crossed my fingers praying that our jerry-rigged seal would be watertight. I knocked on the hull three times signaling that all was in place. Bruce steadily extracted the broken thru-hull pulling it inside the boat. Only a cup of water spilled in. Our temporary Play-Doh seal worked and as much as I wanted to jump out of the muck, I stayed at my post, keeping the container firmly pressed in place. *What's taking so long?*

Bruce then cleaned the hole and gently tapped the emergency soft wooden bung into the breach. From the safety of the deck, Kendall handed down to me the new plastic thru-hull all gooped up with silicon sealant. On the count of three, I removed my cover and pushed the new fitting into the hole, dislodging the wooden bung as it entered. As soon as Bruce saw the threaded plastic pipe poking through the wall he grabbed it and spun on the retaining nut securing the new thru-hull in place. He still needed to reattach the ball valve and hose to the head before I could surface. *Can you hurry this up?*

Remaining in the water another eternally long five minutes, I waited for a crocodile nibble while Bruce tightened the hose clamps and checked for leaks. My imagination spun out of control envisioning rows of razor sharp teeth waiting to strike just beyond my vision. I nearly jumped out of my skin when I heard three sharp raps on the hull. I didn't need a second invitation and in record time raced for the swim step.

Before I even shed my snorkel gear on deck, Bruce came up from the galley with two cold Cokes and a bottle of 12-year-old Nicaraguan Rum. "People back home think all we ever do is lounge around the cockpit drinking Rum and Coke. I'd sure hate to disappoint them," he remarked with a grin.

Blue clinked Pink's full tumbler and toasted to staying afloat yet another day.

CHAPTER 31

PUNTA MALA

"Your dreams are just on the other side of your grit."

-Anonymous

T WAS THE SECOND WEEK IN MAY AND THE PANAMA CANAL BECKONED. WITH Willie Nelson's lyrics playing in my head...I knew it was time to get "on the road again."

We all gathered around the table to plan out several leisurely day hops down the Panamanian coast. It all sounded like fun until I looked over the charts and saw a massive headland jutting off the coastline, seemingly guarding the Bay of Panama. It looked like a daunting point to sail past. *How bad can this be?* I thought. Then my eyes rested on the name; Punta Mala. Uh-oh... "Bad Point." *Why is there never a Punta Tranquillo?*

As soon as we announced our plans it seemed like the radio chatter immediately turned to the harrowing stories of those who had clawed their way around this rugged point with huge seas, opposing currents and for the majority, a collection of horrific experiences. OK, Bad Point stood in our way to the canal. *Just deal with it*, I ordered myself as I read the latest email from our cruiser friends who had just conquered the beast. Call me chicken, but I'm not looking for any tall tales to tell.

With the sun's last rays sparkling upon the darkening water, we were escorted into our next anchorage by frolicking dolphins... always a good omen. I tucked *Chewbacca* in well away from the swell line, conscious of the good-sized breakers crashing on the beach. Was it the sound of the breakers or the thought of Punta Mala looming ahead that caused me to toss and turn all night?

I woke up early, determined to change my overcast mood. I fixed a corned beef and egg scramble for the crew and set up our cockpit table to feast in the clear morning light. I was all smiles until I looked up and saw Punta Mala breaking through the fog in the distance. Even from a half day sail away it loomed forbidding and arrogant. A hands-on-hips bully stood between *Chewbacca* and our prize... the Panama Canal. Black clouds gathered above its brow. Our path was blocked.

I kept taking long, deep breathes to ease the mounting anxiety from my body. I remembered reading Max and Stella's email about their rounding of Punta Mala and the icy feelings returned to my body:

Dear Chewie,

The good news is that we're alive.

Here are our thoughts on rounding Punta Mala and what went wrong the first time:

1. We only relied on Don's weather report and didn't pull weather faxes on our own or pay enough attention to the local conditions. So, when Don said, "Winds from 10-15 knots, this is about as good as it gets," we went for it.

2. We were following a day behind Atlantis and relied a little too much on their experience. Meaning, they had told us it would be awful, and since they never turned back, we tried to tough it out longer than we should have. Unfortunately, Atlantis had radio problems early during the rounding, so we never found out that this rounding was their worst experience ever. Also, we kept hearing Don's words in our heads, "This is as good as it gets", so thought we had to make it as we'd never get better conditions. We couldn't imagine being out there in WORSE conditions.

3. We got out too deep. We were actually able to pass Punta Mala, but then we couldn't turn north due to the wind and current and we never again made any positive progress. We kept going on the only heading we could make,

with the hopes that as we got farther out into the Gulf of Panama, we'd get flatter seas. This was a mistake. The farther off shore we got, the deeper the water, the huger the waves. Really HUGE. VERY SCARY HUGE. That's where things really got bad for us. Past Punta Mala, there is no more land protection from the north winds. There we took the brunt of the north wind, the big seas and the ripping current. When we realized we'd been fighting for almost 5 hours in the worst conditions we'd ever experienced, and we were actually being pushed backwards, we turned around. Punta Mala had beaten us and beaten us badly. We think Atlantis could make the passage because they are a much bigger boat so they could overcome the force of the current and were always able to make headway. Yet, they had a terrible experience. Their genoa track was ripped right out of the deck, shearing off six or eight stainless steel bolts. They fought in the awful gale conditions for almost two days battling around Punta Mala. They were exhausted, literally beat up and bruised and very, very, wet. In hindsight, we did much better by turning back, experiencing no major damage.

We tried it a second time:

1. We had now carefully read and committed to memory the guidebooks advice. "When heading north a yacht should time the rounding of Punta Mala on the rising tide which slows down the southerly flow. During daylight hours, a yacht can stay very close to the shore of Punta Mala keeping in 18-25 feet of water (low tide depths) to avoid the strong current further offshore. We followed this advice closely.

2. We were prepared for gale conditions. So, EVERYTHING was lashed down, above decks and below. All hatches were properly dogged down. We'd taken in a lot of water the first time because our v-berth hatch was not properly dogged down. After we fixed that, we still got water in via the chain locker.

Even in "perfect conditions" it was an ugly passage, but we survived. YOU CAN MAKE IT.

Stella's words "YOU CAN MAKE IT" gave me the strength to move forward.

All the preparation for this voyage reminded me that we were most likely going to get walloped. I didn't want to be the subject of another "trash" story trying to get past this dreaded point, so we waited as day after day Punta Mala disappeared in and out of the gloom. White caps whipped up and died down and squally weather descended and then cleared up. A weather front that promised to put the wind right on our nose and make for an impossible rounding had settled in over our heads... and we waited some more. May turned into June.

I knew timing and patience were everything when passage making, and according to our guidebooks, the winds would be light and variable in June. I hoped they were right. Waiting for the right weather could mean a pleasant passage or the passage from HELL. It could mean keeping your mast and sailing another day or losing your boat altogether. The waiting was never easy.

I reflected on all the major places where we had played the waiting game. Point Conception, along the California coast, Cabo Corrientes in Mexico, the Gulf of Tehuantepec, also in Mexico. Cabo Santa Elena, Cabo Blanco, Punta Burica, all in Costa Rica; and now the "Granddaddy" of them all, PUNTA MALA. If we wanted to go through the Panama Canal we had to face the Bad Point!

Day 10 came and went as we continued to wait out the weather. This was no isolated storm cell but a major weather pattern pinning us down within reach of our goal.

Journal Entry:

"Cruisers sure do a lot of waiting. Waiting for bread to rise, waiting for a storm to pass, waiting for that optimal weather window, waiting for the wind to die down or to pick up, waiting for the seasons to change, waiting for boat parts, waiting for a tidal change and waiting for officials. Patience is indeed a virtue, but damn I'm ready to go!"

Day 14 and Bruce stepped onto *Chewbacca's* top sides before the sun was even awake. The wind was still. Is that what woke him up? He came below and shook my arm. "The deck is wet with dew." My eye roll replied, *so what, big deal, dew.* "Come on!" he replied to my silent scoff. "Dew means settled weather. We're going NOW!" I woke everyone up just as the first hint of grey light was tinging the eastern sky. Bruce was already above yanking the sail cover off and clipping the halyard in place. I poked my head out of the cockpit and noticed the swells once running into the bay were noticeably absent, the wind gone.

The wait was over. D-Day was here. I should have been nervous, but I had too many things to do. There was a charge in the air. This was a "GO" and I found myself running from task to task to make this happen. The girls got busy closing the hatches, putting away anything that could fly around and laying out the chart. I didn't know what our window of opportunity was to sneak around this point, but I knew I didn't want to hang out here for another two weeks. Bruce donned his worn gloves and hoisted the anchor while I pointed the bow towards Punta Mala... all before the sun had even finished breaking the horizon.

Bruce's plan was to stay on the 5-fathom line, about 100 yards offshore, hoping to stay out of the prevailing southern counter current that would endeavor to push us back. We tucked a triple reef in the main and hoisted our handkerchief of a storm jib. We were battened down and prepared for the worst. I had to stop thinking "Punta Mala...Bad Point... Punta Mala...Bad Point..." This was my first real glimpse of the cape, because until this morning it had always been shrouded in swirling cloud cover. The rising sun was illuminating the point and somehow it didn't look so BAD. The wind that was always on our nose had now shifted comfortably behind us. The water remained smooth as we raced our way along the coast. We closed in on Punta Mala and were so close to the beach I could make out several abandoned concrete bunkers surrounded by razor wire. I kept a close eye on the depth sounder as we skirted just outside of the surf line. I replayed *Dream Catcher's* experiences through my mind's eye hoping we were following the right path. I held my breath as we drew ever closer to the point, scanning the horizon nervously for any change in sea conditions and looking skyward to check for squalls. The girls were content in the cockpit, finishing their granola breakfast and all I wished for was the cup of coffee I missed in this morning's fire drill to get moving.

We were just coming upon Punta Mala to our port side when I heard Bruce say, "If it's going to turn shitty, this is when it will hit the fan. Hang on." He eased the tiller into a gentle left turn and we began our rounding of the Bad Point.

You could have heard a pin drop aboard our little boat. I was afraid to breath. As we "turned the corner" and headed towards the Canal, I didn't know what to expect. Several of our friends had gotten this far only to be pummeled and blown out to sea unable to round the point. *Had we waited long enough?* I was standing by ready to retrim the sails as we slowly changed our heading hugging the coast northward. Our heading was changing but the sails kept trim. *Something wasn't right…or was it, too right?*

The blessed tail wind that had pushed us eastward along the coast had now shifted with us, propelling us northward just where we wanted to go. Unbelievable. The counter current shifted in our favor too, and instead of clawing our way around as so many others had, we boomeranged around Mala. A beautiful 12-knot breeze snuck behind us and *Chewbacca* clipped along at a comfortable eight knots. I was giddy as it appeared our waiting had paid off. With the wind still aft, we shook out 1 reef in the mainsail and changed over to our larger headsail. I hardly believed our good fortune. We rocketed around Punta Mala and accelerated into the double digits. The Gods smiled on our little ship that day as we flew downwind towards the Panama Canal.

We had arrived safely at the crossroads of the world.

CHAPTER 32

PLEASE DON'T CRY

"I hated the maze of bureaucracy with a passion, but I've found the best way to deal with it is to smile and act stupid."

-Kim Harrison, Author

"BRING UP THE Q FLAG," BRUCE CALLED DOWN TO THE GIRLS. I WAS STILL A bit groggy in the early morning light which I blamed on the absence of my morning Joe. I motored up the fairway drawing closer to the famed Bridge of the Americas as both girls dashed into the cockpit carrying a rectangle of yellow cloth. The Q Flag.

Traditions die hard in the sailing world and I learned it was best to just go with the flow. In the 14th century the Mediterranean ports established a mandatory quarantine on all ships entering their ports. The word quarantine comes from the Italian quaranti giorni, meaning "Forty days." When the Bubonic Plague swept through Europe, the Port of Venice required ships to anchor away from the city for 40 days before they could unload passengers or cargo. They thought 40 days would be sufficient for any disease to be identified or burn itself out. All newly arriving ships had to fly a yellow flag signaling that they were under quarantine, so up the halyard went our Q flag. *Oh, I hoped we wouldn't be stuck on our little boat for 40 days!*

Bruce had barely secured the mooring rope around our bow cleat when a water taxi pulled alongside *Chewbacca*. A man flashed us an ID badge hanging around his neck and pointed to the yellow flag fluttering in the breeze. The girls were excited to have an official guest aboard. They took their places on the cabin top and quietly observed the exchange as he settled in the cockpit with a stack of forms spilling from his clipboard. Bruce and I answered all the questions to his practiced English concerning our "cargo." "Do you have any fresh, frozen or canned meat products onboard? How about any livestock?" This guy must have been new to confuse our 33-foot catamaran for a cargo ship. *I really should have gotten that cup of coffee when I had the chance.* I soon surmised that maybe this wasn't the Port Captain but the Customs Inspector. He ran down his checklist used for cargo ships, completing them with an X across the pictured farm animals and initialing the bottom of every page. Besides filling in our names and our boat name, not much was relevant to a cruising boat.

After an hour, we finally saw the bottom of the stack of forms. Adjusting his seat in the cockpit, the official looked down through the companionway and into our salon. It took a few seconds for his eyes to adjust to the darkness before he spied Rey chattering away in his cage. His eyes lit up. "Perico?" The official now switched to rapid fire Spanish and talk turned towards "quarantine, veterinarian visits, certified health examination and immunization shots." I figured this visit was leading to some kind of fee for our free parrot.

Deciphering the Spanish, Kendall and Quincy realized that Rey might be confiscated, and they might never see him again. Quincy bolted into the salon from where she was sitting and took Rey from his cage, holding him close while tears rolled down her cheeks. Even the most jaded storm trooper of officialdom crumbles under a child's tears and this bureaucrat was no different. With her chin quivering, Kendall stepped in front of Quincy and stood firmly in front of the inspector. He held his palms outward as if warding off an impending attack. Thinking quickly, he consulted paperwork as if looking for divine guidance. Looking up he asked if this was a native bird. "Yes" Quincy responded emphatically, tears continuing to spill from her eyes. "The islanders on Isla Parida gave Rey to us. We raised him since before he even had feathers," Kendall interjected in a shaky voice. Looking relieved the inspector stammered, "Oh, that's different. This is a Panamanian resident not subject to quarantine laws. Sorry for the confusion." Satisfied that he had dodged a bullet, he continued his tour of *Chewbacca's* interior.

His gaze stopped short on a small cage sitting atop the ice box. "Monkey?" he asked, pointing with his clipboard, eyebrows extending upwards under his ball cap. Once again, Kendall inserted herself between the confused official and the cage. "No, no… that's our baby black squirrel. Ardija, ar-di-ja," Kendall enunciated in proper Spanish. "His name is Rascal. He's Panamanian too!" The inspector returned his gaze to his clipboard and leafed through the printed forms. "Let's see; cow... chicken... pig... dog... cat... no squirrels mentioned here. I guess he is OK," he added unclicking his pen and sliding it into his shirt pocket signaling that he was finished with his tour. With obvious relief on both sides, Bruce signed the paperwork and paid our $10 inspection fee. I suspected that the poor bureaucrat didn't want to search the boat further for fear of finding more stowaway pets.

"Bienvenidos a Panama, welcome to Panama" the inspector shouted with a wave as the panga whisked him ashore. "I bet our menagerie is a topic of conversation around his dinner table tonight," Bruce chuckled with a wave. Now that our Health Inspection was completed we were legal to go ashore and the girls lowered the Q flag. Civilization beckoned.

"I hope we've got mail from home," but be careful what you wish for, because when we arrived to check in at the Port Captain's office there was a letter from the U.S. Internal Revenue Service waiting for us.

Living in a perpetual summer, it was hard to tell the seasons apart, but somewhere up north spring had blossomed, and April 15th had come and gone. In the past, tax day felt like a relentless pendulum swinging through our lives signaling it was time to bear our souls and pocketbooks to the high accountant. Time to split the booty. Like a good responsible citizen Cane, Bruce and I religiously completed our tax forms while we were gainfully employed, yet with no 9-to-5 job and no paycheck, it made little sense to file our 1040 income tax forms. Living life upon the sea had turned April 15th into just another spring day.

I figured what was the use. We made no wages and our interest income from our buddies at Wells Fargo was laughably below the reporting limit. I was wasting time filling in the little shaded boxes when the last line always rounded to zero. Nothing owed, no refunds. Even the handy IRS booklet claimed that if we earned below the set poverty level we didn't have to file income taxes.

It took the bureaucratic grind mill only eight months to determine we were AWOL. They were missing our measly 1040 form in what must have been the Mt. Everest of paperwork. Impressive. The manhunt was on.

A business-like form letter was churned out and directed to our mailing address, 3,000 miles from our actual Panamanian hideout. Its purpose was to enlighten us of the possible error or oversight on our part, and a chance to make amends and be friends once again. *"Failure to file by February 7th"* - which was already four months past- *"would lead to severe penalties, interest on back taxes, and confiscation of personal property."* OK, no mention of blood yet.

Bruce got to a pay phone and tried to explain to a disinterested government employee that according to their own printed instructions, we didn't need to file due to our diminutive income level. Through a volley of questions, the voice at the other end of the line concluded that this was true... but first, we would have to verify that we didn't generate income above the specified limit. To provide evidence of this we would have to file the 1040 income tax forms in question, thereby establishing that we didn't have the requirement to file the 1040 form. Once the status of our poverty was confirmed, the IRS would send us a form establishing that we had no requirement to file that year's filing that we filed to prove such. OK, these are people you don't want to mess with.

We went straight to the U.S. Consulate and found the necessary forms and mailed them into the black hole of the IRS, postmarked from Panama. I hoped someone there was saving the ornate postage stamps I had carefully selected depicting the anniversary of the Canal. Somehow, we were granted a silent reprieve - they stopped sending threatening letters to confiscate our home and all our worldly belongings - and we were free once more. Impoverished, but free.

I called the Admeasurer's Office to start the Canal transit process of physically measuring our boat. I began the conversation in Spanish and was surprised to hear the secretary greeted in Spanish but was surprised to hear her reply in perfect English. Whew, I didn't want to have any miscommunications with my Spanglish when booking what could possibly be the most important passage of our lives.

The official arrived a day later and produced a small pile of forms to fill out and his all-important tape measure. Bruce assisted in measuring the length and width of *Chewbacca*, right down to the nearest inch. Even though everyone under 50 feet paid the same rate and the width of your boat didn't matter, they wanted to know if you could fit in the locks with that 920-foot super tanker nestled tightly to your stern. Next, we worked on filling in the forms for draft, motor type, cruising speed, gross tonnage, bow thrusters, crew list, etc. Luckily most of the forms dealt with types of cargo, frozen meat, and if any of the crew were currently carrying any communicable diseases. Fortunately, he put a big X through them and moved on.

For our crew list, I wrote in our names, ages, passport numbers and positions held. Juan was pleased to see we had a Health Certificate for our parrot, but he was concerned we had nothing for Rascal the squirrel. All animals required a Health Certificate to pass through the canal. He motioned for us to hand him back the stack of forms and I could see the girls' chins began to quiver. With a stroke of his pen he amended the crew list by adding one more name... *RASCAL WINSHIP*; position: *SAILOR*.

After reviewing all the forms one final time and passing them over to Bruce for his signature in about a dozen places, we freed the Canal Commission of any liability should they happen to crush our little home in one of their locks. In less than an hour he was gone leaving us with another thick stack of required documentation.

The next day we tramped from office to office crisscrossing the city to complete our paperwork. First, to the bank to pay our transit fees, second the Maritime Office for the required cruising permit, then the Port Captain's office to obtain our International Zarpe, and finally the Immigration Office where I heard the distinctive whap, whap, whap, whap as our passports and boat documentation were stamped, signed and sealed. We were on our way!

CHAPTER 33

THE BIG DITCH

"My path has not been determined. I shall have more experiences and pass many more milestones."

-Agnetha Faltskog, Musical Artist

WELCOME TO THE EIGHTH WONDER OF THE MODERN WORLD.

As evening fell I found myself immersed in another history lesson. We gathered around the salon light as Bruce cracked open *The Path Between the Seas*, the novel by American historian, David McCullough. Bruce continued reading of man's genius, perseverance and dominance of the world around him captured in words and photographs on the pages.

The Panama Canal opened its gates to maritime traffic on August 15, 1914 just over 400 years after Vasco Nunez de Balboa first dreamed of a route connecting the two seas. After many false starts by the French, the United States began construction in 1904 and finished the project 10 years later at a cost of $382 million. The first yacht to transit the canal was a 60-foot sailboat named *Lasata*, and she passed through these locks on August 14, 1914. And here was *Chewbacca*, nearly a century later, following in her wake.

We were about to transit from the Pacific to the Atlantic Ocean through a series of rivers, man-made canals, and the mighty Gatun Lake. Like walking up a set of stairs, the three locks raise ships 85 feet above sea level where they reach Gatun Lake, and chug across the Continental Divide. Then they're lowered through three locks into the opposite ocean. This shortcut across Panama saves about 8,000 miles versus going around Cape Horn. And now it was our turn to enter the canal.

Chewbacca was suited up with blatant disregard to her diminutive 33-foot waterline. Hanging unattractively at her sides, ten heavy car tires protected her polished fiberglass hull from grinding against the rough concrete walls of the locks. She was also burdened with 500 feet of rented rope and extra provisions for the monumental passage. But that extra baggage was nothing compared to the 1,800 pounds of extra crew onboard. Besides the four of us, joining the circus were my parents, our niece and two fellow cruisers. *Chewie's* waterline sunk four inches below normal. And despite the high spirits onboard, she wallowed like a fattened cow heading to slaughter.

Francisco, our Canal Advisor, literally leapt aboard at 9:00 a.m. sharp. I cringed at the thud of heavy work boots landing on our thin decks, but soon forgot about the black skid marks that his steel toed boots left on our white gel coat. Francisco enthusiastically introduced himself to everyone onboard. Settling into the co-pilot chair across from Bruce, he laid out a computer printout of the day's canal schedule with *Chewbacca* circled in red ink. It listed the exact order and precise time each ship was scheduled to go through each lock. With his VHF radio and Canal Advisor title, Francisco was in charge now and he motioned for Bruce to pull into the fairway leading to the first lock.

The air was charged with excitement and anticipation, mixed with some anxiety about the dangers we had heard about when attempting to transit the canal in a small boat. We were about to embark on a voyage that would take us not only to a new ocean, but to new cultures and new adventures. I felt like James T. Kirk of the USS Enterprise about to go into warp speed.

Following Francisco's confident instructions, Bruce steered *Chewbacca* into the wide channel towards the impressive Bridge of the Americas. The Miraflores Locks were first. We held back and watched as a Titanic-sized freighter was swallowed up in the 1,000-foot-long chamber. It took up the entire front portion of the lock with only inches to spare on each side of the chamber. This left just enough room for three smaller boats to squeeze in behind, stacked side by side. We took our turn, carefully sliding alongside a deep-sea fishing boat and handed over our lines. They were, in turn, tied to a Canal Authority Tugboat which was tied to the wall. The heavy doors closed, muddied water churned and up we went. While ascending, the noise was deafening, and all my senses were on high alert. History flooded around us as 52 million gallons of brown water churned against *Chewbacca's* hulls and we ascended 28 feet. Everything went like clockwork. It happened so fast, I hadn't fully comprehended how momentous the occasion was. "OK, one down and five more to go," said Bruce as Francisco nodded his approval at the flawless ascension. We promptly took our lines back and motored ahead to the next chamber, ready to stack in again.

Once more we were bound together, inching to the top of a concrete wall. The locks observation deck was crowded with tourists and all eyes were on our little ship as we reached the top and untied from our companions, no worse for the wear. It was the same feeling as climbing out of a roller coaster seat grinning like a fool. "Shit, I'm glad that's over. You want to do it again?" Francisco wasn't fazed a bit and pointed towards the next lock, where we would meet up again with the group for the last boost upwards.

Transiting the canal is really just a 50-mile river boat cruise; except for the stair step like locks on each side. Gatun Lake, with its many islands, lay ahead and we motored along through lush untamed jungle. For this part of the journey there was nothing to do but sit on the deck and enjoy the ride. Francisco directed Bruce through the channel markers and by late afternoon we were winding through the Banana Cut, a shortcut for small shallow draft vessels like us. *Chewbacca's* top motoring speed of eight knots was cut down to four and a half with our heavy load so we elected to take a two-day transit instead of the one-day transit customary for larger vessels.

We had lost our race with the sun and Francisco directed us to a mooring ball in Lake Gatun. We had no sooner tied up when a pilot boat swooped by, plucked Francisco off, and whisked him away. Bruce popped the cork off a bottle of Argentinian vino espumantes sparkling wine and seven glasses and two juice boxes were held aloft toasting to our first day of transit. I scrambled below to dig out dinner for the hungry crowd. I'd spent the previous day preparing several meals and stacking the food in the icebox. Out came la cena (dinner) Panamanian style. Ceviche; raw fish stewed in lime juice with herbs, garlic and onion. Patacones; pan fried sliced green plantains and empanadas; dough stuffed with cheese, ground meat and vegetables. Platters of fresh fruit and cheese with assortments of crackers rounded out the feast as everyone fanned out to relive the momentous events of the day under the glow of the deck lights. It was just before midnight before I collapsed into slumber.

I was first up, and slipped into the cool fresh water of Lake Gatun to indulge in a brisk skinny dip around *Chewbacca*. I got two laps in just before the pilot boat zoomed into view at 6:00 a.m. sharp. I quickly climbed the swim step, grabbed a towel and ducked below to check on breakfast. This time Francisco stepped carefully onboard as the pilot boat charged away, leaving *Chewbacca* bouncing up and down in its wake. Once seated, Francisco casually called down the companionway, "Señora, do you know there are crocodiles in these waters?" *Shit, I hate crocodiles*. He unfolded a fresh printout of the canal schedule and with his ever-present smile directed Bruce into the fairway.

The word amongst cruisers was that the most dangerous lock was coming up and I pushed the thought out of my mind and instead I embraced the engineering marvel that would see *Chewbacca* resting in a new ocean before the day was out. At last the water swirled olive green around us as the final steel door of Gatun Locks opened onto the Caribbean Sea.

We had done it. We had safely transited the Panama Canal but before we had time to revel in our accomplishment, as if on cue, we were greeted by a tropical downpour. Anyone who wasn't squeezed under the cockpit awning was immediately drenched to the bone. After six years in the gentle embrace of the Pacific Ocean, we were now in the clutches of the feistier Caribbean Sea. I hoped this cold greeting wasn't a bad omen. Thankfully, like all tropical squalls, it soon passed and there was time for thanks and celebration before Francisco leapt onto a passing pilot boat and was whisked away forever.

CHAPTER 34

ESCAPE TO THE KUNA YALA

"There are no wrong turnings. Only paths we had not known we were meant to walk."

-Guy Gavriel Kay, Author

I N THE FIRST BLUSH OF DAWN, WE SET A COURSE DUE EAST. THE WIND PASSING over the sails was the only sound in the quiet morning as I watched the rugged Panamanian coast slowly slip by. In addition to all our worldly possessions, *Chewbacca* carried canned and packaged stores to last 120 days, plus 35 gallons of water, 25 gallons of fuel, 50 pounds of ice and 72 rolls of toilet paper. Morning gave way to afternoon, and somewhere off on the distant horizon lay the 365 picturesque islands of the San Blas Archipelago, home to the Kuna Indians.

The Kuna were compelled to migrate to these offshore islands because of a hostile natural environment including floods, malaria as well as conflicts with other tribes. However, they were not completely shut off from the outside world as throughout the centuries they encountered Spanish conquistadores and pirates who used their outer islands as a base for attacks on the rich ports of Portobello and Nombre de Dios.

As if surviving the onslaught of pirates and marauders wasn't bad enough, the Panamanian government attempted to eradicate the Kuna culture by suppressing many of their traditional customs in the first decades of the 1900s. This attempt at integrating the Kuna into the Spanish culture was bitterly resisted. The Kuna's isolation combined with their will to maintain their unique way of life lead me to believe that living in the islands would be a fascinating study in cultural anthropology. While I had seen many Kuna living in Panama City, being able to visit them in their villages would add another more personal dimension. There was always excitement onboard when a new land and people were about to be encountered, and especially so as we neared the Kuna Yala.

On our second day out I was just clearing a picnic lunch from the cockpit when I spotted my first glimpse of the islands. Initially they were hazy and indistinct smudges on the horizon. But as the hours passed, these mirages took shape and I finally made out a single palm-studded island surrounded by a ribbon of pale sand. My eyes hurt from pressing the binoculars to them every few minutes but sailing in these reef strewn waters required vigilance. Bruce double-checked our course as black afternoon thunderheads gathered overhead.

From the charts, the island resembled a donut with a small bite taken out of it. Our goal was to pass through the bite and anchor in the middle. I am always nervous when entering an unfamiliar anchorage and entering one with the threat of a downpour and black out conditions only added to the challenge. I lined *Chewbacca* up as if we were landing a small plane on a tiny runway and as I approached from the southwest it became obvious that what I assumed was one island, was actually two. A tiny motu not much bigger than someone's backyard, boasted a lone palm tree standing sentinel to a much larger horseshoe shaped island hidden behind. Whoa, real time perspective is so much more accurate than a chart. I was forced to perform a quick U-turn and realign *Chewbacca* with the narrow entrance in a maneuver Bruce called "butt-puckering eyeball navigation."

The space between this little island and the cut in the reef wasn't much wider than *Chewie* and times like this drove home the disadvantages of our catamaran being twice as wide as a conventional sailboat. Maybe we should have had a sign like truckers have that declared WIDE LOAD. Bruce took his position on the bow pointing the way while Kendall and Quincy were perched high in the rigging reporting water color. They knew a dark blue hue signified deep water while the light blue or green was shallow water and spelled danger. "*Blue, blue go on through. Brown, brown, run aground,*" was a jingle the girls had grown up with. Little breakers from the reefs foamed and gurgled white on either side of the entrance as we scooted into the embrace of the bowl-shaped lagoon.

The cold hand of a breeze wrapped itself around my neck and sent a shiver through my body. The scent of rain was in the air and I called the girls down to the deck. They easily clamored down the rope ratlines to safety, but I could tell they were a little disappointed. The ratlines formed a ladder to climb high up the mast and were a favorite perch for our nimble girls, but not the safest place during a storm.

Life got more interesting as we evaded Mother Nature's obstacles only to be confronted by a human wall calmly awaiting our arrival. Six dugout canoes, or ulu's as the Kuna call them, stood in our path, pitching about in the increasingly squally conditions. Like days of old, they knew sailboats carried prized goods from the "new world" including flashlight batteries, sewing needles and fish hooks. I was as focused on dropping our anchor as they were on trading their prized handicrafts with us. I politely waved and tapped my empty wrist indicating that we would go ashore later. Funny, I was pointing to where I would normally wear a wrist watch, which was something that had zero meaning in the Kuna Yala. My greeting was returned with enthusiastic smiling, waving and tapping on their own wrists.

I refocused my attention and followed Bruce's hand signals, maneuvering *Chewbacca* deeper into the lagoon in search of a parking spot. The anchor was perched on the bow roller and I turned Chewie into the wind bringing us to a complete stop. *Come on, let's get this down before the storm hits!* Bruce surveyed the surroundings and then pointed a finger to the stern. I shifted into reverse and slowly applied power. I heard the familiar rattle of chain as he lowered the anchor into the translucent water. Quincy counted off the feet as the links clattered overboard. The girls had tied plastic zip strips to the anchor chain at various intervals. One strip was 25 feet, two strips marked 50 and three strips signified 75. I powered back as Bruce paid out all 100 feet of chain in anticipation of the looming storm. Fat raindrops began splattering on my back, but we weren't secure yet. Bruce cleated the chain off and I felt our anchor bury itself into the plush, white sand. Bruce twirled his finger skyward and I revved the engine up, setting the anchor deeper and testing the hold. Once secure we exchanged a thumbs-up, and I shut down the engine.

The rain came down in sheets, yet the young men in the ulus surrounding us remained. Kendall conveyed to them in her best

Spanish that given the foul weather we would meet them on the beach the next day to look at their handicrafts. As they paddled away, the deluge instantly swallowed them up in a liquid curtain, leaving us all alone. As Bruce rigged up our canvas rain catcher, the girls hurriedly set buckets in all the proven places to catch even more precious water and I retreated below. Tucked deep within *Chewbacca's* storage bin we had 120 bags of roasted Panamanian peanuts. I dug out bag number one. There were 119 more bags, or four months of treats, if we rationed ourselves wisely. Time to celebrate our arrival.

Bright and early the next morning, we eagerly rowed ashore to explore the village. I'd researched the fascinating culture of the Kuna people and in accordance with their customs, our first visit was to the village chief. The Sahila is responsible for administering the day-to-day political and social affairs, as well as the repository to sing the history, legends and laws of the Kuna. We introduced our family and paid our respects with a customary gift. Our small bag of sugar was graciously accepted, and we were welcomed onto the island which was about the size of two city blocks.

The Kuna Indians are accepting of visitors, but their laws prohibit any non-Kuna from permanently settling on Kuna land or marrying a native. Because of this last decree, the Kuna culture and bloodlines have stayed pretty much intact. However, this lack of genetic variety has created some interesting side effects including the fact that Kunas are the second shortest race next to the African Pygmies and they exhibit a high degree of albinism in their population. According to Kuna mythology, Albinos are a special race with the specific duty to defend the moon against a dragon which tries to eat it during a lunar eclipse. Only the Albinos are allowed outside on the night of an eclipse and use specially made bows and arrows to shoot down the dragon.

The Kuna also adhere to several other customs that initially seem incredibly archaic to our western culture. For example, a Kuna woman is not given a name until she has had her first menstrual period. In a private ceremony to mark this step into womanhood, a local medicine man selects her name and her jet-black hair falling to mid back is cut just below her ears. This may sound as if the society is one in which women have a very reduced role, however it is just the opposite. The

Kuna society is matrilineal where women control both the land and the money. Considering Panama is a country where male swagger reigns, it was refreshing to witness this unique perspective empowering their women.

I stepped onto the sandy path weaving my way in between bamboo and thatched huts and was greeted warmly by several Kuna women wanting to show me their intricately sewn molas. The word mola means blouse which the Kuna have turned into an art form. The intricate patterns sewn into the blouses can be traced back to the custom of body painting. After colonization by the Spanish and contact with missionaries, the Kuna started to transfer their geometric designs from their naked bodies onto fabric. Several layers of different colored cloth are sewn together, and the design is then formed by cutting away parts of each layer exposing the different colored fabric below. The edges of the layers are then turned under and sewn down creating intertwining geometric patterns into themes that are often influenced by ancient history and nature. This reverse applique technique is found nowhere else in the world.

The Kuna women are traditionally the mola makers, but what if a family didn't have a girl to sew molas? To accommodate that role and carry on the tradition, a son is selected and raised as a daughter. In fact, many of the islands Master mola makers were transgender Kunas. There is no stigma attached to this tradition and the transgender Kunas are openly accepted and play an integral role in Kuna society.

Taking in the colorful and intricate designs being displayed by the Kuna women, it occurred to me I was window shopping in the most magical of settings. Instead of treading on a concrete sidewalk along Rodeo Drive or Michigan Avenue, my bare feet were caressed by the warm sands of paradise. I knew from my homework that molas on Chimiche were crafted by exceptional talent and I was tempted to reach deep into our "trading bin" for several. I admired my new acquisition depicting a colorful lobster surrounded in a matrix of complex geometric patterns as Bruce handed over his prized swiss army knife and a packet of fish hooks in trade.

Deep yellow rays of the afternoon sun filtered through the palm trees and hunger drove the girls to search out the old man who baked

Kuna bread. I had heard most islands had a baker and the smell of fresh baked bread lead us right to him. I placed our order for the next batch and watched as he slipped a dozen elongated dough balls into an old 55-gallon oil drum that served as his oven. He adjusted the oven temperature by stacking more coconut husks to fuel the fire and we waited patiently for our treat. The mini loaves resembled skinny hotdog buns, and when spread with peanut butter, the warm dough became a relished afternoon treat. By the looks of pure pleasure on the girl's faces, an outsider would think they were digging into a triple decker hot fudge sundae.

For the next month I would return to the beach day after day and sit back on my elbows surveying the gorgeous expanse of ocean dappled with picturesque tropical islands. Feeling blissful, I relished the warm soft sand under my legs and the priceless view. I often wondered how much someone would pay to spend even a moment on a deserted beach such as this. One afternoon I was woken from my daydream by the clanking of chain and rolled over to spy a mega yacht just outside the lagoon. After lowering a launch and landing on the beach, three uniformed crew members quickly assembled a temporary resort not five yards to my left. The empty beach must have spread out for a quarter mile on either side of me, but I guess I landed on their chosen spot. One crew member nodded to me then neatly lined up eight teak deck chairs in the pillowing sand, while another draped fluffy monogrammed beach towels on the back of each chair. The third busily prepared iced refreshments and arranged plates of food to sit atop matching tables. I watched in amazement as another launch approached ferrying six guests ashore for their two-hour taste of Paradise. I quietly picked up my well-worn towel and met up with Bruce and the girls farther down the beach and joined in on their improvised game of bocce ball using different colored shells.

Although our accommodations aboard *Chewbacca* were a fair step down from the 100-foot yacht, here I was soaking in the same breathtaking islands while sitting on the same stretch of beach yet, unlike my better dressed companions… I had all the time in the world.

CHAPTER 35

ISLAND LIFE

"But what is happiness except the simple harmony between a man, and the life he leads?"

-Albert Camus, Philosopher

I HAD A GOOD FEELING ABOUT THIS PLACE. LIKE THE SEA OF CORTEZ, OUR surroundings were striking but unlike the harsh desert landscape, gently swaying palm trees waved, sending an inviting whisper across the water. As if a spell had been cast over me I found myself slipping quickly and contentedly into the island life. Days turned into weeks and weeks into months. If we needed a field trip there was nothing quite so magical as pulling the dinghy onto a new uninhabited island and stepping out. The girls worked out math problems in wet sand and read aloud to the sounds of distant surf. Exploration is thought provoking and our intellect expanded along with the vision of our world.

Island life was so peaceful that my greatest concern was getting conked on the head by a falling coconut as we idly swung in our hammocks. At first, I doubted the possibility of confronting death by coconut until I heard one fall and hit the ground with an audible THUD. I had read somewhere that a falling coconut could reach 55 miles per hour when it hit the ground. Imagine being hit by a bowling ball traveling at freeway speeds. No wonder every year it's estimated that 150 people die from falling coconuts. Most of them were laying down, enjoying a siesta from which they never awoke. Now, I made sure to check for these unassuming grenades high overhead before stringing up my hammock.

Initially, I laughed when I heard someone ask, "How many coconuts is that?" But here it was actually true. Coconuts were still used as currency in the local island stores where a kilo of rice could be purchased with four coconuts. A can of SPAM cost 12 coconuts and a small bottle of cooking oil set the customer back 6 coconuts. It was literally a cash crop. Now I understood why visitors were warned to NEVER remove a coconut from an island. You were literally robbing a local of cold hard cash.

Between school work and spearfishing Kendall and Quincy kept busy searching the nearby waters for empty conch shells. They were eager to create their very own conch trumpet to herald new arrivals just as we had been welcomed. After a week of scouring the sandy bottom and surf line for that perfect shell, the girls received a conch horn making lessons from a veteran cruiser. Hacksaw in hand, Bruce carefully trimmed off the tip of the shell to reveal hidden chambers inside. The girls took turns cleaning and sanding the mouth piece smooth and with a little practice they mastered their new instrument! Excited to share their new talents, the girls kept a keen eye seaward to spy any new boats entering our idyllic waters. When a new boat arrived, the race was on to see who could welcome them with the longest horn blow.

The kayak that Bruce had wrestled aboard a bus in Puerto Vallarta, Mexico was pressed into continuous service with the girls paddling it into the shallower reaches of the reef to explore where the *Blaster* with its low hanging outboard engine couldn't venture. A family snorkel around the island always yielded wonderous surprises. A squadron of curious iridescent squid, a pair of menacing barracuda or a refrigerator-sized Goliath Grouper lurking in the shadows. Afterwards, we'd canvas its shoreline searching for shells, pale green beach glass, crazy shaped driftwood and other treasures tossed upon the plush white sand. Kendall discovered a talent for photography and drawing. She had an eye for beauty in natures simple designs; an interesting piece of coral fragment, scattered shells or the curve of palm trees as they bowed towards the aquamarine water. As Bruce and I swung in our hammocks, I'd spy her stalking birds, butterflies and hermit crabs, either with a camera or sketch pad in hand. Meanwhile, Quincy was dressed in her bath towel cape, wielding a palm frond sword with a plastic dagger tucked in her belt. Her mission was to track down and slay every dragon and troll she encountered. The tiny deserted island became a place of self-discovery and revelry.

The next morning, the sound of a scraper could be heard as Bruce cleaned the bottom of *Chewbacca* free from the tenacious fuzzy sea growth we had accumulated. Looking over the side into the clear water I saw a shadowy figure pass alongside him. "Shark!" But as I grabbed for the boat hook I realized the shadow was that of a large Green Sea Turtle (*Chelonia Mydas*) slowly circling *Chewbacca*. It appeared disoriented and lethargic bumping clumsily against our hull. Coming face to face he looked Bruce in the eyes as if asking for help. I called for the girls to come quick. In a flash they jumped into their snorkel gear, slipped quietly into the water and began conversing with their new friend in gentle voices. Upon closer examination, Bruce noticed a polypropylene line was wrapped tightly around a green flipper and cutting deep exposing the white flesh. I quickly abandoned any boat projects for the day and set about gathering first aid supplies for our injured friend. I hoped that maybe if I could clean and disinfect the wound, this handsome creature would recover and perhaps even forgive mankind for their carelessness.

Bruce and the girls guided the turtle to shore while I followed up in the dinghy with the first aid supplies. At the water's edge, we counted "one-two-three," and lifted him in unison out of the surf. I gently cut away the fishing net with kitchen shears and disinfected his laceration with peroxide. I then smeared a generous amount of antibiotic cream on his wound and sealed the area with a waterproof coating of zinc oxide. While I worked, the girls poured bucket upon bucket of seawater over our friend to keep him cool, all the while whispering endearments. With my triage complete, they lifted our friend back into the surf and pointed him to open water. We swam together in companionable silence until he took a breath, dove and disappeared into the depths. I felt blessed to have had the chance to do a good deed for this magnificent creature.

A week later, I turned the page in my journal and noticed Mother's Day printed in bold blue letters next to the date. I was feeling a bit blue myself. I missed my mom. It seemed a bit self-serving if I made that day's homeschooling topic, "Honoring your loved ones on Mother's Day," so I just stewed in quiet contemplation. Maybe the girls deserved a day off from school.

I claimed my traditional morning spot on *Chewbacca's* starboard bow with only my coffee to keep me company. The morning sun was disappearing behind a dark blanket of clouds adding to the chill in the air and my melancholy mood. It was then that I noticed a large sport fishing boat anchoring not far off. Their port of call said Corpus Christi, emphasized by a large Texas flag flying proudly off the stern.

It had been stormy the past few days and I wondered how their passage was. I turned my back and allowed my mind to wander through the darker recesses of my thoughts, so I didn't hear the dinghy motoring up until I was shaken from my stupor by "HAPPY MOTHER'S DAY." A ginger haired woman was at the dinghy controls and offered a friendly wave as she pulled alongside *Chewbacca*. "I have a small gift for y'all from Texas," she said passing me a perfect, pink Ruby Red grapefruit. I brought it to my nose and inhaled deeply taking in the fresh clean aroma and thanking her for her kindness. At least someone here had a calendar with all the important Hallmark holidays. "I heard you have two young ladies aboard," she continued, reaching into her canvas bag and pulling out a book entitled *Marley and Me*. A Yellow Labrador Retriever graced the cover. "This is a great book and there's nothing like sharing one on a stormy day." We talked for a few more minutes until rain drops started splattering on the deck and it was time to retreat indoors. I ducked below to see the girls deep in play and Bruce at the navigation station tinkering on a project. I stealthily retreated to my bunk and slowly peeled back the pale pink skin of my prize. Savoring every segment of the fragrant fruit, I turned the pages of the true story about a couple and their mischievous pup.

The simple pleasures of life enveloped me.

Happy Mother's Day to me.

CHAPTER 36

THE GREEN FLASH

"Enjoy the beauty of the sunset and nature's farewell kiss for the night."

-Sharon Rene, Author

LIVE YOUR DREAMS! IT S ALL ABOUT HAVING THE TIME TO FOCUS ON WHEREVER *your mind takes you.* What a lovely reflection. I repeated it out loud to myself as I walked across *Chewbacca's* warm deck. One advantage to living away from civilization and being completely unplugged from our frenzied culture is that I had time to investigate even the smallest wanderings of my mind. It gave me great satisfaction. I dangled my feet over the side and reflected on the day's events while my only companion was the setting sun radiating golden shimmers across the still water. I took a deep breath and fixed my gaze to the west awaiting the fabled green flash that is said to mysteriously appear just as the sun is setting. In some folklore it is said that he who has seen the miracle can look into his own heart and that of another, so that he will never make a mistake in love. I'd always been curious about this sailor's tale and contemplated if it truly existed. For weeks, I made a point of being on deck just as the sun touched the horizon and I waited for that moment when one of the wonders of nature would reveal itself to me. So far nothing. Lucky for me, I had the time.

I took in the placid scenery, enjoying the moment and then…there it was. A flash of pure green light laid atop the molten sun just as it sank into the blue. Did I imagine it? It was there but for only a split second. A flash of green. "So, it's true, its real," I whispered to myself, the image still burned into my eyes. I didn't want to move and break the spell, but I had to share this with someone. I raced below to tell my family as the sun continued to slip further below the horizon, taking my proof with it.

The girls looked up from their play trying to decipher what I was jabbering about. Kendall wanted to go on deck right then, excited to see the sun turn green. Quincy faced her dad and asked skeptically, "Why did the sun turn green?" Bruce looked up from his book and made his fist sink slowly behind the salon table. I knew he lived for these teachable moments and I smiled as he began the explanation. "That's the sun setting below the horizon. See how its light rays are refracted or spread out?" He spread his fingers so only the index finger was pointing above the table. "One by one the colors that make up the sunlight disappear until we are left with just the green one…but only for a second." Bruce defined this as an optical phenomenon. I preferred to think of it as magic, and like many intimate encounters with nature, it continued to be a rare privilege to behold.

I am fascinated with people who study something with a focus, a passion, becoming an expert in one defined area, so naturally, Jane Goodall is a hero of mine. I would have named our first daughter after her, but then Bruce would have claimed naming any sons after Jane's most famous chimpanzees, Freud and Frodo. I didn't dare call his bluff. I made it my mission, my passion, to study the watery world surrounding me… and right in my backyard were the fish, creatures and corals inhabiting the reef nearest *Chewbacca*.

Like scientists, cruisers named the reefs, sandbars, hidden coves and fishing holes in our community. Names such as the *Japanese Gardens, Sand Dollar Reef, Grouper Rock, Barracuda Reef, Sand Spit Island, Nurse Shark Bank* and *Dog Snapper Grotto* all had meaning. They conjured up the lay of the land and what reef fish, creatures or coral lived there. And of course, everyone loved *Chewbacca Reef*.

After school I snorkeled the reefs to check on my newfound friends. Day after day I became aware of the same fish living under the same rock, inhabiting the same hole in the coral or sleeping in the same spot in the sand. A group of Blue Tangs was always found at one outcropping and a brilliant Queen Angelfish made her home in another group of rocks on the slope of the reef. Fairy Basslets always gathered on the channel side of the reef, under a favorite rock shelf, while the side closest to *Chewbacca* was favored by the iridescent blue Damselfish. The neighborhood often changed after a storm when some fish, like my favorite Spotted Drum fish we had been watching for weeks, was swept away. I searched for his whereabouts for days until I discovered him one reef downwind, happy in his new digs.

My daily excursions and ensuing enthusiasm were contagious and soon the entire crew of *Chewbacca* became avid observers of the undersea world in our neighborhood. Everyone took the challenge to identify all the reef fish and in a few weeks our pocket-size *Guide to Caribbean Reef Fish* was dog-eared and worn. We each had our favorites. Where I loved the inquisitive squid, octopus and the Smooth Trunkfish, Kendall and Quincy sought out the rare Highhats and Honeycomb Cowfish. Bruce was more partial to bringing lobster and crab to the dinner table, so he liked to investigate who might be wedged between the rocky ledges and crevices on the reef's outskirts.

After a few months of study, I knew the name of every fish, creature and coral that inhabited our neighborhood. Curious about what took place on the reef after dark, I began slipping into the black water to snorkel the familiar alleyways at night. With a full moon overhead, it wasn't as eerie as I anticipated, and the glow illuminated a whole new collection of reef citizens that I dubbed the "night crew." While the day shift slept, the night crew maintained the vitality of this wondrous habitat under the secret shroud of nightfall. Thus began the ritual of family night dives each month when the moon was at its ripest. I liked to hover over the coral heads as they feasted on the plankton passing by on the currents. Kendall went in search of her favorite queen parrotfish who secreted a mucus from its mouth to form a protective cocoon around herself for the night. "She's in her sleeping bag" Kendall reported when she surfaced. Bruce and Quincy, always on the prowl for something to grace the table, kicked their fins slowly through the water looking for any lobster emerging from their hiding places or crawling along the sandy bottom in search of food.

Besides attaching names to our pets, I started naming our familiar fish friends. Some of the larger fish were recognizable and a slightly walleyed triggerfish named Bob was my favorite. Every morning and evening Bob made his rounds through the anchorage visiting each boat, fishing for handouts. Nobody dared to spear Bob; it was an unspoken rule of the anchorage… until one day a new boat arrived, and they didn't get the message in time. Poor Bob showed up as the guest of honor at our Monday night potluck. Sorry Bob.

One still morning we donned our Lycra suits, grabbed our dive gear and spear guns and piled into the dinghy like any ordinary family going to the grocery store in their minivan. We decided to snorkel close to the outer reef and explore the cracks in the reef wall forming coral alleyways that acted as fish highways, connecting the shallow inner waters to the deep ocean outside.

Kendall and Bruce were absorbed in coaxing out the colorful reef fish that lived amongst the coral closest to the water's surface. Covered in iridescent blue dots, the Yellowtail Damselfish swirled like confetti, aggressively defending their territory by charging and nipping at gloved fingers. They could observe the inhabitants of this part of the reef without even submerging their heads.

I was puttering along behind Quincy when she suddenly stopped kicking. She hung motionless while holding her fist to her forehead, flashing me the peace sign and wiggling her two fingers. That's the sign for lobster. She had spied his red twitchy antenna poking out of a cave and took a deep breath. She descended 15 feet to assess her prey then surfaced for another breath, gave me a nod, cocked her spear and kicked down aggressively, going in for the kill. Quincy rebounded with her spear wiggling and a huge grin. She'd scored that evening's first serving of hors d'oeuvres! I gave a yell and waved to Bruce and Kendall signaling that we were taking her catch back to the dinghy.

The lobster was a big one and its body weighed down Quincy's arm. She swam on her back with her catch skewered on her spear like a triumphant flag. With every kick, we moved closer to the *Blaster* bobbing on the surface, passing one alleyway, then another. The cold current chilled me each time we passed these thoroughfares to the ocean. I could see ribbons of sunlight piercing the darkness and dancing along the narrow canyon walls in rhythm to the waves above. The undulating shadows coalesced into a solid shape and wove its way towards me. Shit. That was no shadow. A Caribbean reef shark (*Carcharhinus perezii*) was coming straight at us!

My heart pounded, and I grabbed for Quincy, pushing her arm up even higher, making sure that the spear and lobster were clear of the water. Maybe if he couldn't smell the lobster he wouldn't want it, or us! DAH-DA DAH-DA…the music from *Jaws* throbbed in my head. We were kicking on the surface with a fresh kill… not a good combination. He was close enough that I could feel his cold grey stare. Neither of us blinked. I couldn't even breath. He passed by us as if bored, then turned sharply and came back for another look. I wanted to stand up and lift Quincy clear out of the water, but that was impossible. If I took her spear to defend us that would be like shaking live bait in front of a hungry tiger. Everything slowed down as *Jaws* brushed by at arm's length. I clutched Quincy tighter, squeezed my eyes shut and braced for impact.

But abruptly, the shark bolted to the left and was gone in a streak of grey. Unaware of the unfolding situation, Bruce and Kendall had decided to swim back to the dinghy to check out our catch and their movements must have scared *Jaws* off. Not waiting to explain our encounter, Quincy and I rocketed towards the safety of the *Blaster*. In unison, we threw ourselves and the lobster onto the dinghy floor. Suddenly I didn't feel like spending the rest of the afternoon in the water.

The hunting party ran me back to *Chewbacca* and then went off in search of another adventure.

I was soaking in the silence when I spied a large panga threading its way between the reefs. An old man and his son returned my friendly wave and pulled alongside to show off their lucky catch. Instantly sadness throbbed through my body as my eyes rested on its gunnels. Taking up the width of the boat was a giant sea turtle. She had a noose around her neck, and another on her hind flippers. I was close enough to see a tear falling from her eye and I had to turn my head and brush one away from my own. Like the octopus, sea turtles tugged at something deep within me. I understood that this was a gift from the sea and that her meat would feed an entire village for a week, yet it grieved me to see such a magnificent and rare creature imprisoned and destined for the butcher's block. My chin began to quiver and for an instant I fantasized that I could set the turtle free. I would jump into the panga, untie her, and tip her over the side… but I didn't. I could only put the scene into perspective. What I viewed as an injustice, was for the islanders, a lucky catch. I knew it was not my place to pass judgement on these fishermen whose survival depended on the sea just because I considered their catch to be off limits. Maybe our rescue of the sea turtle months before would offset the death of this one. But the thought was of small consolation, and did little to quell my sadness.

That evening the four of us sat shoulder-to-shoulder on *Chewbacca's* warm deck waiting for the sun and ocean to once again kiss each other good night and reveal their magic of the green flash.

CHAPTER 37

JUNGLE ORPHANS

"Clouds come floating into my life, no longer to carry rain or usher storm, but to add color to my sunset sky."

-Rabindranath Tagore, Author

T HE SEASONS CHANGED LIKE CLOCKWORK. MOTHER NATURE EXHALED, AND THE wind barreled in. The Christmas Trades signaled the arrival of the dry windy season and they blew into paradise right on schedule. Once the trades took hold the winds ramped up to a steady 25-30 knots turning our travel between the islands into a miserable, windward bash. We also depended on the rain for our fresh water supply and that too ceased as the constant winds chased the clouds away. Summer had vanished and likewise, it was our turn to scoot.

Bruce reluctantly pulled up our chain and Quincy neatly flaked it into the plastic milk crate strapped down by the mast. Kendall waited for the command and confidently shifted the engine into forward while I steered *Chewbacca* away from paradise towards civilization and our growing to-do list. I looked around one last time at the brilliant blue water moving smoothly past and took in the familiar islands as we slipped away. I felt like it was Sunday evening, when a happy, fun filled weekend was still fresh in my mind, but the inevitable work-a-day Monday morning was closing in fast.

We had stayed until the bitter end and our last meals were dipping into the GOK can pile. In three days, we would be tied to the marina dock, hooked up to electricity and fresh water. Water from the dockside hose bib meant I wouldn't be out in a midnight downpour filling my containers and unlimited electricity meant I'd get to hear the blessed whirl of my coffee grinder. There would be real stand-up hot showers, easy provisioning close by and no all-night anchor watches. After six months living on the hook I thought; *What's not to like about this set-up?*

Before we reached the marina, we made a stop to answer a most peculiar invitation to the island of Linton. "They live with sloths?" asked Kendall excitedly as I clipped the VHF microphone back into its holder. The girls had listened intently to Roger's voice inviting all the cruisers to his home on Isla Linton for a potluck. Although we hadn't met our hosts before, their reputation for kindness and generosity was legendary in the Panamanian cruising community... especially the fact that they lived with sloths. Roger and Cathy were former cruisers themselves, and as well as being a wealth of information about the local area, they took on the roles of rehabilitating injured or orphaned sloths. Kendall and Quincy were especially intrigued by the idea of sharing one's house with these slow fuzzy creatures.

It was only a day sail to Linton and by late afternoon we were tying *The Blaster* up along a decaying, wobbly dock next to four other dinghies. We walked along the grassy shoreline until we found the gate entwined by twisting vines and thick hedges, like the nearly hidden entry to the *Secret Garden*. We stepped through and as we ascended the hillside on a winding wooden staircase, the groomed and tamed jungle escorted us upwards to a teak veranda overlooking the bay.

Half way up the steep flight of stairs a couple of happy, healthy looking dogs greeted us enthusiastically. They had luxurious, shiny coats, unlike the painfully skinny, flea infested dogs that normally lingered around small villages. The girls were amazed that the dogs wore collars and looked loved, not merely barking property, chained up and used to discourage trespassers. We came to find out that these used to be stray village dogs, mangy and starving mutts, before Roger and Cathy adopted them. Now transformed and the picture of health, Lurt and Tess were happy, tail wagging, loving pets.

On each side of the glass entry a giant Panamanian flag mirrored by an equally impressive American flag waved in the tropical breeze. We were warmly welcomed inside and there was no shortage of conversation as the ex-cruisers and cruisers shared local experiences and information. Floor to ceiling bookshelves lined the main room and it was a feast for the eyes. I had not seen a library for quite some time, and the sight of so many books was breathtaking. Books on any subject you'd care to browse were at my fingertips. I was overwhelmed by the cozy and comfortable feel of their lovely home perched high on the rugged hillside. It had the ambiance of a sanctuary, a cottage by the sea...a place of escape. Roger built their retreat 30 years before. Working side-by-side, he and Cathy created an island of tranquility nestled above the bay. The views were breathtaking.

But who cared about a view when there were real live sloths in the house? Kendall and Quincy were thrilled when Roger introduced them to Hurricane, Lightning and Thunder. So, the story was true. These two-toed sloths (*Choloepus didactylus*) shared the house with their owners and we looked in on these nocturnal mammals wrapped in fleece blankets, fast asleep in their guardian's king-size bed. By night they literally cruised the huge junglegym tree fort that Roger had built for them in a spare bedroom. They kept themselves busy wandering from branch to branch and munching on leaves threaded throughout their makeshift, artificial jungle. Full grown, these sloths were about the size and color of an adult German Shepherd complete with two large canine teeth. Roger gave the girls a lesson in two-toed sloth facts while they sat patiently petting these most peculiar creatures:

- *Sloths are built for life in the trees.*
- *They sleep 15 to 20 hours a day.*
- *Sloths are identified by the number of long claws they have on each front foot.*
- *There are two-toed and three-toed sloths. Two-toed sloths are slightly larger than their three-toed relatives.*
- *Sloths have large stomachs with several chambers to ferment the large amount of plants they eat. Two-toed sloths eat primarily leaves, but also shoots, fruits, nuts, berries, bark, some flowers and even small rodents.*

Now adults, their baby pictures hung on the wall as a reminder of their survival. The photographs revealed tiny, injured creatures that were left for dead and had no hope for survival. One had machete slashes across his face, another was hit by a car. All of them were orphans. Roger and Cathy nursed them back to health and over the years became the regions experts on these fascinating animals. Their large, heavily forested property became a safe habitat where other wild sloths felt free to congregate. Roger counted as many as 14 sloths at one time nestled in the trees and bamboo stands on his property. They were safe and undisturbed, if they stayed in the confines of this oasis. However, beyond the walls laid the road, wild jungle and most menacing of all… man.

It seemed like the marina could wait. Bruce and I enjoyed meeting fellow cruisers at Roger and Cathy's, while the girls were content helping care for their new sloth friends. They lay seemingly inert wrapped in their blankets only to grasp at a passing hand in search of a dangled hibiscus bud. Their new friends seemed to graze almost continuously, and the girls were always ready to wave a leaf, long bean or a sweet hibiscus flower in front of their snouts and carefully feed them. They watched as the sloths were bathed, which was no easy feat lathering up an animal with six-inch claws.

What started out as a single day detour turned into a week. We were all reluctant to go, but just as a flock of scarlet macaws announced the coming day, Bruce pulled anchor and I pointed *Chewbacca* towards the marina.

I was so looking forward to being tied up at the marina, but be careful what you wish for. Living in a marina is like parking in a drive-in theater. Row upon row of boats stacked in for efficiency. It's nothing like swinging free in an anchorage with a deserted island as your back yard… And we had next door neighbors.

It was 3:00 a.m. Lightening ripped across the blackened sky and rain hammered upon *Chewbacca's* deck, so I barely heard the staccato knock on the hull. I emerged from below and was hit by a downpour in full force. The night was so black I didn't notice the shadowy silhouette looming across the dock. Just then lightening cracked and lit up the camouflaged face perching night vision goggles atop his head. He stepped forward. I instinctively stepped back. The figure swung something over the lifelines. "Sorry it's so late ma'am, but we found this in the jungle and the Chief said we should bring it to you." I reached out to steady the soggy cardboard box. "We couldn't leave him there to die, once we found him... again." I recognized the clipped but warm voice of a United States Navy SEAL we had met earlier that evening. "Thank you, Sergeant, "We'll see if he survives the night," I stammered as I peered into the box.

The U.S. Navy had a deal with the Panamanian government that allowed the SEALs to conduct jungle warfare training at the former army base known as Fort Sherman. The surrounding dense rain forest adjacent to the marina was perfect for their needs and as luck would have it, their stay coincided with our own. Most of the SEAL's comings and goings were in the dead of night, so we had little idea of what they were doing under the cover of darkness, however several times our family was invited to join them on short day jaunts into the rain forest where they shared their jungle survival knowledge and a few details of their interesting lives.

My mind flashed back to the turn of events that all began earlier that evening when we were at the marina club's bar. The Master Chief caught Bruce's attention and asked if there were toucans in the jungle. This would be like asking if there are polar bears in the arctic. Duh? But this was the highest-ranking enlisted man in the U.S. Navy, and a trained Navy SEAL to boot, so where Bruce's retort would normally take a sarcastic turn he simply replied, "Absolutely!" I had to jump in, "You typically see them flying mid-level in the canopy, usually in pairs. They're about yea big" I added, holding my hands apart approximating the size of a penguin.

But this wasn't what they saw. The chief continued describing what his team had encountered the previous night while crawling through the muddy jungle floor during their latest nighttime maneuvers. "It was a little featherless bird, all beak, hopping around the jungle floor. Could it be a baby toucan?" Bruce praised them for not eating it on their survival training. "Too bad it's so late, because it won't likely survive the night in the jungle with jaguars and boas slinking around." Not another word was spoken. The Master Chief caught the eyes of the three guys at the end of the bar happily minding their own business. He snapped his fingers and cocked his head signaling them back into the dark, creepy, crawly jungle to find the bird. For most it would have been deemed a foolhardy endeavor.

A bulging set of black eyes belonging to a scrawny, featherless bird with way too much beak stared intently back at me as I peered into the box. He leaned precariously forward because of his extra-long appendage. Sure enough, it was a baby toucan. I assumed he was washed out of his nest during the torrential downpour that afternoon and had a one-way flight to the ground.

I called for Quincy and our little dinosaur like bird with his silly looking, top-heavy head was whisked inside and wrapped snug in a dry towel. We warned the girls that our little guy might die, and that the first 24 hours were the most critical.

The next day, low and behold, "Sherman" as we came to call him was still alive. Quincy mashed up bananas and he gobbled them down. She mashed up papaya and he gobbled that down. In fact, he gobbled and gobbled everything set before him.

Bruce headed out early to the internet café to search the web for information on the care and feeding of our exotic little guy. He connected with a toucan breeder in Florida and they began corresponding about toucan care. Turns out our boy was a Chestnut-mandibled Toucan (*Ramphastos ambiguus swainsonii*) and when he matured, his beak would be chestnut colored with a bold bright yellow stripe. For now, though, he was a scrawny, reptilian looking creature. The breeder told Bruce that the preferred food is "Toucan Chow" available at any exotic bird store in the good old U.S. of A. Bruce had to explain that we were literally at the "end of the road" down in Panama and there were no exotic pet stores in our neck of the woods...unless you counted the fact that our whole back yard was one big exotic pet store. The breeder confessed, "OK, you can use any puppy chow, it's really the same thing in a different package." I had to hand it to American marketing. A half dozen phone calls later and I found puppy chow in Panama City. It was just on the other side of the country. Back and forth the e-mails flew and we learned more about toucans than we ever thought possible. The closest I had come to a toucan was the Fruit Loop cereal box bird from my childhood and now we had one living with us!

As if overnight, Sherman sprouted feathers and graduated from his cardboard box to a large cage on our stern teak deck. Bruce sewed up a cover for his new enclosure, so he stayed dry and shaded. As Sherman grew he became loud and demanding, especially at mealtimes and soon I was up at dawn every morning hand feeding him chopped up mango, papaya, banana and puppy chow. It soon became apparent Sherman was even more handsome than any wild toucan. He had grown a luxurious coat of radiant, deep, coal black feathers. His yellow bib and brilliant green crown shone. The markings around his eyes resembled black eyeliner applied by an expert and his bandy blue legs and feet finished off his designer outfit perfectly.

His beautiful physique was due in part to the supplemental high protein puppy chow as well as the seemingly around the clock feeding. I'm sure nature wasn't quite as accommodating. I measured his feedings carefully but without the added kibble to fill him up, I would have been a slave to his nonstop eating habits. The saying, "She eats like a bird" is an out and out lie. Sherman did not pick or peck at his food nor was he a dainty or hesitant eater. He dove into his dish of papaya and banana 5 times a day with unbridled gusto, seizing the pieces of fruit between his growing beak and deftly flinging his head back and gulping the morsel down. I wondered where he learned this? If the offered cuisine was not to his liking, or if he was bored, he showered anyone near him with pieces of fruit. I swear he wore a smug look and his eyes gleamed with amusement at his own antics watching us duck and dodge. He was so impressed with himself.

Sherman soon imprinted on me and we became best of friends. When I opened his cage he immediately hopped to my hand and laid his head in my palm, signaling for me to stroke the top of his head with my other hand. Over time he grew so docile and tame that he often fell asleep while I petted him.

One day, Sherman suddenly discovered he had a voice.... and could sing...and what a song it was! "yo-YIP, a-yip, a-yip" sounded more like a rear axle going out on a car than a bird song. It was a tune only his real mother could love. His nasal caw rose from a short cough to a full out shriek as his call cut through the still morning air like a siren, answering his brother toucans deep in the rain forest.

Sherman, like all birds was an early riser and at dawn he "thrilled" the marina with his music. I am not a morning person, but Sherman soon had me trained. After the first few weeks of trying to sleep through the first chorus just inches from my head, I flew out of bed, snatched the already prepared chopped fruit out of the ice box and dumped it into his cage. "There, that will hold you for a little bit longer" I sleepily muttered before stumbling back inside. I felt as if I was the mother of a newborn baby…and I was!

Sherman might have been born an elusive wild bird, but he was determined to have the gaze of every bystander, the admiration of every bird lover, and the eye of every camera. The word soon spread that *Chewbacca* had a real toucan living aboard. Cruisers stopped by and even local Panamanians gathered by the back of the boat for a close encounter with a live toucan. Rather than glimpsing a rare view through a spotting scope, there was Sherman in all his magnificence right before their eyes, oftentimes perched on Quincy's gloved hand.

We came to the realization shortly after trying to teach our handsome toucan to fly that maybe he needed to have a better home with more freedom of movement than we could provide. On one of our exploration trips around the area we discovered a working ranch nestled on the shores of Gatun Lake. The owners were dabbling in eco-tourism and had built a retreat with rooms, community kitchen and some private separate bungalows for rent. As a tourist attraction, they built a rain forest zip line and had mountain bikes and horses for rent. But what really got our attention were the large aviaries they erected that housed several species of toucans that were also in various stages of rehabilitation.

We met with the manager and discussed the possibility of Sherman "bunking" there to complete his rehabilitation. In a few months, Sherman's "roomies" had taught him to fly well enough that he was able to be released back into the wild.

Not long after we released Sherman, another member of the SEAL Team stopped by *Chewbacca* gingerly carrying a cardboard box. When I came up on deck I thought, "Uh-Oh." "Ma'am, I have another orphan for you. I found it by the airstrip, sitting in the grass. It looks hurt," explained the clean-cut young man. I peeked over the ragged edge of cardboard and there sitting desolately on its bottom was a gray bundle about the size of a small house cat. But as my eyes adjusted I recognized a very listless female sloth. "A SLOTH! A wild three-toed sloth. OK, I'll see how she does. Let's hope she lasts the night." This sounded all too familiar I thought to myself. "Thank you" I said wondering what I had gotten myself into... again.

I prayed she would survive. She was beautiful, matted fur and all. She refused water and I simply wrapped a towel around her quivering body and tried to comfort her. Kendall took the first shift and gently whispered encouragement to our newest charge. She instinctively spoke to her in soothing, soft tones. They gazed at each other and a connection was made.

In the morning, I held my breath. The sloth was still sitting in the same spot in her box, arms covering her head with knees drawn up, hugging herself. She was alive, and my heart melted. "Let's see what we can do with you little girl" I said softly. After examining her from head to toe we decided to bathe her and afterwards we set to work gently picking blood swollen ticks from her dense, wiry hair. Another bath and she still showed no resistance to our handling. Wrapped up she looked like any swaddled newborn, warm and content. We placed a call to the only people we knew who had experience nursing sloths from the wild. On the other end of the line were Roger and Cathy sharing with us their expert sloth advice.

As it turns out, three-toed sloths (*Bradypus variegatus*) are super finicky eaters and dine exclusively on only one type of leaf. Luckily for us, the broad Cecropia leaf is easily identifiable and plentiful. We sent the girls out to scour the surrounding rain forest daily.

After tearing up the young and more tender spring green leaves, I created a mash and slowly hand fed our newest guest, scooping the leaves onto a finger and pushing the sloppy concoction into her mouth. Kendall called this precious girl Stella Luna, named after a fruit bat in one of her favorite children's books.

Word spread and Stella, like Sherman, soon became famous. Her health improved, and she quickly became a member of our family, much like a dog or cat…but way slooooower. Their scientific name *Bradypus* is Greek for "slow feet." A very accurate description earned by being the world's slowest animal only reaching a top speed of 0.003 miles per hour. We were confident in our ability to rehabilitate this wonderous girl, especially with Roger and Cathy as an excellent source of expertise. They were only a phone call away if we had any questions and I had many.

Sloths are fascinating creatures and not much is known about their life in the tree tops. But as the months unfolded, our observations of Stella and wild sloths that lived in the nearby jungle piqued my interest and I learned some of the more interesting facts about this endangered mammal:

- *Sloths have no facial muscles and like dolphins they don a permanent endearing smile.*

- *They have one speed; a ponderous crawl and are incapable of going faster or hurrying up hence they are easily struck by cars as they cross a road. They move a mere six-to-eight feet a minute.*

- *Though they couldn't be clumsier on land, sloths are surprisingly good swimmers.*

Stella recovered after a few weeks of constant care and soon settled into a daily and nightly routine. When not munching on leaves, sloths sleep a lot and Stella was content to snooze 15 to 20 hours per day. She was most active at night and while the rest of us slept she would ever so slowly roam the bowels of *Chewbacca*. By day she divided her time between sleeping in the girl's clothes cubby or hanging upside down in the cockpit on ropes Bruce had strung up for her. I hid leaves around the boat, so she would have to forage and go looking for her food like she would have to do if she was in the wild. I think she thought of me as her tree branch and she spent a fair amount of time holding onto me around my neck or waist like a human toddler when I went about my business. She liked contact with us and loved being held close, although in the wild, adult sloths are mostly solitary.

Around the marina, the girls had earned quite a reputation for nursing injured animals, anything from birds with broken wings to geckos missing toes. We couldn't turn any animal away and Bruce laughed that our tiny house was turning into a jungle animal shelter. Over the years we fostered several small parrots, a free roaming sloth, a cheeky toucan and a mischievous squirrel.

Stella recuperated fast, but she would need further rehabilitation if she was to be released back to the rainforest. Roger and Cathy offered to adopt her and eventually she would have the jungle home she deserved. The goodbyes were long and tearful.

CHAPTER 38

OUT OF LUCK

"The world is indeed full of peril and in it there are many dark places."

-J.R.R. Tolkien, Author

W E WERE ON OUR WAY BACK TO MY FAVORITE PLACE ON EARTH AND I HAD NO inkling we were being stalked. *Chewbacca* loped along happily under sail on our way to the San Blas Islands with a fresh early morning breeze off the beam. I was standing watch and when I swept the horizon behind me I spotted the white dot of a sail in the distance. It was a beautiful day to be underway and a popular stretch of coast to be traversing, so I was not surprised that we had company.

As time passed, the speck in our wake became a blob. A few hours later the blob materialized as a large sloop with a deep red hull gobbling up our wake. I hailed the vessel on the VHF radio but got no reply. As the minutes ticked by the boat seemed to hone in on us like a fighter jet moving in to get a missile lock on its intended victim's tail. "Whoever they are hon they are breathing right down our necks and…" I didn't even finish my sentence before Bruce reached over to give the autopilot two clicks to starboard. *Chewie* scooted 10° to the right and I relaxed a bit with more sea room between our boats. "It's a big ocean, no need to be this bunched up," said Bruce as he grabbed the radio mic to hail the phantom vessel, but again the airwaves were silent.

Like a bat out of hell, the "attack boat" blazed by us. When she passed, she was still close enough that I could see there was no one in the cockpit. Zip. Not a human on deck. What kind of person in command of a vessel kept no watch? I wondered if everyone was OK on the mystery ship. Noting the name on the transom, I again called over the VHF radio and was again greeted with an eerie silence.

Someone was ALWAYS topsides on *Chewbacca* keeping watch day or night when underway. Whether we were sailing along the coast four miles from shore or crossing the open ocean with land several hundred miles away, we followed the same rules. I was shaken and couldn't fathom setting the autopilot on *Chewie* and letting her go where she may, unsupervised. So much could go wrong with that scenario.

If only this was the last we would hear of this boat and its master, the notorious Captain Louie.

That next morning, as *Chewbacca* and her crew lay blissfully at anchor whiling away another idyllic summer day, our VHF radio suddenly jumped to life. A friend's classic, beautifully restored wooden ketch was just rammed by another sailboat while at anchor. Our friends continued to describe the hit and run culprit as a red hulled sloop. Could it be the same boat that blazed by us with no one on watch? Bruce dubbed this mystery boat "the ghost ship," but I more correctly christened it "an accident waiting to happen." The topic of irresponsible boat handling was the hot piece of conversation around the potluck table and bonfire that evening. "Yummy, this is scrumptious," swirled around our gathering as much as; "Can you believe that careless bastard?"

Three weeks later, news travelled through the fleet of a sailboat limping into the harbor in Cartagena in need of repairs to a splintered bowsprit. Come to find out, the same madman that had damaged our friend's boat in the San Blas, had bashed into another. Captain Louie had struck again. When would his luck run out?

Lady Luck can be on your side or decide to slap you "up side of the head" if you are not careful. A month later news burned up the air waves of a boat that had steered itself onto the rocks fringing the Panamanian coastline and had sunk to the bottom in a matter of minutes. Evidently nobody was on watch. The captain had escaped with only the swim trunks he was wearing and his passport. You guessed it. Captain Louie's luck had finally run out.

But some people just seem to have all the luck. Ava and Ricardo were veteran cruisers and their pretty little sailboat could be spotted year-round tucked amongst the San Blas Islands. Ava was a gifted seamstress and she had found a lucrative niche while living in paradise. Her creations incorporated the brilliant Kuna Indian's molas into western style clothing and other decorative items and her successful cottage industry was widely admired and her unique designs were sought out and prized by cruisers. Ricardo likewise had talent and had made a successful and profitable living as a musician in his native Colombia before retiring to full time cruising life. They had it all.

One evening over dinner, Ava announced they were setting sail for Florida. They had sold their sailboat *Fancy Free* and were delivering her to the new owners. I was still processing the fact that they were giving up the good life when Ava said they were heading to town to return their rental car that next morning and to pick up the last of their provisions for the long sail north. She asked if we would like to ride to town. Oh, hell yes. One way into town in a car beat both ways on a chicken bus any day. Our food supplies were getting a little thin and maybe I could learn a thing or two from these seasoned cruisers.

The bank was our first stop and as Ava was conducting her business with the teller she motioned Quincy to her side then bent down and whispered something in her ear. Quincy unzipped a pocket in her cargo pants while I watched Ava stash what looked like a rubber-banded roll of bills in her pocket. Quincy turned, and Ava unzipped a pocket in her other pant leg and inserted another wad. As weird as it sounds, this wasn't all that unusual to distribute cash amongst several people, albeit it was usually exclusively among family members. Quincy thought nothing of this procedure and stood there as another bundle found its way into another pocket.

The rest of the day wasn't very relaxing for me as we moved about the store filling our shopping carts. I kept Quin glued to me and saw dollar signs every time I looked at her. It was raining when the six of us were disgorged from the bus and stood on the roadside with our cargo. We still needed to schlep everything down to the rickety dock, into the dinghy and ferry it all back to *Chewbacca* before our already soggy boxes deteriorated.

As Bruce and Kendall unpacked our supplies, I whisked Quincy over to *Fancy Free* to unload her of her worrisome burden. I stared in disbelief when Ava pulled out rolls of hundred-dollar bills from each pocket that had been carried by our little "mule" through the mean streets of Colon! This was a town of 70% unemployment, where a laborer was lucky to make $8 a day and rumor on the street was that for $50 you could make someone go away... FOREVER. This was not a nice town. What would someone do to our little girl if they knew she was carrying $20,000 on her? I was speechless. I believed that Ava and Ricardo had stepped across the line of etiquette, but luck was on our side and Quincy was safe and we had survived the day.

The next evening, we coasted up to *Fancy Free* for an impromptu farewell party as the soothing sounds of jazz wafted on a gentle breeze from the open portholes. I imagined Kenny G. was entertaining the crowd and waiting for my request. Moonlight flooded across the teak deck illuminating the way as I stepped down the companionway steps into their salon. Ricardo stopped his playing long enough to raise my hand to his lips for a kiss. Ever the suave and charming host, he bowed gallantly at the girls, tousled their hair, shook Bruce's hand and resumed his playing. I heard the chink of ice as it came tumbling from the icemaker into our glasses as Ava prepared our drink orders. *Fancy Free's* cabin was filled with cruisers who had come far and wide to say farewell. As Ricardo continued to soothe us with jazz, the laughter of good friends and good music flooded the night and was an appropriate sendoff for such a renowned couple. Waving from the *Blaster* we wished them the best of luck on their passage north.

Several months later, we heard through the cruiser grapevine that *Fancy Free* had reached Florida safely, however she wasn't delivered to her new owners. Instead *Fancy Free* was seized by the U.S. Drug Enforcement Authorities who had received a tip. Concealed within her hull were neatly bagged kilos of cocaine. Lots of them. I was shocked that our family had been deceived and betrayed by the cunning wolf disguised so skillfully in sheep's clothing. Both Ricardo and Ava were sent to prison ending the fairytale, and like Captain Louie, their luck had also run out.

CHAPTER 39

THE KUNA CONNECTION

"The only thing I like better than talking about food is eating."

-William Morris, English Poet

"HE'S HERE!" KENDALL HOLLERED, AS SHE MADE HER WAY FROM THE FRONT TRAMP back to the cockpit. Sure enough, the outline of a panga could be seen plowing along with confidence between the reef strewn islands. The girls cleared the back deck of our lawn chairs and put down a fender while I brought my calculator, paper, pen, old shopping list and new list into the cockpit. It had been three weeks since Juliano's last visit and I was looking so forward to receiving fresh supplies. I had used our last egg and the last of the powdered milk to make muffins that morning for breakfast and even the GOK canned food pile was getting sparse. Once more we awaited the "Kuna Connection."

On our first venture into the San Blas, I decided to provision for a four month stay at anchor in the deserted islands. I constructed a very loose menu by listing our typical canned meals and guessing how many times a week we could stomach them. I was looking at 120 breakfasts, 120 lunches, 120 snacks and 120 dinners. The kids translate this to be: 1,540 plates, 1,540 assorted bowls, 720 pots and 4,320 utensils they must wash, dry and put away. Homeschooling math on a boat always led away from theory and focused on real life applications.

As quartermaster, I had to shop for food, cooking supplies, gasoline and propane for four months... and oh yes, don't forget toilet paper. Tackling this chore alone was mind boggling so I gathered the troops. Logistically it was easier to lug four grocery carts up and down the aisles than 12 so we stretched our shopping over the course of a few days. The first trip to the supermarket was dedicated to buying only canned and jarred goods. The next was for dry goods such as flour, beans and rice. Last was meat and cheese with fresh produce purchased just before we cast off. If it wasn't on the list, it didn't make it in the cart. My rules. But I suspected "daddy's cart" was a little heavier than warranted.

Provisioning while coastal sailing wasn't such a big deal. Stash a couple weeks of canned goods in the lockers and buy fresh food as you go. Easy. But once we left the well-worn supply route and entered the far reaches of the Kuna Yala territory, provisioning became more challenging. I used to tell the girls that getting supplies to the dark side of the moon might be easier.

The San Blas Islands are about as remote as you can get. We were so far off the beaten path that the locals depended on a few small trading boats to bring in goods from either Colombia or Panama. If our timing was just right we could sometimes catch a Colombian trading vessel passing by and purchase limited supplies of gasoline, canned food and a few tired looking fruits and vegetables. We couldn't rely on these serendipitous encounters as our sole supply chain and happily we didn't have to.

The anchorage was abuzz, and I noticed other sailboats preparing for Juliano's welcomed visit. There was a civility to his visit, an unspoken rule to await your turn, not charge over to someone's boat and interrupt this important flow of commerce. The order seemed to follow the seniority of the anchorage and we were third in line on this trip. I waited patiently for the familiar sky blue panga and driver to slowly approach *Chewie's* stern. Once tied off, I was as eager as a child on Christmas morning to see what Juliano had brought for us. But in the Kuna Yala there are no clocks, no schedules, so Juliano took time with Kendall and Quincy to practice their Spanish and learn a few new Kuna words before the bargaining began.

"Buenos Dias Señor Bruce, Señora Abril y niñas," said Juliano in slow deliberate Spanish. Like us, Spanish was not his first language so slowing down the cadence of our shared tongue was welcomed. Juliano took out my grocery list which was a duplicate of the one I had resting in my lap. "OK, I bring you almost everything you ask for, except no find this brand of, what do you call it, chili?" He handed me the label

I had torn from a Hormel can several weeks before. "But I bring some beans for Mr. Sid and he no want them. So, if you like, I sell them to you?" Juliano added as he handed me several cans of frijoles negros, (black beans) to inspect. OK, it wasn't exactly what I wanted, but close enough. Flexibility is the essence of the cruising life and at this point I was about as pliable as Gumby on a sweltering summer day.

Juliano started down the list while his helper dug into the bowels of the panga and produced our items:

- *1 gallon of cooking oil*
- *15 pounds of white flour*
- *5 pounds of course yellow corn meal*
- *12 boxes of UHD radiated milk*
- *1 tin of powdered milk*
- *3 packages of individually wrapped American cheese slices*
- *10 pounds rolled oats*
- *10 pounds of sugar*
- *2 boxes of margarine*
- *1 jar of yeast*
- *1 package of salt*
- *10 packets of chicken broth*
- *1 pound of dried kidney beans*
- *1 pound of brown lentils*
- *3 pounds of white rice*
- *6 cans of tomato paste*
- *6 cans of sweet corn*
- *1 case of original SPAM*
- *1 case of Turkey SPAM*
- *1 jar of dry roasted sunflower seeds*
- *1 package of white sesame seeds*
- *1 package of black sesame seeds*

- *5 pounds of potatoes*
- *1 propane tank to switch with our empty one*
- *5 gallons of gasoline*

Lastly, a flat of 36 eggs were passed gently over to the girls. It was a miracle they survived the journey unbroken. "Cuidado niñas." The girls mimicked "careful" as they accepted the fragile cargo aboard *Chewie*. Next, Juliano set up a makeshift scale and weighed cabbage, onions, green peppers, carrots and handed over eight Red Delicious apples still wrapped in tissue paper from their original cardboard packing box. Bruce's eye brows raised, "Wow, here we are in the back waters of Panama, eating imported apples from Washington State!" Juliano carefully passed over a full propane tank and Bruce handed him our empty one. He also fished out the girl's new school notebooks and a package of colorful felt pens for each of them. Next, he produced 20 loaves of Kuna bread each resembling a big fat brown cigar. "Just baked this morning," he grinned as the girls cheered in delight. After he checked off all the items on the list, he then showed us his special offerings. I loved this part because you never knew what coveted item was stashed under the seats or wedged between the sacks of vegetables. After years of working with cruisers, Juliano had gained an inkling for the luxury items that comprised the less basic goods, such as pancake syrup, boxed wine, jarred apple sauce, pretzels, peanuts and cake mixes. Juliano reached down and pulled out a six-pack of genuine A&W Root Beer! He had no idea what it was, but we did. Sold!

Sometimes Juliano brought out an unidentifiable cut of beef, and he'd hack off however much we wanted, and the rest went back into his cooler for the next customer. Today there was a cooler dedicated to whole chickens. He smelled each one as it passed by his nose and handed it to his helper who chopped off the feet and head before handing it to me. The girls loved watching as these discarded parts were tossed into the water. Soon a Nurse shark would arrive to vacuum these tidbits off the sandy bottom. The sharks had learned to follow Juliano from boat to boat looking for a free handout.

Once our business was completed, I paid and handed Juliano another list to be delivered in about three weeks. We chatted amicably for a few minutes about local Kuna news and then his traveling tienda motored on to the next customer. When he left the anchorage a few hours later, his empty panga was riding high in the water. Market day was a wonderful day in the neighborhood!

I knew from my family's appreciative comments that it was the little treats that made mealtime memorable, especially during passage making. Little luxuries may cost a bit more, but they boosted morale when the cupboards started to thin out and the fresh veggies had long disappeared. As I gained more experience provisioning, I squirreled away treats such as jarred pickles, relishes, green olives, applesauce, chocolate chips, almonds, raisins, cake mixes, pretzels, popcorn, canned fruits, peanut butter, jams, chutneys, capers and salsas. I also bought enough yeast, white flour, whole-wheat flour and cornmeal to make breads, pizza crust, muffins and cakes from scratch every day. I was suddenly a rock star when I added a handful of sunflower seeds, a cup of dried cranberries or shredded coconut to any freshly baked staple.

But life for the quartermaster wasn't without challenges. *What! Weevils in my rice supply!* I checked the pasta and my coveted flour inventory. Sure enough, those were contaminated too! While mostly unheard of in the States, this was a common occurrence in developing countries. There were no stores nearby to replace our staples so we'd either go hungry or find a way to roll with it. I developed a technique for picking the wiggly weevils out of the rice at least. I found that instead of sorting through the dry rice piece by piece I could rinse the grains in a pot of water and allow the little critters to float to the surface. I then easily spooned them out, but no matter how careful I was, some inevitably ended up in the cooked meal. After a while I accepted the idea that they were just added protein, although Quincy was led to believe I always added a little oregano to my steamed rice! After cruising in foreign lands with lower quality control standards, we acknowledged that sooner or later, even if the package was just purchased, we were going to have bugs.

To the girls' great amusement, we discovered that trading food was as acceptable as book swapping and the market boomed between cruising boats. It worked something like this: Cruising boat "A" would be leaving the San Blas and planning to store their boat for several months at the marina. "Was anyone in need of 15 pounds of flour and 10 pounds of sugar?" Or, in another scenario, cruising boat "B" bought a case of chili and decided they didn't like it; "Would anyone want to buy or trade for something?" When I discovered that I had a lifetime supply of poppy seeds, I split the huge container and traded it for six jars of Spanish olives.

Now, what did I have to trade for a bottle of gin?

CHAPTER 40

BOATYARD BLUES

"Time is money."

-Benjamin Franklin, American inventor

T HE FIRST IMAGES THAT CAME TO MIND WHEN I HEARD "COLOMBIA" WERE THOSE of drug lords, violence and, of course, Romancing the Stone.

Swinging at anchor outside the beautiful colonial city of Cartagena was magical, yet just across the bay its modern, high-rise skyline was a jolting contrast to the turquoise waters, tranquility and natural beauty of the San Blas Islands. After so many months of solitude I wondered if I was ready for civilization. The rude sounds of traffic on the pavement and the clip clop of horse's hooves on the cobblestone mingled with the ever present loud, abrasive music and the hum of human activity. My quiet world was shattered.

But the city far surpassed my expectations with its European architecture, culinary delights, diverse culture and exceedingly friendly people. Excerpts from my email home read:

"From palm-fringed islands to concrete towers. I hate this place.

There's so much more to Cartagena than the wild traffic, constant noise and high-rise buildings. The city is drenched in history and everywhere I look there are reminders of the Spanish, English, Dutch and African cultures who have settled here and melded in with the native population. This place is interesting and full of flavor. I'm really loving this place"

In the early morning, a walk along the waterfront or atop the city wall was invigorating with the cooling trade winds blowing steadily off the Caribbean Sea. Parts of Colombia may have been in turmoil but Cartagena, like a jewel tucked away by the sea, remained a refuge. I knew that this would be the perfect place to bone up on history and take in some culture while Bruce thought this to be an ideal spot to undertake a major refit for our 20-year-old catamaran. It was time to go to work.

My heart stopped beating. I couldn't breathe. Our home was soaring over my head, water streaming off her hulls as the boatyard crane plucked her from the water. I focused on the thin cable hoisting *Chewie* and thought back to the waiver I signed just moments before. It said that if anything went wrong with the lift, we were to "hold the boatyard harmless." So, in other words, if they dropped our home, it was our problem. Three mammoth rusty cargo ships formed a canyon surrounding our little boat and she had to be lifted... UP and OVER. OK, breathe. I exhaled as they set her down carefully on makeshift wooden stands. *Whew, I'm glad that's over.* I didn't realize how badly I was shaking until I held the camera up to my face to take another picture.

I looked at the boatyard as a full-time job. A dirty, messy, exhausting and hazardous job. One that would easily soak up 14 hours a day for the next month. Bruce estimated that we had two months of work ahead of us, but our budget mandated that 30 days in the yard was all the time we had.

It is hard to keep kids safe and occupied in a boatyard. There is no more a caustic and chemical laden place on earth... especially in a foreign country where environmental laws range from somewhat lax to non-existent. Ungloved hands, no eye protection and flip flops were standard operating procedure for the locals perched on crude, cobbled together scaffolding. *Chewbacca* was too dirty, noisy and hot to take refuge in, and besides that, climbing up and down a ladder was a hazardous venture all on its own. I wondered how were we going to keep the girls engaged and out of harm's way while we worked?

While grabbing lunch in the small cantina inside the boatyard, opportunity knocked and outgoing Kendall answered the call. She was recruited to help out as an assistant to the sole lady proprietor who was also the chef, waitress and cashier. Kendall peeled vegetables, wrapped silverware, set tables and served lunch to the rough, but polite boatyard workers. She received a free lunch and 50 cents per hour, but the compensation wasn't about earning a paycheck for her services. At age 14 Kendall's immersion in this foreign world allowed her Spanish to grow by leaps and bounds and she even developed a Colombian lilt to her adopted language. As a bonus, she also learned to cook Colombiano style, utilizing ingredients fresh from the mercado to concoct the most delicious and flavorful sauces, soups and stews.

While Kendall was in the restaurant most of the day, Quincy assisted me with her own project list. Week one, she wielded a battery powered screw gun and unscrewed all the teak planks on our back deck. Week two, she sanded each plank smooth. Week three, she oiled each plank and by week four she was screwing them back into place.

Through recommendations of fellow cruisers, Bruce hired a foreman and a work crew to take on the major jobs, however he stayed involved in case questions arose and to keep the project on schedule. The team was excellent. They started work on time and stayed on the job until quitting time. Every task, no matter how mundane, was tackled with zest. The jingle from *Snow White* came rolling off my tongue each morning as our crew filed through the narrow chain link boatyard gate. "Hi-ho, hi-ho, it's off to work we go."

Like a Fortune 500 executive, Jorge kept his crew rotating through varying tasks, keeping them stimulated, rather than letting monotony get the upper hand and possibly lead to sloppy work. Sanding and grinding is hard labor but undertaking this work in the humid tropics was especially challenging. Jorge had his crew encircling *Chewbacca* throughout the day and mixed up the doldrums with some work under the boat, and then back on the topsides. Around and around, up and down they went, grinding and sanding in one of the hottest and grittiest conditions imaginable, yet their faces and body language were always etched with enthusiasm. It probably helped that Bruce and I worked right alongside them sanding and grinding. We were just as tired and disheveled as they were when we all filed out the boatyard gate at day's end.

While *Chewbacca* was laid up, we rented a small furnished high-rise apartment in an area of town called Boca Grande. Instead of the historic cobblestone streets of Cartagena that I had fallen in love with, this area was its flashier cousin, drawing Colombian tourists to its beaches and resort style living. It didn't have the old-world charm of the walled city but had a cultural vibe all its own.

But not everyone lived a charmed life. Throughout our cruising years the girls sometimes couldn't help but be exposed to life in the raw. Nowhere was this more apparent than in large cities where life's inequalities and injustices stood out. A prostitute exiting the marina, a homeless young boy getting high by sniffing glue to stave off hunger, older men exploiting the young local girls who were seeking a better life and looking for a way out of their country, and the ancient trades of pick pockets, beggars and shysters abounded.

At times, I wondered if all these real-world experiences would take away some of the girls' innocence. But reading one of Quincy's letters to her grandma proved that they took all they saw and heard in stride:

> *"Dear Grandma. I hope you are all right! I am doing fine, I like Cartagena a lot. There are lots of things to do and see. We are docked at a real marina and to get on and off Chewbacca we must walk a plank like pirates. Dad, Kendall, me and 2 people on another boat went to see a real fort! The fort had tunnels and we had to use flashlights to see. It was fun! Mom had to stay on the boat because she got Dengue Fever and we don't want her to die. Hope you are well. Love Quincy."*

Each night we dragged ourselves back to the apartment to scrub off layers of sweat and dirt, rinse out our equally filthy clothes and hang them out to dry on a line strung from the balcony. Bruce and I would then collapse in a heavy heap while the girls made grilled cheese sandwiches. Our dinner menu seldom varied, mostly because the apartment had a sandwich panini press and it was something the girls could make unsupervised. I'm sure the man at the little neighborhood store thought that white bread, Kraft cheese singles and butter were the only foods we Americans ate.

Our work lists steadily shrank as the weeks passed. When the end was in sight, we started to raid the bank ATM a little at a time so that we weren't withdrawing a billion Colombian pesos all at once. The criminals knew a boatyard bill could mean a significant windfall, so we forked over the small fortune a little at a time. We had heard accounts from other cruisers of taxi drivers colluding with criminals to rob unsuspecting gringos of their freshly withdrawn cash, so we went so far as to enlist a trusted local friend to drive us to a different ATM each time to avoid becoming victims.

As a bonus, my artistic side decided to design a more stylized boat name. This was the only part of *Chewbacca's* refit that didn't require any brawn. Like finally getting to arrange the furniture and hang pictures after a major home remodel, it was my favorite phase.

As the stencil was peeled back to reveal our new *Chewbacca* lettering and the last of the bottom paint was applied I hardly recognized our boat. Like a thoughtfully renovated home, she had morphed into a more functional and comfortable cruising catamaran with a little more curb-side appeal. She was a handsome sight.

The girls squatted on their haunches and calmly watched as the crane lifted *Chewbacca* off her saw horses and high into the air, moving her back to the water where she belonged. I was sweating bullets, but for the girls, this was just business as usual.

Our home swayed in the breeze as four Colombians maneuvered her UP and OVER again, setting her into the water between two rusted, hulking, steel freighters. I tried not to think about the breeze that had sprung up. What happened if they dropped her? Oh yeah, that would be on us. What happened if one of those guy's stumbles or just let's go of their rope? Oh yeah, tough luck. I resumed breathing only when she gently settled in the water on her new boot stripe.

At last our little ship was safely back in the water and we were free. I hopped aboard and started the engine, letting it warm up while Bruce checked the thru-hulls for leaks. Everything looked good. Kendall brought out our little hand drawn map with GPS waypoints to get us back to the marina, while Quincy checked to make sure the binoculars were handy and that the radio was working. It felt good to have the crew of *Chewbacca* back aboard our beloved home.

CHAPTER 41

FAMILY AFFAIR

"The sea, once it casts its spell, holds one in its net of wonder forever."

-Jacques-Yves Cousteau, Explorer

WE WERE RETURNING TO MY FAVORITE PLACE IN THE WHOLE WIDE WORLD. *Chewbacca* slipped easily through the water with her new slick bottom paint and we set course for Panama to once again drop our anchor in the clean, turquoise waters of the San Blas Islands.

I brewed a cup of coffee and thought back to that misty October morning when we left San Francisco to give the cruising life a try. Bruce and I were game for a big adventure and Kendall and Quincy, just seven and five years old were eager to show their Beanie Babies the big ocean. One year had become two, then three and somehow stretched into ten.

Our first few years of cruising as a family had been punctuated by more than a few hair-raising experiences, but all-in-all it had been an idyllic wandering marked by our girls' emergence from childhood into adolescence and beyond. They lost baby teeth along the coast of Mexico and Guatemala. They changed shoe sizes every few months in Honduras, El Salvador, Costa Rica and Panama, and sprouted inches after crossing through the Panama Canal. While in Colombia, Kendall leapt into young adulthood. One morning she emerged from her bunk and sported a brand-new body, seemingly overnight.

Sailing back to Panamanian waters again I wondered where the time had gone. We had all come of age on this adventure.

All too soon the South American coastline disappeared behind us. With the sun hanging low in the late afternoon sky, we started our nightly passage routine and noticed as we tucked a precautionary reef in the mainsail that two extra sets of hands set the cringle down a notch and threaded the ties in place. Somewhere along our journey we had lost two passengers and gained two very capable new crew members.

The early night watch began, and Quincy stepped below to assemble the evening snacks. After placing the basket of goodies on the cockpit bench she took her place to stand watch alongside Bruce. She confidently snapped her safety harness into the chair and rearranged her binoculars on the strap hung around her neck. These were the official tools of the "Watch Commander" and she wore them with pride. Quincy was in her element, one-on-one time with her dad and they chattered away the time.

The near full moon had risen, chasing away the nearby stars when it came my turn to stand watch with Kendall. She was now able to gauge the wind strength, direction and sea state and she entered these estimates along with our latitude and longitude neatly into *Chewbacca's* log book. Bruce chose to doze in the cockpit while Quincy shuffled below to her new bunk next to Kendall's bed. To accommodate her growing frame, Bruce cut a hole in the hanging locker for her legs, added a piece of plywood topped with foam and she now had her own custom bunk. She squeezed into her nook like an Olympic bobsledder slipping into her torpedo capsule…feet first. Our watch wove through the night and it was good to have Kendall's company.

Our first full day at sea I found myself sitting on the front tramp wrapped up in Harry Potter's very last adventure. I was shielded from the sun by the largest jib and a cooling breeze drifting over our starboard side. With one book to read between the four of us, we each were allotted a 90-minute turn before passing it to the next reader. "I solemnly swear not to talk about what I just read," was the oath we all took. I was bewitched as the richly woven narrative unfolded.

Bruce was giving another one of his "lessons at sea" which entailed showing the girls how to calculate speed through the water and plot our course on our paper charts. Suddenly the fishing line trailing off the back transom pulled taught signaling a change in the lunch menu. Boat school never stops, and a biology lesson ensued as Kendall gutted our catch and Quincy filleted it. I battered and fried fish fingers and rounded up the ingredients for a zesty tartar sauce. Quincy joined me in the galley and helped prepare a fruit salad as Kendall sliced into a block of cheese. Our highly preserved Kraft singles, also referred to as "plastic cheese" by the girls, were held in reserve until our fresh provisions dwindled. Teamwork made the time pass quickly and the miles clicked steadily by in our wake.

After lunch Kendall brought up the cloud book and attempted to match the shapes and patterns in the sky to those on the pages. As a family we were constantly scrutinizing the conditions at sea and tried our best to predict the weather. That evening when the sun set it was a glorious blazing crimson. Red sky at night; sailor's delight.

The second night loomed leaving Bruce and Kendall to take the first watch. Quincy raced below knowing that she had a date with Harry Potter. I was hot on her heels knowing that I could slip in a treasured three hours of uninterrupted sleep. I didn't have to set an alarm because I knew that all too soon there would be a gentle tug at my foot signaling me to "suit up."

Like clockwork the girls rotated watch with Bruce… and I slept through it all. Bruce pretended to doze in the cockpit allowing Kendall and Quincy to take the watch. He heard them whispering to each other with excitement about their new roles. Sitting across from each other in the cockpit chairs they confidently checked our course every seven minutes, scanned the horizon and swept a complete circle, binoculars pressed to their faces. This was a milestone towards full-fledged crew members as they were in command of their home. They had been handed the responsibility of keeping *Chewbacca* on course and keeping us all safe.

Sunshine woke me and I realized I had been gifted with a full night's sleep. I emerged bright-eyed bringing granola and cut-up papaya for breakfast to my blurry-eyed watch crew. Their fatigue from the second night's passage soon evaporated at the first color of sunrise. Our destination was somewhere over the horizon and the energy level on *Chewbacca* visibly heightened even though I was the only one fully rested.

By lunch, dark smudges appeared on the horizon, foretelling shadows of the Panamanian mainland. We were happy with our progress and anxious to get the hook down. Quincy excitedly dug out the Panamanian flag while Kendall pulled down the Colombian flag that had flown above *Chewbacca* for the past year. Together they hoisted up our aged Panamanian flag once again.

We were still hours from closing in on land and the girls eagerly volunteered to stand another watch. This opportunity to take complete responsibility with no adult topsides would be a test. When we emerged an hour later, we were still on course, sails trimmed and no dangers in sight. They smiled with pride knowing they had passed the test. Kendall gave us a formal watch report and then turned *Chewbacca* over to her parents. I could see them growing a few inches taller.

With only a couple hours of light left I began to recognize various clumps of islands and the closer we drew the more distinct and detailed the scenery became. The VHF squawked to life as our friends spotted our lone stick on the horizon. "Yes, that would be us," I exclaimed. I grabbed the binoculars and made out seven masts half hidden behind a cluster of palm trees. We homed in on our waypoint that marked the entrance of the channel and I felt as if I was driving down a familiar lane towards a favorite hideaway.

Together we doused the large headsail and tied it down on the front tramp. Then we slowly let down the main, flaking it neatly and tying it down atop the boom. With many capable hands working, the process was quick and smooth. We would fold and bag the sails once anchored, but for now we were content to soak up the familiar landscape. Quincy coiled the cockpit lines and hung them in place as Kendall disengaged *Han* and I took the tiller in hand. Both girls were anxious to take their place up in the rigging to keep careful watch on the water color. We had snorkeled this area the previous summer and though we knew the reefs well, it paid to be cautious. In a strong voice, Kendall shouted "Mom, come to port a little bit, the water is getting lighter on the starboard side and I can make out the bottom." I adjusted our course, trusting her judgment. *Chewbacca* moved into deeper blue water again and I gave her a thumbs-up. Recognizing the seascape, Quincy called out Sea Horse Reef, and when *Chewbacca* was abreast of the Japanese Gardens they whooped with joy. I felt like we were greeting old friends.

Once past the outer reefs, Quincy climbed down and posted herself on the front tramp keeping her eyes peeled for "stuff in the road" which meant any floating debris or sudden change in water color. She sported a big grin that said she was happy to be in such beloved territory. My pulse quickened as we approached our small slice of paradise. This was to be our home for the coming season and the thought brought pure joy to my heart.

We were swept with emotion as friends waved and the sound of conch horns filled the air welcoming us back. I asked myself what made the perfect anchorage; a tropical island with the ideal balance of isolation and civilization, new sites for explorations with a pinch of peace and adventure. Some anchorages felt "right," and this was one of them. The bottom was ideal...flat, with deep fine sand rising gently to shore with a protective reef encircling the anchorage. It was the ultimate place for a temporary home base. I knew from experience that what seemed a perfect anchorage today, next week or even next month could turn 180 degrees with the changing seasons, but for now, this place was close to perfection. My journal entry that evening simply read:

"I could stay here forever."

Kendall quickly climbed down from the rigging and managed the engine controls while I maneuvered *Chewbacca* slowly into position to anchor. Our drill was well rehearsed, and not a word was spoken as Bruce took his place as the human windlass and Quincy stepped in to help. I brought *Chewie* into the wind and her forward momentum stopped, then Bruce lowered the anchor with a soft splash. Kendall carefully shifted the engine to reverse and Bruce paid the chain out slowly through his threadbare gloved hands. Quincy held up 1 finger for every 50 feet of chain paid out and I felt the anchor flukes burrow deep into the sand and *Chewbacca* stopped abruptly... held fast. Quincy expertly tied a rolling hitch to the anchor bridal, cleated each line to the bow cleats and then set out the last bit of chain. Her well-worn kiddie garden gloves were now too tight for her teenage hands and

I saw Bruce watching her with pride as she secured the knots. When *Chewbacca* settled comfortably at anchor we converged on the bow and took in the crystal clear, blue-green water. We were home.

I returned to the cockpit to shut off the instruments and engine when my gaze rested on our daughters, each responsible and confident, blooming before our eyes. Kendall filled in the last line of the log, noting our arrival time, how deep we were anchored, how much chain we had out and our latitude and longitude. As she raised the pencil above her entry and closed the logbook, I didn't know it then, but *Chewbacca* and her crew had completed their final passage.

CHAPTER 42

JOURNEY'S END

"And so, for a time it looked as if all the adventure were coming to an end; but that was not to be."

-C.S. Lewis, Author

THAT NIGHT THE MILKY WAY SPLASHED ACROSS THE SKY LIKE SILVER GLITTER spilled upon black poster board. Under the brilliant canopy of stars, we spread out our sleeping bags on the front tramp and gazed upward counting the brilliant streaks of shooting stars. I was so filled with contentment, I didn't even know what I would wish for.

By now the girls realized that although their home was small, the backyard just outside their door was more expansive and vaster than most could ever imagine. I often caught them, legs swinging off the front trampoline drinking in the sprawling landscapes and I knew this journey would never end.

We had spent a nearly a year anchored in paradise, and now it was time to determine where next our journey would take us. Were we going back to South America or north to explore the Caribbean further?

Anyone could call a family meeting aboard *Chewbacca* and tonight it was the girls' turn. Kendall led the conversation although she kept looking at Quincy as she unfolded her notes, so I knew they must have collaborated on the subject matter at hand. *They must have something serious on their minds*, I thought as she cleared her throat and began. "You know we appreciate the cruising life and all that we've done together." I squeezed Bruce's hand not sure where this was going, but my heart already knew… "but Quincy and I would like to go to school…to a real school and have friends, friends that don't leave, and…well…be American."

I turned to Bruce. "You know, they can't be Peter Pan forever," I quietly said with a deep sigh as we leaned into each other. Bruce waved the girls closer for one big group hug. They needed the reassurance that this new revelation was all OK as much as we did. We'd had a beautiful decade together in Neverland but now we knew it was time to let the girls create their own adventures.

Sitting in my favorite spot on *Chewbacca's* bow sipping my morning Joe I captured the first light of dawn. The islands and I were slowly waking up together. I was trying to come to grips with Kendall's fateful words. The sun was beginning to warm the air, and the water surrounding me gradually changed hues becoming a brilliant turquoise. The palm trees became a vivid green set against the deep yellow sand. *Chewbacca* rested in unarguably the definition of paradise. We had obtained our life long goal. We had indeed found paradise.

All alone in the quiet solitude, I let the beauty surrounding me soak through my pores and settle into my bones. I pulled my knees to my chest and let out a peaceful sigh. Below decks, the girls were stirring and beginning their morning banter. I could hear Bruce in the galley reheating the kettle.

Just then the real revelation washed over me like a warm tidal wave. We had found paradise, but it wasn't a point on a map that had defined our paradise. Paradise was the journey itself. This adventure had been a voyage of self-discovery and personal growth rich beyond measure: It was a precious gift we had chosen to give to ourselves.

Now it was time to put events in motion that would close this chapter of our life.

Later that week Bruce slowly pulled up the anchor to the sounds of conch shells being blown. Our friends were sending us on our way in familiar style. As I threaded *Chewbacca* between the reefs and islands I allowed the tears to rain down my cheeks. The girls were high in the rigging pressing the beautiful images to their eyes. They didn't want to ever forget these magical years, but their faces were excitedly turned to the future.

A profound sense of happiness swept over me as I realized I had fulfilled my own vow to become an equal partner with Bruce in our sailing adventure. We made a formidable team at sea as well as on land. I steered *Chewbacca* along the deep blue waters of the Eden Channel and around Punta San Blas where together as a family we hoisted the sails and travelled towards another fresh adventure.

A month later, once again my tears fell freely as I watched our beloved *Chewbacca* disappear in the rear-view mirror of the taxi as we silently drove away...leaving her behind forever.

EPILOGUE

We sold *Chewbacca* to a couple who sailed her to all our favorite places in Panama and as far as we know, our beloved Chewbacca is still out there cruising!

The last personal item Bruce removed from *Chewbacca* was my worn and faded journal. I opened to the last dog-eared page where the entry simple stated: "To be continued."

It did not take us long to fall back into American life. Kendall and Quincy excelled at school and after graduating from high school continued on to university. Kendall earned her undergraduate degree in English and another in Spanish and Quincy earned a degree in Criminal Justice.

I often catch Bruce reading cruising blogs about traversing America's Great Loop and exploring the 5,600 miles of waterways within our own borders. When he tapes a savings thermometer on the back of the bedroom door, I'll know I'd better get ready for another love affair with the sea and I'm all in!

ACKNOWLEDGMENTS

We are extremely grateful to all our cruising friends who shared idyllic anchorages with us, who rode out many a storm with us and who lifted our spirits when we faced adversity and to all those who lived the cruising life alongside us… Peter & Jennifer, Eric, Christine & Kai, John, Amy, Jordan, Kendall & Ally, Jake & Sue, Les & Diane, Neil & Esther, Dave & Kim, Jim & Leslee, Rick & Marsha, Papa Grumps & Mimi and the couple who first ignited the fire; Lin & Larry. Thank you doesn't seem enough to express the inspirational role you played in our family's life changing odyssey.

To my mom & dad who went rogue and immigrated to Australia with two young children. I owe you one.

To John & Mary who watched us sail into the sunset, once to the South Seas and again when we set off on our great escape with our girls. As lifelong friends, we always picked up where we left off as if no time had passed at all.

Special thanks to Elizabeth who listened to our story and then read the first raw draft and edited countless others. We are grateful for your editorial insights, encouragement and honesty when something was "meh."

To Larry & Evelyn who read our book over and over and over again, adding valuable comments and telling us what topics piqued their interest.

To Carrie; we hope your desire for travel was sparked in part by your time aboard *Chewbacca* and we hope you choose to have an adventure of your own.

To our dear friends, Roger & Binnie for exemplifying the very best in mankind.

To all our family and friends, and any we may have omitted, thank you for your enthusiastic support throughout our journey and welcoming us home.

Authors' note:

The boat names and names of crew mentioned in the telling of our story have been changed to honor their privacy.

GLOBAL CREWING ROUTE

HAWAII

ATLANTIC
OCEAN

TAHITI

PACIFIC
OCEAN

CHEWBACCA ROUTE MAP

ABOUT THE AUTHORS

Bruce and April Winship were young and newly married when they decided to go looking for a little adventure. With little to no experience they hopped on a sailboat bound for Tahiti, and after two years of crewing on different sailboats throughout the South Pacific, Central and South America, they returned home with a burning passion to rediscover paradise on their own boat… this time as a family.

Set Sail AND *Live Your Dreams* is the story of how Bruce and April overcame adversity, financial hurdles, and a steep learning curve to create the adventure of a lifetime for themselves and their two young daughters. Their voyage of discovery exposes the hardships of almost losing their boat on a reef, the challenges of homeschooling to the joyous moments spent anchored at uninhabited islands for months at a time.

We hope *Set Sail* AND *Live Your Dreams* will inspire you to launch an adventure of your own, whether big or small, by land or sea… to drift off the beaten path, even for just a little while.

For more photos and information about our adventure visit our website at www.setsailandliveyourdreams.com.

April & Bruce Winship